The Fraternal Atlantic, 1770–1930

This book examines Freemasonry in the eighteenth- and nineteenth-century Atlantic world. Drawing on fresh empirical evidence, the chapters position fraternalism as a critical component of Atlantic history.

Fraternalism was a key strategy for people swept up in the dislocations of imperialism, large-scale migrations, and the socio-political upheavals of revolution. Ranging from confraternities to Masonic lodges to friendly societies, fraternal organizations offered people opportunities to forge linkages across diverse and widely separated parts of the world. Using six case studies, the contributors to this volume address multiple themes of fraternal organizations: their role in revolutionary movements; their intersections with the conflictive histories of racism, slavery, and anti-slavery; their appeal for diasporic groups throughout the Atlantic world, such as revolutionary refugees, European immigrants in North America, and members of the Jewish diaspora; and the limits of fraternal "brothering" in addressing the challenges of modernity.

The chapters in this book were originally published as a special issue of *Atlantic Studies: Global Currents*.

Jessica L. Harland-Jacobs is Associate Professor of History at the University of Florida, USA; her research focuses on the British Empire and comparative imperialism.

Jan C. Jansen is a professor of global history at the University of Duisburg-Essen, Germany. His research interests include comparative imperial history, refugee history, and the history of the Atlantic and Mediterranean worlds.

Elizabeth Mancke studies the geopolitical impact of European expansion on systems of governance. She is a Canada Research Chair in Atlantic Canada Studies at the University of New Brunswick, Canada.

The Fraternal Atlantic, 1770–1930

Race, Revolution, and Transnationalism in the Worlds of Freemasonry

**Edited by
Jessica L. Harland-Jacobs, Jan C. Jansen
and Elizabeth Mancke**

LONDON AND NEW YORK

First published 2021
by Routledge
2 Park Square, Milton Park, Abingdon, Oxon, OX14 4RN

and by Routledge
52 Vanderbilt Avenue, New York, NY 10017

Routledge is an imprint of the Taylor & Francis Group, an informa business

Introduction, Chapters 1–4 and 6 © 2021 Taylor & Francis
Chapter 5 © 2019 Andreas Önnerfors. Originally published as Open Access.

With the exception of Chapter 5, no part of this book may be reprinted or reproduced or utilised in any form or by any electronic, mechanical, or other means, now known or hereafter invented, including photocopying and recording, or in any information storage or retrieval system, without permission in writing from the publishers. For details on the rights for Chapter 5, please see the chapter's Open Access footnote.

Trademark notice: Product or corporate names may be trademarks or registered trademarks, and are used only for identification and explanation without intent to infringe.

British Library Cataloguing-in-Publication Data
A catalogue record for this book is available from the British Library

ISBN13: 978-0-367-65406-1
ISBN13: 978-0-367-65408-5 (pbk)

Typeset in Myriad Pro
by codeMantra

Publisher's Note
The publisher accepts responsibility for any inconsistencies that may have arisen during the conversion of this book from journal articles to book chapters, namely the inclusion of journal terminology.

Disclaimer
Every effort has been made to contact copyright holders for their permission to reprint material in this book. The publishers would be grateful to hear from any copyright holder who is not here acknowledged and will undertake to rectify any errors or omissions in future editions of this book.

Contents

Citation Information	vii
Notes on Contributors	ix

The fraternal Atlantic: An introduction *Jessica L. Harland-Jacobs, Jan C. Jansen and Elizabeth Mancke*	1

PART I
Revolutions

13

1	From a cosmopolitan fraternity to a loyalist institution: Freemasonry in British North America in the 1780s–1790s *Bonnie Huskins*	15
2	Brothers in exile: Masonic lodges and the refugees of the Haitian Revolution, 1790s–1820 *Jan C. Jansen*	42

PART II
Race

65

3	A secret brotherhood? The question of black Freemasonry before and after the Haitian Revolution *John D. Garrigus*	67
4	"Perfectly proper and conciliating": Jean-Pierre Boyer, freemasonry, and the revolutionary Atlantic in eastern Connecticut, 1800–1801 *Peter P. Hinks*	87

vi CONTENTS

PART III
Tensions **109**

5   Atlantic antagonism: Revolution and race in German-American Masonic
relations, 1848–1861   111
Andreas Önnerfors

6   The great divide: Transatlantic brothering and masonic internationalism,
c. 1870–c. 1930   130
Joachim Berger

Index   149

Citation Information

The chapters in this book were originally published in *Atlantic Studies*, volume 16, issue 3 (September 2019). When citing this material, please use the original page numbering for each article, as follows:

Introduction
The fraternal Atlantic: An introduction
Jessica L. Harland-Jacobs, Jan C. Jansen and Elizabeth Mancke
Atlantic Studies, volume 16, issue 3 (September 2019) pp. 283–293

Chapter 1
From a cosmopolitan fraternity to a loyalist institution: Freemasonry in British North America in the 1780s–1790s
Bonnie Huskins
Atlantic Studies, volume 16, issue 3 (September 2019) pp. 294–320

Chapter 2
A secret brotherhood? The question of black Freemasonry before and after the Haitian Revolution
John Garrigus
Atlantic Studies, volume 16, issue 3 (September 2019) pp. 321–340

Chapter 3
Brothers in exile: Masonic lodges and the refugees of the Haitian Revolution, 1790s–1820
Jan C. Jansen
Atlantic Studies, volume 16, issue 3 (September 2019) pp. 341–363

Chapter 4
"Perfectly proper and conciliating": Jean-Pierre Boyer, freemasonry, and the revolutionary Atlantic in eastern Connecticut, 1800–1801
Peter P. Hinks
Atlantic Studies, volume 16, issue 3 (September 2019) pp. 364–385

Chapter 5
Atlantic antagonism: Revolution and race in German-American Masonic relations, 1848–1861
Andreas Önnerfors
Atlantic Studies, volume 16, issue 3 (September 2019) pp. 386–404

Chapter 6

The great divide: Transatlantic brothering and masonic internationalism, c. 1870–c. 1930
Joachim Berger
Atlantic Studies, volume 16, issue 3 (September 2019) pp. 405–422

For any permission-related enquiries please visit:
http://www.tandfonline.com/page/help/permissions

Contributors

Joachim Berger is Research Coordinator at the Leibniz Institute of European History (IEG) in Mainz, Germany. He studied history and art history in Jena (Germany) and Bristol (UK). Berger's PhD thesis (published 2003) dealt with scopes of thought and action of a German princess in the Enlightenment. His current research focuses on masonic internationalism in Europe (c. 1845–1935).

John D. Garrigus is Professor of History at the University of Texas at Arlington, USA. He is the author of *Before Haiti: Race and Citizenship in French Saint-Domingue* (Palgrave-Macmillan, 2006) and co-author with Trevor Burnard of *Plantation Machine: Atlantic Capitalism in French Saint-Domingue and Jamaica* (University of Pennsylvania Press, 2016).

Jessica L. Harland-Jacobs is Associate Professor of history at the University of Florida, Gainesville, USA. She is the author of *Builders of Empire: Freemasons and British Imperialism* (University of North Carolina Press, 2007), articles and chapters that argue for examining freemasonry using macro-level units of analysis, and articles and a bibliography on the Atlantic dimensions of fraternalism. She is currently researching how empires manage religious diversity, in particular the incorporation of Catholics into the British Empire of the eighteenth and early nineteenth centuries.

Peter P. Hinks has worked extensively in public history and historical editing. He is the author of *To Awaken My Afflicted Brethren: David Walker and the Problem of Antebellum Slave Resistance* (Pennsylvania State University Press, 1997) and, with Stephen Kantrowitz, the editor of the collection of essays, *All Men Free and Brethren: Essays on the History of African American Freemasonry* (Cornell University Press, 2013). His research and writing are now focused on southeastern Connecticut, especially for the late eighteenth century.

Bonnie Huskins teaches history at St. Thomas University, USA, and the University of New Brunswick, Canada, where she is also an Adjunct Professor and Loyalist Studies Coordinator. Her current research projects include Loyalist sociability patterns, the imperial life and career of British military engineer William Booth, and Loyalist Freemasons in northeastern North America.

Jan C. Jansen is a professor of global history at the University of Duisburg-Essen, Germany, and principal investigator of the research project "Atlantic Exiles: Refugees and Revolution in the Atlantic World, 1770s–1820s," funded by the European Research Council. His publications include *Erobern und Erinnern: Symbolpolitik, öffentlicher Raum und französischer Kolonialismus in Algerien, 1830–1950* (Oldenbourg, 2013);

Decolonization: A Short History (Princeton University Press, 2017) (co-authored with Jürgen Osterhammel); and *Refugee Crises, 1945–2000: Political and Societal Responses in International Comparison* (Cambridge University Press, 2020) (co-edited with Simone Lässig).

Elizabeth Mancke is Professor of history and the Canada Research Chair in Atlantic Canada Studies at the University of New Brunswick (UNB), Canada. Her research interests address the impact of European overseas expansion on governance and political systems, from local government to international relations. Her most recent book is *Violence, Order, and Unrest: A History of British North America, 1749–1876* (co-edited with Jerry Bannister, Denis McKim, Scott W. See; University of Toronto Press, 2019). At UNB, she is heading a team to build an open-source database of all the legislation of the colonies that became Canada from 1758 to 1867.

Andreas Önnerfors is Associate Professor in the History of Sciences and Ideas at the University of Gothenburg, Sweden. He has specialized in the cultural history of the eighteenth century, in particular secret societies, cultural encounters, and press history. His publications include *Freemasonry: A Very Short Introduction*. (Oxford University Press, 2017).

The fraternal Atlantic: An introduction

Jessica L. Harland-Jacobs, Jan C. Jansen and Elizabeth Mancke

ABSTRACT
This introduction to the volume on "The Fraternal Atlantic" places the eighteenth-century emergence of freemasonry within the context of the dynamic Atlantic world. It highlights three characteristics that persisted into the twentieth century: the importance of freemasonry to sociability across borders; the tensions within freemasonry between cosmopolitan fraternalism and the turbulent political waters of the modern era, often leading to exclusive practices; and the plasticity of freemasonry that facilitated local adaptations and resiliency. A focus on freemasonry and the fraternal Atlantic offers a bridge between the early modern and modern eras, from the Age of Revolutions to movements for international cooperation after the First World War. It likewise mitigates the tendency of Atlantic scholarship to compartmentalize into various sub-Atlantics, instead seeing the Atlantic world as a zone of interaction with broader global connections.

Fraternalism was a key element in Atlantic history. Ranging from confraternities to masonic lodges to friendly societies, fraternal organizations cultivated kinship-like bonds among their members – a form of "symbolic" or "fictive kinship," as cultural anthropologists and social scientists have come to call it.[1] The personalized links forged by these associations stretched across vast spaces, political boundaries, and cultural systems. They were enmeshed within the diverse forces that shaped the Atlantic world: they figured prominently in imperial and then national political cultures; they supported people through various forms of mobility, both voluntary and involuntary; they served as crucibles of cosmopolitan thinking, as well as of ideologies that legitimized hierarchies along lines of class, race, or gender; they intersected with and reinforced professional, political, ethnic, or religious networks stretching across the ocean; and they became involved in the turmoil of Atlantic revolutions, wars, and the struggles around slavery and its abolition.

While scholars have pointed out the abundance and significance of fraternal associations in the Atlantic world, until recently most studies in this field have remained encased in national or local frameworks.[2] We are only beginning to see the transoceanic and transcontinental scope of the phenomenon. Thanks to new work that uses larger units of analysis (empires, oceans, continents, and regions), it is becoming increasingly clear that fraternal organizations were particularly well suited to building large-scale networks.[3] Whether imperial, Atlantic, or global, such brotherhoods were often based on universalizing, cosmopolitan ideologies that posited the local club, lodge or chapter as a place for fraternal sociability and friendship that could transcend religious, political, social, national, and cultural boundaries.

This volume on "The Fraternal Atlantic" offers six essays that explore the role that fraternal associations and networks played in integrating and dis-integrating the Atlantic world. It focuses on the most widespread, significant, and long-lasting fraternal association, freemasonry, or, more precisely, freemasonries. As the essays emphasize, beneath the powerful commonalities of freemasonry emerged diverse adaptations that could divide as well as unite freemasons. Although freemasons trace their roots to medieval stone masons' guilds, the emergence of freemasonry as a fraternal organization open to men from any trade or profession occurred in the late seventeenth and early eighteenth centuries in Scotland and England.[4] In 1717, freemasons from English lodges formed the first grand lodge, what would become the Grand Lodge of England, and in 1723, a Scots Presbyterian minister living in England, James Anderson, published *The Constitutions of the Free-Masons*, which was soon translated into other languages.[5]

By the 1720s, masonic lodges could be found in many places in the Atlantic world – Ireland, France, and British America – seemingly in response to the accelerating population growth and economic activity across the Atlantic basin.[6] In the three decades of peace after the War of the Spanish Succession (1702–1713), natural reproduction in the French and British settler colonies saw populations doubling every twenty to twenty-five years, a phenomenon Benjamin Franklin analyzed in a 1755 pamphlet entitled *Observations Concerning the Increase of Mankind, Peopling of Countries, etc.* Highly productive farms fed not just their growing local populations, but also the expanding slave societies of the Caribbean. The transatlantic African slave trade expanded rapidly, supplying labor to grow the cane and process the sugar on an industrial scale, catering to a seemingly insatiable demand for sugar and its derivative products, most particularly molasses and rum.[7] In these decades, the French Caribbean colony of Saint-Domingue, which figures in three of the essays, became the top sugar producer in the world.[8] To facilitate the movement of people and goods, port cities in the Atlantic world, whether New York, Louisbourg, Liverpool, Cap-Français, Philadelphia, Baltimore, Boston, Rio de Janeiro, Cartagena de Indias, or Lisbon, became vibrant cosmopolitan spaces. Most ports supported the publication of newspapers, provided financial services, and engendered a consumer revolution that tapped into trade networks moving goods and people on a global scale, so that cotton and tea out of Asia become everyday items in the Atlantic world.[9]

Within this dynamic world, freemasonry offered men a way to belong, to find "brothers" in strange port towns. As the dislocations of war and revolution convulsed the Atlantic world in the late eighteenth and early nineteenth century, followed by Europe's disgorging of millions of emigrants into the Americas and Antipodes, membership in freemasonry became a way for thousands of men to weather the political, social, and economic changes whether at a personal, national, or international level. Studying freemasonry – and fraternalism writ large – in this Atlantic context promises to be highly beneficial for the well-established scholarly field of Atlantic history.[10] As the articles collected here demonstrate, the topic points to still largely understudied systems of networks along which people and ideas moved across the Atlantic world and brings to light an important element in the Atlantic history of mutual aid and charity, to mention but two major aspects. On a more abstract level, the history of freemasonry (and fraternalism) helps address certain blind spots of Atlantic history scholarship. Cutting across particular divisions that gave structure to the Atlantic world, be they based on kinship, religion, profession, politics, nationality or ethnicity, the study of fraternal networks mitigates the tendency in Atlantic scholarship to compartmentalize in separated sub-Atlantics (e.g. British, French, Dutch, Iberian, Catholic, Irish, Black Atlantic).[11] Likewise, with fraternal organizations always being part of a worldwide network, their study can help to respond to the criticism that Atlantic history perspectives tend to isolate the region from its manifold connections with the wider world.[12]

Yet, perhaps the most valuable benefit of the topic is that it encourages us to ask and pursue precise questions for specific contexts that might help us to move beyond the plausible and seemingly self-evident conclusion that everything was, in the end, interconnected. Examining freemasonry in a wide range of geographic and chronological contexts, these articles cover the period from the late eighteenth to the early twentieth centuries. They, thus, zero in on a period in which the early modern Atlantic world underwent particularly dramatic transformations, with its social, political and cultural systems being tested and reconfigured, the lines between freedom and slavery redrawn, and migratory patterns altered.[13] Each of the studies weaves the topic of fraternalism into some of the major threads of Atlantic history during this transformative period: What role did fraternal organizations play for revolutionaries and their adversaries? What does studying the history of freemasonries tell us about the complex local political cultures of the Atlantic world from the "age of revolutions" to the "age of internationalism"? What was the significance of masonic membership (or claimed masonic membership) to men of various races, ethnicities, and social positions? How did fraternalism intersect with the conflictive histories of racism, slavery, and anti-slavery? What was its appeal for diasporic groups throughout the Atlantic world such as refugees of the Haitian Revolution and European immigrants in North America? How did fraternal associations provide frameworks for professional networking and interactions across imperial borders? What were the limits of fraternal "brothering" and connectivity across the Atlantic?

By addressing such questions based on fresh empirical evidence, the articles explore to what extent the Atlantic world was shaped by fraternalism, and how, in turn, fraternalism was shaped by the Atlantic world. In the six case studies presented here, there are connecting threads that stretch from eighteenth-century Saint-Domingue to the movement for international freemasonry in the early twentieth century. Three related themes run through all of the essays: first, the importance of freemasonry to sociability across borders; second, the tensions between freemasonry's official commitment to cosmopolitan fraternalism and its members' engagements in the multivalent political cultures of the revolutionary and post-revolutionary Atlantic world; and, third, the resulting multiplication of *freemasonries* across the Atlantic world and beyond. This introduction uses these connecting strands to sketch out how freemasonry reflected interdependent developments in the Atlantic world – revolution, migration, nationalism, racism, internationalism – and how people used freemasonry to mediate their relationship to these developments.

Extensive sociability

Freemasonry was not only a fraternal, but also a voluntary association, that is, an organization based on the idea of free and individual membership whose existence was dependent neither on the state nor the church. The masonic brotherhood was part of what historian Peter Clark has labelled the "associational revolution" of the eighteenth century.[14] Shaping a semi-private, semi-public space for conviviality, leisure, and friendly intercourse, these associations gave way to modern clubs and societies in the following century. As burgeoning places of sociability, they have been widely credited as the backbone of local civil society. But seen in an Atlantic context, sociability proves to be not only highly relevant for local communities and intimate relationships, but also for building and maintaining networks that could sustain people as they moved across great distances. In its ideology and its practices, the masonic brotherhood – as other fraternal organizations – championed wide-scale networking, both ideological and physical, while remaining firmly rooted in local contexts. The articles thus challenge us to rethink the ways in which the (allegedly) secluded and intimate worlds of face-to-face interaction within lodges intersected with broader structures of the Atlantic world.

The cases examined here demonstrate the truly transatlantic extensity of its network. When a member arrived in a new place, he could anticipate the possibility of being accepted as a masonic brother, as though he were family. In his "'Perfectly proper and conciliating': Jean-Pierre Boyer, freemasonry, and the revolutionary Atlantic in eastern Connecticut, 1800–1801," Peter P. Hinks describes how the captured Saint-Domingue soldier and future president of Haiti was taken in by a group of freemasons in Norwich, Connecticut. Masonic relations complemented, substituted for, at times replaced, the family networks that underlay so many Atlantic merchant networks in the early modern era.[15] Masonic brothers – not unlike a cousin, a great aunt, an uncle, a godfather – provided introductions into local communities, and often bed and board. The transatlantic spread of freemasonry in the eighteenth century and its commitment to cosmopolitanism legitimated the forging of networks even across imperial borders.[16] Jan C. Jansen notes in his essay, "Brothers in exile: Masonic lodges and the refugees of the Haitian Revolution, 1790s–1820," pre-revolutionary French Saint-Domingue's thriving masonic landscape was well-connected beyond the imperial metropole. Drawing their members from a milieu of merchants, colonial administrators, sailors, and planters, Saint-Domingue's lodges forged links with freemasons not only across the French Atlantic, but also in the British West Indies, North America, and the Danish Caribbean. These masonic relations often followed legal or illegal trade routes. In the years before the Haitian Revolution, particularly intense masonic relations sustained the burgeoning commerce between Philadelphia and Saint-Domingue.

Masonic sociability helped people survive the buffeting of political upheavals, whether as refugees from the American, French, or Haitian revolutions, or as refugees from the political uprisings of 1848 in Germany. As Jansen notes, "A Masonic certificate provided access to a universe of informal social networks that shaped the eighteenth-century Atlantic world, thereby helping people communicate and move about during a time of uncertainty." Indeed, the importance people placed in masonic papers may indicate that people feared dislocation in the Atlantic world far more than we have realized. One of the early acts of political refugees upon resettling was to establish a new masonic lodge. Loyalists in the new colony of New Brunswick established Hiram Lodge No. 17 in 1784, just months after disembarking from the military transports that had evacuated them from New York. Refugees of the Haitian Revolution quickly reshaped and rebuilt Saint-Domingue's lodge network across their places of refuge in North America, the

British and Spanish Caribbean, and Louisiana. As Jansen argues, due to their ubiquity and manifold uses, masonic lodges were among the most important social infrastructures within the Saint-Domingue diaspora.

The importance of lodges as hubs for transatlantic refugees and exiles lasted well into the nineteenth century. Andreas Önnerfors shows in his study "Atlantic antagonism: Revolution and race in German-American Masonic relations, 1848–1861" that émigrés from the 1848 uprisings in Germany made similar use of freemasonry as a means to ease their resettlement to North America. His analysis of the German-speaking lodge Pythagoras No. 1 in New York cautions us against limiting the diasporic uses of masonic networks to forced migrants. In New York City alone, the port of entry for more immigrants than any other North America port, there were over 30 German-speaking lodges, a majority of which were run by non-refugee immigrants. The studies presented here underscore the role of masonic (and other forms of) sociability in the Atlantic history of migration, both voluntary and compelled, and invite other scholars to research this understudied aspect of Atlantic history.[17]

Masonic cosmopolitanism under pressure

While masonic sociability was more extensive than most other forms of social interaction in the Atlantic world, it was often limited, in practice, by the complexities of Atlantic political culture, which intensified starting in the late eighteenth century. Freemasons espoused political cosmopolitanism and counselled their members to avoid entanglement in political disputes that would pit masonic brothers against one another. But neither individuals nor associations could shield themselves from the era's political upheavals. Each study speaks to fissures among freemasons, sometimes within lodges, often transnationally, that resulted from this tension. In "From a cosmopolitan fraternity to a loyalist institution: Freemasonry in British North America in the 1780s–1790s," Bonnie Huskins examines the shift in the ethos of freemasonry in the British Empire, through a case study of Hiram Lodge No. 17, organized in Saint John, New Brunswick shortly after loyalist refugees from the American Revolution arrived in 1783. She traces how the political disputes during Saint John's founding decade involved masons and publicly spilled over into masonic relations, prompting the Grand Lodge of Nova Scotia to revoke the warrant for Hiram Lodge No. 17 in 1796. She argues that it is an example of an early casualty of the shift within British imperial freemasonry from an emphasis on political cosmopolitanism to an emphasis on loyalty. During the American and French Revolutions, British officials feared that masonic lodges could foster and harbor seditious behavior, thus compelling grand lodges to engage in more self-policing, including the revocation of warrants, as happened in New Brunswick.

Fissures within freemasonry caused by political disputes are also clearly evident in the case of freemasonry in colonial and revolutionary Saint-Domingue and its Atlantic ramifications. The fact that the most radical of the Atlantic revolutions took place in one of the most "masonized" societies in the world, makes this case particular intriguing. In "A secret brotherhood? The question of black freemasonry before and after the Haitian Revolution," John D. Garrigus engages with the recurring idea that revolutionary agents, most notably Toussaint Louverture, had been freemasons and that, consequently, masonic lodges had served as incubators of political change and emancipation in Saint-Domingue. Pointing to the membership practices in pre-revolutionary Saint-Domingue, he concludes that there is no evidence for any significant involvement of free people of color in official freemasonry. Rather, the colony's lodges reflected how the white population increasingly rejected the aspiring class of prosperous free people of color in the decades leading up to the revolution. Revolutionary events did usher in some changes. After the 1793–94 abolition of slavery, a few lodges did accept black or biracial members – a revolution by pre-revolutionary standards. But, Garrigus contends, men of color never came to a significant presence in these lodges, and Louverture himself was likely not a freemason.

Freemasonry also became an important network for those who were dislocated in the course of the revolutionary events and, consequently, a field in which the Haitian Revolution reverberated across the Atlantic world. One particularly fascinating example is the experience of and reaction to Jean-Pierre Boyer in Connecticut, one of the few free blacks to access official freemasonry during the Haitian Revolution. As Hinks details, Boyer was carrying masonic papers and ceremonial jewels with him when he fled Saint-Domingue in 1800 and was captured by an American naval patrol. At sea and then on land, Boyer experienced contrasting receptions by groups of local freemasons, revealing how the political upheavals impacted on the allegedly non-political field of fraternal association. With the presence of a foreign black freemason in their midst, Connecticut's lodges were thrust into broader Atlantic conflicts about religion, political revolution, slave emancipation, and racial discrimination. Refugee lodges, with well over a thousand members, also became an organizing backbone for white Saint-Domingue refugees navigating the volatile political landscape of the revolutionary Atlantic. As Jansen shows, many of their political leaders played prominent roles in the lodge network, and their lodges even came to mix messages of universal brotherhood with pro-slavery statements.

The tension between inclusion and exclusion continued to cause fissures within the brotherhood in the nineteenth century, particularly over the issue of race. After the American War of Independence, freemasons in the United States agreed among themselves that each state should have a grand lodge and that within each state the grand lodge would have unchallenged control. Önnerfors analyzes what happened when German immigrants in New York broke with the New York State Grand Lodge, and then asked for and received a warrant from the Hamburg Grand Lodge to organize as Pythagoras No. 1. This "foreign" warranting of a lodge within the state of New York provoked a decades-long transatlantic dispute, with US grand lodges arguing that every state grand lodge had exclusive jurisdiction within the territory of any state. Neither another state grand lodge nor a foreign grand lodge had jurisdiction to intervene in masonic business and certainly not to warrant a lodge in another state. The members of Pythagoras No. 1, in turn, justified their split by invoking freemasonry's aspirations to universalism and building transatlantic bridges with European-based freemasons, as well as criticizing US lodges for their policies against blacks in the Atlantic world.

The American practice of exclusive territorial jurisdiction emerged in part because of the revolutionary break with Great Britain, in part because of the diversity among states. Harmonizing deeply rooted cultural differences among the states so that freemasons could establish a national grand lodge proved an unattainable goal, and hence they compromised on the exclusive jurisdictional autonomy of each state grand lodge. As Joachim Berger shows in "The great divide: Transatlantic brothering and Masonic internationalism, c.1870–c.1930," attempts to elevate cosmopolitanism over differences tested transatlantic freemasonry at the end of the nineteenth century. Rifts between North

American, British and continental European freemasons over religion and racial exclusion complicated these efforts. As in other areas, transnational entanglement, interaction and structures did not override local particularities.[18] Rather, they seem to have been a precondition for spelling out national or regional distinctiveness more forcefully.

Freemasonries

Given the volatile divisiveness that emerged in the Atlantic world at the end of the eighteenth century, masonic cosmopolitanism encountered political, racial, national and other divisions that make it necessary to think in terms of "freemasonries": beneath the powerful commonalities of freemasonry emerged diverse adaptations that could divide as well as unite. While freemasonry may have provided a safe haven from political storms, those upheavals also engendered differentiating changes within freemasonry. In addition to the "diasporic freemasonry" investigated by Jansen and the politicized forms of freemasonry examined by Huskins, Hinks, and Önnerfors, these essays highlight other forms of freemasonry that emerged when masonic fraternalism encountered the shoals of racial difference and discrimination. We see the emergence, for example, of "quasi" or claimed freemasonry on the island of Saint Domingue in the last third of the eighteenth century. Despite being largely excluded from official freemasonry, many well-to-do men of color in Saint-Domingue deployed three symbolic dots under their signatures. As Garrigus posits, the use of these symbols implied membership in a respected fraternal organization, either a confraternity or a masonic lodge. By laying claim to such membership, they asserted their own respectability and sought to underpin their social climbing. Rumors from different places of the Saint-Domingue diaspora suggested that black and biracial men participated in a thriving clandestine market of unauthorized certificates, initiations and masonic degrees. Most of these activities happened under the radar of masonic authorities, and they never entered the historical records, which makes it hard to substantiate stories of independent lodges run by former slaves or free people of color.

Yet, what is clear, despite their racist animosity, white colonial freemasons may have unintentionally laid the groundwork for other, successful claims to brotherly love. It is certainly no accident that shortly after Haiti's independence in 1804, masonic lodges started to operate. The growth of freemasonry was capped by the establishment of an independent Haitian grand lodge in 1824, by the time when President (and freemason) Boyer was seeking diplomatic recognition of Haitian independence. This made Haiti the second pillar of a fiercely independent black Atlantic freemasonry, along with the United States. In 1784, at the end of the American Revolution and after decades of unsuccessful attempts to join colonial lodges, Prince Hall, a free black in Boston, had already established African Lodge No. 1, the mother lodge of what would become a thriving African American freemasonry across the United States.[19] Equipped with their own symbolic reservoir, Prince Hall and Haitian freemasonry became, not unlike their white colonial predecessors, a central source of respectability and identity, as well as a place of brotherly sociability and long-distance networking and communication within the Black Atlantic.[20]

By the early twentieth century, another freemasonry – "international freemasonry" – was emerging in the Atlantic world; once again, tensions evident in the broader political culture, this time in terms of religion and nation, shaded its development. Berger retraces how freemasons participated in the general movement of internationalism in the late nineteenth century. Like other internationalists, masonic internationalists – mainly from continental Europe, but at times also from New York – pushed their agenda on manifold conferences and created institutions to coordinate their activities. Conflicts over religion and race marred these efforts to organize a united masonic international, and ironically, it was the horror of twentieth-century warfare that helped many see that what they shared was more important than what divided them. After the United States entered the First World War in April 1917, overtures for stronger transatlantic ties were embraced.

These studies just begin to tell the story of the proliferation of freemasonries across the Atlantic world from the eighteenth through the twentieth centuries. The thriving of freemasonry in Latin America, West Africa and the South Atlantic brings in new complexities to a history that has often been told primarily from a North Atlantic or Anglo-Atlantic perspective.[21] The Caribbean is increasingly emerging as an area of heightened masonic geopolitics, replicating the complex and shifting imperial affiliations within the Caribbean Sea and the Gulf of Mexico.[22] Indeed, freemasonry took on a diverse array of localized, racialized, regionalized, nationalized, and internationalized forms wherever lodges met as brothers. What, then, allows us to still put them under one masonic umbrella? First, regardless of the adaptations that resulted in response to local circumstances, the claims to cosmopolitan fraternalism remained consistent and often honored in the breach. Even in the most un-fraternal of circumstances, freemasons continued to assert that their brotherhood was the "Center of Union, and the Means of conciliating true Friendship among Persons that must else have remain'd at a perpetual Distance."[23] Second, freemasons were united in their practice of shared rituals and use of a common body of symbols. Third, all freemasons continued to espouse and practice cross-border sociability, in various guises, and interacted for mutual benefit. Fourth and finally, the vast majority of freemasons around the Atlantic world would have agreed that freemasonry was an exclusively masculine space. Though not explored in this volume, the gendered dimensions and implications of freemasonry remain critical subjects of investigation.[24]

Thus, despite the extent of the spread of masonic networks, the manifold exclusions practiced by members while making claims to cosmopolitan brotherhood, and the proliferation of its forms that resulted, freemasonry retained a basic identity and purpose. Masons might, indeed, withhold or withdraw official recognition from an individual brother, as happened with Jean-Pierre Boyer, or from a lodge, as happened with Hiram Lodge No. 17 or Pythagoras No. 1. Nevertheless, members of the brotherhood would definitely have been able to recognize in the ideas and practices of brethren across the vast expanses of the Atlantic world an identifiably masonic fraternalism, one that was, as will be seen, remarkably capacious, vibrant, and elastic.

Notes

1. Terpstra, "Deinstitutionalizing Confraternity Studies," 264; Clawson, "Fraternal Orders," 689; Bullock, *Revolutionary Brotherhood*, 39, 74; Harland-Jacobs, *Builders of Empire*, 17–20.
2. Harland-Jacobs, "Worlds of Brothers."
3. Beaurepaire, *République universelle*; Harland-Jacobs, *Builders of Empire*; Mollès, "'Triangle atlantique'."
4. Stevenson, *The Origins of Freemasonry*; Jacob, *The Origins of Freemasonry*; Bogdan and Snoek (eds.), *Handbook of Freemasonry*; Péter (ed.), *British Freemasonry 1717–1813*; Önnerfors, *Freemasonry*.

5. Anderson, *Constitutions*.
6. For Freemasonry in the North American context, see Bullock, *Revolutionary Brotherhood*.
7. Horn and Morgan, "Settlers and Slaves," 20–24; Hancock, "Atlantic Trade," 330–331.
8. Dubois, *A Colony of Citizens*, 33–38.
9. Steele, *The English Atlantic*.
10. The following paragraph draws largely on Jansen, "Atlantic Sociability." See also Harland-Jacobs, "Worlds of Brothers"; Mollès, "L'histoire globale."
11. See the critique by Canny, "Atlantic History and Global History."
12. Coclanis, "Drang Nach Osten"; Bowen, Mancke and Reid, *Britain's Oceanic Empire*; Vidal, "Histoire globale."
13. The period after the Age of Revolutions is a much less studied period in Atlantic scholarship. For forceful arguments to include them, see Gabaccia, "Long Atlantic"; Fogleman, "Transformation."
14. Clark, *British Clubs and Societies*, 471. On sociability, see also Hoffmann, *Civil Society*; Beaurepaire, "Sociability"; Jansen, "Atlantic Sociability."
15. On family merchant networks, see Supple, "Nature of Enterprise," 410; Bosher, *The Canada Merchants*; and Roitman, "New Christians, Jews, and Amsterdam." On the role of freemasonry within eighteenth-century commercial and diplomatic mobility, see Beaurepaire, "Universal Republic."
16. Harland-Jacobs, *Builders of Empire,* 83–88.
17. On the Sephardic diaspora, for example, see Jansen, "Becoming Imperial Citizens." On other forms of diasporic sociability in the Atlantic world, see Studnicki-Gizbert, *Nation Upon the Sea*, 67.
18. Conrad, *Global History*, 79–89.
19. Hinks and Kantrowitz, *All Men Free*; Kantrowitz, "Intended for the Better Government"; Révauger, *Black Freemasonry*.
20. On communication within the Black Atlantic during this period, see Scott, *Common Wind*.
21. There is a prolific scholarship on the history of Latin American freemasonry. For some recent publications, see Vázquez Semadeni, *Cultura política republicana*; Arroyo, *Writing Secrecy*; Soucy, *Enjeux coloniaux*; and the articles in *Revista de Estudios Históricos de la Masonería*. Scholarship on freemasonry in Africa is still limited. Önnerfors's essay in this volume discusses how contentious freemasonry in Liberia was internationally. See also White, "Networking."
22. See, e.g., Saunier, "L'espace caribéen."
23. Anderson, *Constitutions*, 50.
24. Clawson, "Early Modern Fraternalism"; Harland-Jacobs, *Builders of Empire*, 15–17, 61–62, 88–96, 259–262.

Disclosure statement

No potential conflict of interest was reported by the authors.

Bibliography

Anderson, James. *The Constitutions of the Free-Masons: Containing the History, Charges, Regulations, &c. of That Most Ancient and Right Worshipful Fraternity*. London: John Senex and John Hooks, 1723.

Arroyo, Jossiana. *Writing Secrecy in Caribbean Freemasonry*. New York: Palgrave-Macmillan, 2013.

Beaurepaire, Pierre-Yves. *La République universelle des francs-maçons: De Newton à Metternich*. Rennes: Éd. Ouest-France, 1999.

Beaurepaire, Pierre-Yves. "Sociability." In *The Oxford Handbook of the Ancien Régime*, edited by William Doyle, 374–387. Oxford: Oxford University Press, 2012.

Beaurepaire, Pierre-Yves. "The Universal Republic of the Freemasons and the Culture of Mobility in the Enlightenment." *French Historical Studies* 29, no. 3 (2006): 407–431.

Bogdan, Henrik, and Jan A. M. Snoek, eds. *Handbook of Freemasonry*. Leiden: Brill, 2014.

Bosher, John F. *The Canada Merchants, 1713–1763*. Oxford: Clarendon, 1987.

Bowen, H. V., Elizabeth Mancke, and John G. Reid, eds. *Britain's Oceanic Empire: Atlantic and Indian Ocean Worlds, 1500–1850*. Cambridge: Cambridge University Press, 2012.

Bullock, Steven C. *Revolutionary Brotherhood: Freemasonry and the Transformation of the American Social Order, 1730–1840*. Chapel Hill: University of North Carolina Press, 1996.

Canny, Nicholas. "Atlantic History and Global History." In *Atlantic History: A Critical Appraisal*, edited by Jack Greene and Philip Morgan, 317–336. Oxford: Oxford University Press, 2009.

Clark, Peter. *British Clubs and Societies 1580–1800: The Origins of an Associational World*. Oxford: Oxford University Press, 2000.

Clawson, Mary Ann. "Early Modern Fraternalism and the Patriarchal Family." *Feminist Studies* 6, no. 2 (1980): 368–391.

Clawson, Mary Ann. "Fraternal Orders and Class Formation in the Nineteenth-Century United States." *Comparative Studies in Society and History* 27, no. 4 (1985): 672–695.

Coclanis, Peter A. "*Drang Nach Osten*: Bernard Bailyn, the World-Island, and the Idea of Atlantic History." *Journal of World History* 13, no. 1 (2002): 169–182.

Conrad, Sebastian. *What is Global History?* Princeton, NJ: Princeton University Press, 2016.

Dubois, Laurent. *A Colony of Citizens: Revolution and Slave Emancipation in the French Caribbean, 1787–1804*. Chapel Hill: University of North Carolina Press, 2004.

Fogleman, Aaron. "The Transformation of the Atlantic World, 1776–1867." *Atlantic Studies* 6, no. 1 (2009): 5–28.

Gabaccia, Donna. "A Long Atlantic in the Wider World." *Atlantic Studies* 1, no. 1 (2004): 1–27.

Hancock, David. "Atlantic Trade and Commodities, 1402–1815." *The Oxford Handbook of the Atlantic World, 1450–1850*, edited Nicholas Canny and Philip Morgan, 324–340. Oxford: Oxford University Press, 2011.

Harland-Jacobs, Jessica. *Builders of Empire: Freemasons and British Imperialism, 1717–1927*. Chapel Hill: University of North Carolina Press, 2007.

Harland-Jacobs, Jessica. "Worlds of Brothers." *Journal for Research Into Freemasonry and Fraternalism* 2, no. 1 (2011): 10–37.

Hinks, Peter P., and Stephen Kantrowitz, eds. *All Men Free and Brethren: Essays on the History of African American Freemasonry*. Ithaca, NY: Cornell University Press, 2013.

Hoffmann, Stefan-Ludwig. *Civil Society, 1750–1914*. Basingstoke: Palgrave Macmillan, 2006.

Horn, James, and Philip D. Morgan. "Settlers and Slaves: European and African Migrations to Early Modern British America." In *The Creation of the British Atlantic World*, edited by Elizabeth Mancke and Carol Shammas, 19–44. Baltimore: Johns Hopkins University Press, 2005.

Jacob, Margaret C. *The Origins of Freemasonry: Facts and Fictions*. Philadelphia: University of Pennsylvania Press, 2007.

Jansen, Jan C. "Becoming Imperial Citizens: Jews and Freemasonry in the British Caribbean (Early 19th Century)." In *The Sephardic Atlantic: Colonial Histories and Postcolonial Perspectives*, edited by Sina Rauschenbach and Jonathan Schorsch. Basingstoke: Palgrave-Macmillan, forthcoming 2019.

Jansen, Jan C. "In Search of Atlantic Sociability: Freemasons, Empires, and Atlantic History." *Bulletin of the German Historical Institute* 57, no. 2 (2015): 75–99.

Kantrowitz, Stephen. "'Intended for the Better Government of Man': The Political History of African American Freemasonry in the Era of Emancipation." *The Journal of American History* 96, no. 4 (2010): 1001–1026.

Mollès, Dévrig. "Le 'triangle atlantique': Emergence et expansion de la sphere maçonnique internationale, une analyse statistique (1717–1914)." *Nuevo Mundo/Mundos Nuevos* (25 November 2014). http://nuevomundo.revues.org/67498.

Mollès, Dévrig. "L'histoire globale et la question maçonnique: Éléments pour une analyse." *Revista de Estudios Históricos de la Masonería Latinoamericana y Caribeña* 6, no. 1 (2014): 4–32.

Önnerfors, Andreas. *Freemasonry: A Very Short Introduction*. Oxford: Oxford University Press, 2018.

Péter, Róbert, ed., *British Freemasonry 1717–1813*. London: Routledge, 2016.

Révauger, Cécile. *Black Freemasonry: From Prince Hall to the Giants of Jazz*. Rochester, VT: Inner Traditions, 2016.

Roitman, Jessica Vance. "New Christians, Jews, and Amsterdam at the Crossroads of Expansion Systems." In *Migration, Trade, and Slavery in an Expanding World: Essays in Honor of Pieter Emmer*, edited by Wim Klooster, 119–140. Leiden: Brill, 2009.

Saunier, Eric. "L'espace caribéen: Un enjeu de pouvoir pour la franc-maçonnerie française." *Revista de Estudios Históricos de la Masonería Latinoamericana y Caribeña* 1, no. 1 (2009): 42–56.

Scott, Julius S. *The Common Wind: Afro-American Currents in the Age of the Haitian Revolution*. London: Verso, 2018.

Soucy, Dominique. *Enjeux coloniaux et franc-maçonnerie à Cuba au XIXe siècle: Un renouveau historique à la lumière des archives du Grand Orient de France*. Pessac: Presses Universitaires de Bordeaux, 2016.

Steele, Ian Kenneth. *The English Atlantic, 1675–1740: An Exploration of Communication and Community*. New York: Oxford University Press, 1986.

Stevenson, David. *The Origins of Freemasonry: Scotland's Century, 1590–1710*. Cambridge: Cambridge University Press, 1988.

Studnicki-Gizbert, Daviken. *A Nation Upon the Sea: Portugal's Atlantic Diaspora and the Crisis of the Spanish Empire*. Oxford: Oxford University Press, 2007.

Supple, Barry. ""The Nature of Enterprise." *The Economic History of Early Modern Europe*. Vol. 5." In *The Economic Organization of Early Modern Europe*, edited by Edwin Ernest Rich and Charles H. Wilson, 394–461. Cambridge: Cambridge University Press, 1977.

Terpstra, Nicholas. "Deinstitutionalizing Confraternity Studies: Fraternalism and Social Capital in Cross-Cultural Contexts." In *Early Modern Confraternities in Europe and the Americas: International and Interdisciplinary Perspectives*, edited by Christopher Black and Pamela Gravestock, 264–283. Burlington, VT: Ashgate, 2006.

Vázquez Semadeni, María Eugenia. *La formación de una cultura política republicana: El debate público sobre la masonería: México, 1821–1830*. México: Universidad Nacional Autónoma de México, 2010.

Vidal, Cécile. "Pour une histoire globale du monde atlantique ou des histoires connectées dans et au-delà du monde atlantique?" *Annales: Histoire, Sciences Sociales* 67, no. 2 (2012): 391–413.

White, Owen. "Networking: Freemasons and the Colonial State in French West Africa, 1895–1914." *French History* 19, no. 1 (2005): 91–111.

Part I
Revolutions

From a cosmopolitan fraternity to a loyalist institution: Freemasonry in British North America in the 1780s–1790s

Bonnie Huskins

ABSTRACT

British Freemasons accommodated the revolutionary politics of the eighteenth-century Atlantic world until the 1790s, when the British waged war against revolutionary France and suppressed internal radicalism and associations they defined as seditious. British Grand Lodges reoriented to overt displays of loyalty, such as adopting royal patrons, and consolidating their authority over Freemasonry. This transformation from an elastic and cosmopolitan fraternity to a loyalist institution was highly embattled. This essay examines this shift within "Hiram Lodge No. 17" in Saint John, New Brunswick. Lodge members became embroiled in political conflicts in the colony's first election in 1785. A decade later, members sparred with Masonic officialdom, after Nova Scotia's provincial grand lodge adopted the anti-revolutionary turn of British Grand Lodges. It clamped down on fractious lodges, including Hiram Lodge, a case demonstrating the complex relationship between fraternal organizations and the dynamic political culture of the late eighteenth- and early nineteenth-century Atlantic world.

Introduction

British Freemasons were involved in many of the revolutionary ruptures of the eighteenth-century Atlantic world. This accommodation of radical politics eroded by the 1790s as the British Parliament and Ministry contemplated war against France, and turned their attention to suppressing internal radicalism, most particularly the United Irish Rebellion, as well as any associations they defined as seditious, which included Freemasons. The British Grand Lodges engaged in a rebranding exercise to show their loyalty, involving such strategies as adopting royal patrons, eradicating competitors, and consolidating their authority as the only legitimate governors of Freemasonry. On the ground, however, the transformation of Freemasonry from an elastic and cosmopolitan fraternity that accommodated rebellion and dissidence, to a loyalist institution that deliberately associated itself with the "defining features of the British state," including loyalty to monarch and empire, Protestantism, and a celebration of British cultural and political superiority, was highly embattled.[1]

Against this backdrop, this essay sheds light on the uses of Freemasonry by American Revolutionary War Loyalists who organized themselves in Masonic lodges in British North America. It examines the contested shift away from political cosmopolitanism, in this context by focusing on one lodge, "Hiram Lodge No. 17," established in 1784 in Saint John, New Brunswick, the largest settlement in a colony created in British North America in 1784 due to the arrival of Loyalist exiles after the American Revolutionary War. Lodge members became engaged in developing the institutions of government, running as opposition candidates in the colony's first election. The election quickly became conflicted, but members remained engaged despite Masonic charges that dictated that members should not be involved in political disputes. A decade later, lodge members also sparred with Masonic officialdom, as the provincial lodge in Nova Scotia sought to impose the new, anti-revolutionary lead of their parent lodges and clamped down on Hiram Lodge and other lodges it considered fractious. In sum, the case of Hiram Lodge No. 17 clearly demonstrates the complexities of the relationship between fraternal organizations and political culture in the late eighteenth- and early nineteenth-century Atlantic world.

The authority exerted by Masonic hierarchies in this period reveals that the fate of individual and provincial lodges was partly determined by developments in the larger fraternal Atlantic. To understand why Hiram Lodge members engaged in political unrest and were forced to surrender their warrant, one must adopt "multiple and intersecting units and scales of analysis," consisting not only of "nations, empires and worlds" but also of "localities."[2] This essay thus adopts a "cis-Atlantic" approach, examining local developments in Saint John within the context of a "wider web of connections (and comparisons)."[3] It also draws attention to the "limits of expansion" within British Freemasonry, i.e. the "schisms" among members, "ruptures" between local and parent bodies, and the "processes of disconnection" leading to the eradication of lodges like Hiram Lodge No. 17.[4]

Historians are beginning to appreciate the "prospects and potentials" of studying Masonic networks in imperial and Atlantic World contexts.[5] Jessica Harland-Jacobs shows how British freemasonry connected people across oceans by offering services and sociability, and by "encouraging an 'imperialist' identity that helped consolidate the British Empire."[6] Freemasons also articulated a "pronounced cosmopolitan attitude" which "sought to ignore confessional, political, social, national, and continental boundaries." Fraternal values and virtues were enabled by Freemasonry's efficient transnational structure. As Jan C. Jensen has noted, "Only a few other non-religious movements of the time adopted institutional structures of a comparable intercontinental scope."[7]

There are few academic analyses of Freemasonry in British North America. Michael Eamon, in his recent book *Imprinting Britain*, incorporates Nova Scotia Masons into his analysis of print culture and sociability in eighteenth-century Halifax and Quebec City, while Hannah M. Lane examines the relationship between evangelical churches and Freemasonry in the early nineteenth-century Canadian-American borderlands of New Brunswick and eastern Maine.[8] Chris Raible discusses Antimasonry in early nineteenth-century Ontario, while Gregory Klages engages in a comparative analysis of the Freemasons and Orange Order in late Victorian rural Ontario.[9] And sociologist J. Scott Kenney brings us into the present-day by reflecting on the contemporary meaning of Freemasonry in his analysis of lodge members in Newfoundland and Nova Scotia.[10]

Scholarship on Loyalist Freemasons is also spotty. Studies of American Freemasonry during the Revolutionary War tend to illustrate the heavy involvement of Patriots in the fraternity: it is estimated that 29 percent of the 241 men who signed either the Articles of Association, the Declaration of Independence, the Articles of Confederation, or the Constitution, or who served as generals in the Continental Army or as Washington's aides or military secretaries, were Freemasons.[11] Stephen C. Bullock's work provides myriad insights into the evolution of revolutionary and post-revolutionary Freemasonry within the United States, but he does not extend his focus to the Loyalist lodges.[12] In her review of the American literature on Freemasonry, Harland-Jacobs notes that that Freemasonry had a "significant presence among Loyalists, a point that eighteenth-century historians have insufficiently addressed."[13] And Neil L. York reminds us that "[n]ot every Mason became a Revolutionary, and some became or remained Loyalists."[14]

This study of Hiram Lodge in Saint John, as well as a previous analysis of Loyalist lodges in Shelburne Nova Scotia, owes a great debt to the scholarship of Jessica Harland-Jacobs and David G. Bell. Harland-Jacobs's identification of a shift in British Freemasonry from a cosmopolitan fraternity to a loyalist institution is the scaffolding on which this essay is based.[15] Bell's research provides the necessary local context on Loyalist history in New Brunswick. In his book *Loyalist rebellion in New Brunswick*, Bell is the first scholar to identify a relationship between political dissidence and membership in Hiram Lodge No. 17.[16] Also useful are the institutional studies written by Masonic historians, most notably William Franklin Bunting's *History of St. John's Lodge, F. & A. M. of Saint John, New Brunswick, Together with Sketches of All Masonic Bodies in New Brunswick from A.D. 1784 to A.D. 1894* (1895), A.J.B. Milbourne's research on Loyalist Freemasons in the Maritime colonies, a history of Freemasonry in Nova Scotia penned by Ronald S. Longley and Reginald V. Harris, and a brief overview of Hiram Lodge No. 17 compiled by Stuart MacDonald, based largely on the research of Reginald V. Harris.[17] Aside from these selected works, this essay is based largely on the manuscript collection of the Nova Scotia Grand Lodge Ancient Free and Accepted Masons. This collection consists of minutes, correspondence and other records from the Nova Scotia Grand Lodge in Halifax as well as the individual lodges, including Hiram Lodge. Access to evidence generated by both the provincial and local lodges has provided insight into the escalation of conflict between the two, resulting in a more polyphonic analysis.

British Freemasonry and loyalist Masons

The fate of Hiram Lodge No 17 in Saint John must be placed in the context of British Freemasonry and its expansion into Britain's American colonies. British Freemasons essentially adapted the infrastructure, regulations, and rituals of the medieval stonemasons' guilds as they declined in the sixteenth and seventeenth centuries due to the decline of castle and cathedral building, the expansion of the marketplace, urbanization, population growth, and migration. In order to survive, the guilds turned to the patronage of aristocrats and gentlemen as "free and accepted" brothers. This marked the transition from "operative" to "speculative" Masonry. Speculative Masons operated in an "increasingly cosmopolitan London society, where enlightened thinking and polite social practices led to the creation of a new form of Masonic brotherhood."[18] They subsequently adapted the guilds into a system of lodges with parent or "grand" lodges. In 1717 the first "grand" lodge was formed in England – the Premier Grand Lodge of Free and Accepted Masons – followed by grand lodges in Ireland (1725) and Scotland (1736). What had formerly been operative regulations became Freemasonic constitutions. Hand signals, grips and handshakes, initially used by stonemasons to identify each other and retain trade secrets, helped to transform Freemasonry into a secret society. The guilds' three basic degrees – Entered Apprentice, Fellow Craftsman, and Master Mason – which had initially marked their initiation and passage through their trade, was adapted by speculative Masons as a means of progressing "by degrees toward a veiled yet constantly unfolding wisdom and enlightenment."[19]

The Enlightenment and the revolutions of the Three Kingdoms – England, Scotland, and Ireland (1640–1660 and 1688–1689) – had a profound impact on the emergence of British Freemasonry. After the Glorious Revolution (1688–89), which witnessed the establishment of the first cabinet government in England, Freemasonic societies emerged as schools of parliamentary and constitutional government, according to Margaret C. Jacob. Their regulations, now termed "constitutions," turned them into "microscopic, and contractually founded and constitutionally governed, civil societies." Moreover, the historical roots of Freemasonry identified by James Anderson in 1723 privileged the development of "strong constitutional and court-centred government." Whig leaders became Freemasons and championed constitutional practices such as holding elections, forming representative assemblies, imposing taxes (dues) and holding courts where disputes could be adjudicated. The newly formed grand lodges also required all members to

> submit to the authority of their elected officers and all lodges to pledge their loyalty to the Grand Lodge. [...] the members of the new fraternity submitted to its constitutional government, which embraced stability, while celebrating the brotherhood as a model for a well-ordered cooperative society.[20]

Attempting to avoid the sectarianism of the seventeenth century, Freemasons also promoted enlightened cosmopolitanism, which emphasized the transcendence of political, social, and religious divisions. In 1723, the fraternity was described as the "Centre of Union, and the Means of Conciliating True Friendship among Persons that must have remain'd at a Distance." Religious or political disagreements were discouraged amongst members, their "Charges and Regulations" stipulating that "No private piques or quarrels about nations, families, religions, or politics, must be brought within the doors of the lodge [...] we are resolved against political disputes, as contrary to the peace and welfare of the lodge." One of the less used synonyms for cosmopolitanism in the eighteenth century was "freemason."[21] The question, however, of how cosmopolitanism would be "designed" and where its "boundaries" would be drawn plagued Freemasonry for decades.[22]

Despite an official focus on unity and friendship, the Saint John lodge emerged out of a schism in British Freemasonry between the Ancients and the Moderns. In the mid-eighteenth century, Irish working-class Masons precipitated this rupture when they complained of being denied admission to the London lodges because of their unfamiliarity with ritual changes made by the London grand lodge to "keep out imposters." Subsequently a group, spearheaded by this Irish faction, met to organize their own grand lodge in 1751 – the *Most Ancient and Honourable Society of Free and Accepted Masons according to the Old Institutions* – as a rival to the original grand lodge. They called themselves Ancients and their rivals Moderns, because as members of the lower and middling strata, they claimed to embody traditional or "ancient" notions of "fraternal equality." Laurence Dermott, an Irish journeyman painter and later wine merchant, who had been a member of a Dublin lodge, became Grand Secretary, and urged his fellows, in a new publication entitled *Ahiman Rezon*, to "treat his inferiors as he would have his superiors deal with him, wisely considering that the original of mankind is the same."[23]

The Ancients were effective in using the British Atlantic world to expand their fraternal network. As Harland-Jacobs has noted, "Only recently have historians begun to realize the significance of the Ancients in transforming Freemasonry in the British Isles" as well as their role in "spreading Freemasonry abroad."[24] Their organizational structure was more adaptable than that of the Moderns, permitting the formation of many new locals. Immigrants to Britain's American colonies carried Ancient warrants with them, as well as the desire to create an imperial Freemasonic network. The Ancient order also spread via ambulatory British military lodges, the "most effective mechanism for the globalization of the Masonic network during the eighteenth century."[25] Moreover, Ancients established regional grand lodges to act as intermediaries between local and grand lodges. Ancient Masonic expansion into the colonies was also enabled by recruiting from a larger pool than the Moderns – welcoming the lower orders and middling sort – whereas the Moderns tended to recruit amongst elites. In America, artisans and shopkeepers gravitated to Ancient lodges to "negotiate social position, adjust to dislocation, and even further their political causes."[26]

The American Revolution had contradictory impacts on Freemasonry. On the one hand, it further empowered the middling sort who were already drawn to Freemasonic lodges. People in this stratum took advantage of the American Revolution to push themselves forward and attain more power within their communities.[27] The war, however, also disrupted meetings and divided lodges. These schisms reflected the cosmopolitanism and elasticity of eighteenth-century Freemasonry, which accommodated men of various political stripes. In the end, Ancients survived the uncertainties of war "stronger than ever before," due in part to the decline of the Moderns, the ability of the fraternal brothers to align themselves with revolution and republicanism, and the migration of military lodges and Loyalist civilians into exile, which expanded the range of the Ancients even further.[28] Approximately 35,000 Loyalists and disbanded soldiers arrived in Nova Scotia in the 1780s, many of whom were Freemasons. However, new arrivals in Nova Scotia found the status of Freemasonry uncertain.

With its founding in 1749 as the new capital of Nova Scotia and the Northeast base of the British Navy in North America, Halifax quickly became a "hub of military Masonry."[29] Civilian Freemasons established their first lodge in Halifax in 1750, with Governor Edward Cornwallis as the first Worshipful Master. By the mid-1750s, Masons in Halifax and Annapolis Royal (formerly a French settlement and then the capital of Nova Scotia until the founding of Halifax), applied for warrants from the new Ancient Grand Lodge in London. Petitioners received a warrant in 1757 to establish a provincial grand lodge in Nova Scotia, the first such lodge under the Ancients to be established in the British Empire.

Nova Scotia Freemasonry suffered from many challenges in the ensuing period, however, including the deaths of two Masonic leaders in 1760: Erasmus James Philipps (Annapolis Royal politician and Masonic grand master) and Charles Lawrence (Governor of Nova Scotia). Confusion also emanated from the granting of new warrants and numbers by the Ancients in the late 1760s, rivalry between the Ancients and Moderns in Halifax, and the death of acting governor and Nova Scotia Provincial Grand Master Jonathan Belcher in 1776. These developments left the colony without a grand lodge or a grand master, for the 1757 warrant had become dormant. The arrival of large numbers of Loyalists in the 1780s motivated the brethren of three Halifax lodges – St. Andrew's, St. John's, and Union – to pass a resolution in 1781 to meet in Quarterly Communication and revive the movement for a new provincial grand lodge. After three years of petitioning, the warrant finally arrived on 24 August 1784, precipitating the formation of the Ancient Provincial Grand Lodge of Nova Scotia. Thus, the Loyalists not only transformed the colony demographically and spurred the formation of the colony of New Brunswick in 1784, but also expedited the formation of the provincial grand lodge and over 50 new lodges by 1829. As *The History of Freemasonry in Nova Scotia* notes regarding the new arrivals: "Where there were lodges [...] they joined them. In new areas, they founded them. With this new blood, the lodges of the jurisdiction took on new energy and enthusiasm."[30] The Nova Scotia Grand Lodge exercised jurisdiction over the lodges in New Brunswick until the formation of the Grand Lodge of New Brunswick in 1867.[31]

The first Freemasonic lodge formed in the new colony of New Brunswick was Hiram Lodge No. 17 in Saint John, a settlement located at the mouth of the St. John River (For location of Saint John, see Figure 1). Loyalist barrister Elias Hardy applied to the lodges meeting in Quarterly Communication in Halifax on 6 March 1784 for permission to organize a lodge in Saint John. It granted a dispensation, and on 1 September 1784, Hiram Lodge No. 17 formally opened. One of the first acts of the lodge was to apply directly to the Grand Lodge of England for a warrant. They entrusted their application to Captain Peter McPherson, who was traveling to London, but unfortunately he disappeared and they never heard from him again. By this time the Grand Lodge of Nova Scotia was emerging, so in May 1786 they applied for a warrant from the provincial lodge, which they received on 6 December 1786.[32]

Hiram Lodge was formed largely by Loyalist refugees who had traveled in six fleets from New York City, the "centre of Masonic loyalism" during the revolution and the main departure point for the naval fleets transporting Loyalist refugees to the Maritime region.[33] Many members of Hiram Lodge had been Freemasons in the American colonies. Five Hiram Lodge members had previously belonged to one of the most militantly loyalist lodges in the Thirteen Colonies: Lodge No. 169.[34] Originally formed in Boston, Ancient Lodge No. 169 received its warrant in 1771. When Loyalists evacuated Boston in 1776, they accompanied General Howe's troops to Halifax, carrying the lodge's warrant with them. Two or three years later, the lodge was moved to New York City, where a number of lodge members formed the nucleus of a Provincial Grand Lodge.[35] Furthermore, two Hiram Lodge Masons belonged to St. George's No. 2 in New York City, and 15 had been members of New York Lodge No. 210.[36] This New York lodge followed a similar trajectory to that of Hiram Lodge No. 17, becoming so divided that it was eventually dissolved and some of the members received a new warrant under the title of Jerusalem Lodge No. 4. However, the climate of the new lodge was no better, as some members were expelled, as were members of Hiram Lodge a few years later. The New York Grand Lodge attempted to heal the rift between members, but it appears that the Jerusalem Lodge was beyond help: on 4 March 1794, it was formally dissolved and the property divided between two parties designated as Trinity and Phoenix.[37] Perhaps the former members of No. 210 who emigrated to Saint John brought a legacy of Freemasonic dissension with them.

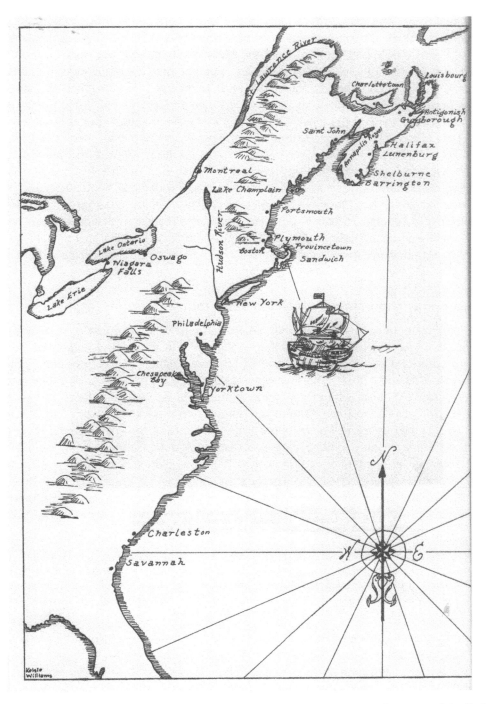

Figure 1. A map of the Eastern Seaboard showing the location of Saint John. Used courtesy of the Shelburne County Museum.

A few Saint John Masons had roots in the larger fraternal Atlantic. A couple of the original members of Hiram Lodge had been members of Scottish lodges: merchant David Prentice from Bathgate Scotland (the lodge number/name was not recorded) and merchant James Cuthbirt, who had been a member of Montrose Lodge in Scotland. Members William Campbell, Captain Peter McPherson and Sergeant John Paul had also been born in Scotland, while Elias Hardy hailed from Surrey, England.[38] Ambulatory military lodges were also operational in Saint John in the same time period as Hiram Lodge. The New Brunswick *Royal Gazette* reports that the brethren of the 54th Regimental Lodge of Free and Accepted Masons assembled on 26 December 1786 to hear a sermon by Rector George Bissett on "The Pleasures and Advantages of Brotherly Unity." Moreover, a letter from Hiram Lodge to the Grand Secretary in Halifax dated 24 September 1788 complained that Lodge No. 230 of the First Battalion of Royal Artillery, stationed at Fort Howe, attempted to initiate a civilian, which went against the regulation that "no military lodge shall make a citizen a mason."[39] Regardless of the complaint, it is clear that military lodges also brought masonic knowledge and experience to settlements such as Saint John.

Freemasons and political conflict in Saint John

Shortly after the first Loyalists arrived in Saint John in 1783, a number of them became involved in partisan politics. According to Bell, of the 74 brothers admitted during Hiram Lodge's 12-year existence, at least 35 were "identifiably in opposition politics between 1783 and 1786."[40] This involvement runs counter to the spirit of the injunction in Anderson's 1723 constitution that a "Mason is a peaceable Subject to the Civil Powers, wherever he resides or works, and is never to be concern'd in Plots and Conspiracies against the Peace and Welfare of the Nation."[41] Similarly, the *Ahiman Rezon* notes that "In the State, a mason is to behave as a peaceable and dutiful subject, conforming cheerfully to the government under which he lives."[42] So why did the Freemasons in Saint John feel it was appropriate to foment political unrest? One must remember that these Freemasons were acting within the environment of Enlightenment cosmopolitanism, which accepted the legitimacy of radical politics. This tolerance was articulated in an "escape clause" in the 1723 constitution:

> if a Brother should be a Rebel against the State he is not to be countenanced in his Rebellion, however he may be pitied as any unhappy Man; and, if convicted of no other Crime though the Loyal Brotherhood must and ought to disown his Rebellion, and give no Umbrage or Ground of political Jealousy to the Government for the time being, they cannot expel him from the Lodge, and his Relation to it remains indefeasible.[43]

This proviso suggests that a Freemason in the eighteenth century could engage in politics up to opposing the state in "open rebellion" without being expelled.[44]

Some of the Saint John Masons may have been politicized while resident in New York City. Elias Hardy, who had been a member of No. 169 and would eventually petition for the formation of Hiram Lodge in Saint John, was one of four scribes chosen by his peers at Roubalet's Tavern in New York to pen a "savagely sarcastic counter-petition" to the "petition of fifty-five." Three other Loyalists, who would become embroiled in the political unrest in New Brunswick, were Tertullus Dickinson, Henry Law, and Samuel Hake, the latter of whom would also become a member of Hiram Lodge.[45] The petition of fifty-five was submitted by 55 prominent Loyalists to British Commander-in-Chief Guy Carleton for assistance in procuring grants of 5,000 acres each in Nova Scotia, which then still included the territory that became New Brunswick. It exemplifying the same logic as the Loyalist Claims Commission would later use – that those who lost the most deserved the most in compensation – these Loyalist gentry argued that their sacrifices for the Crown required significant grants to restore their rightful status, notwithstanding the fact that few if any had sacrificed such extensive estates. They proposed establishing a landed aristocracy in the soon-to-be colony in New Brunswick, in order to create a Loyalist experiment that would be the "envy of the American states." When word of their petition circulated, especially among those awaiting evacuation to Nova Scotia, 628 Loyalists signed the counter-petition. They worried that the land grab in Nova Scotia envisioned by the 55 would mean that others would receive poor land or none at all, reducing them to the status of tenants on the lands of the wealthy. In Saint John and elsewhere, the "affair of the Fifty-Five lived on for years as a mobilizing symbol of what many claimed was a conspiracy to reduce rank Loyalists to the status of landless 'slaves.'"[46]

Loyalists began arriving in Saint John in 1783 with fully articulated complaints about how poorly they had been treated during the revolution, not just by the Patriots, but also by the British government at the treaty table. Loyalists agonized during the long wait from Cornwallis's surrender in Yorktown in October 1781 to September 1783 for the peace treaty: it took one year to negotiate the Preliminary Peace Treaty and then another year before the Treaty of Paris was finalized in 1783. Loyalist Elizabeth Johnson ruminated: "The war never occasioned half the distress, which the peace has done to the unfortunate Loyalists, no other provisions made than just recommending them to the clemency of Congress, which is in fact casting them off altogether." She was referring to Article V of the Preliminary Peace Treaty, which states that "Congress shall earnestly recommend it to the legislatures of the respective states to provide for the restitution of all estates, rights and properties, which have been belonging to real British subjects." This reliance on Congress's recommendation to the states to restore Loyalists' rights and properties had no teeth, and Loyalists would attain little in the way of restitution from the Americans. Moreover, as exiles, settlers quickly became dissatisfied with the extent of the "royal bounty" (provisions and relief supplied by the British government), the quality, location and acreage of their land grants, and how local authorities distributed lots and supplies.[47]

Part of the Freemasons' discontent may also be attributed to their socio-economic profile. Although Loyalist mythology has persisted in painting the new arrivals as the crème de la crème of the American colonies, social historians since the mid-twentieth century have effectively illustrated that the Loyalists were a diverse lot, ethnically, racially, culturally, and economically.[48] Elsewhere I have argued that many of the Loyalists who arrived at the edge of empire were modest migrants from American towns who had expectations of social mobility and wished to establish for themselves a sense of "middling gentility."[49] These social climbers emerged from the same artisanal and middling stratum as the Americans who fought for more power in their communities before, during, and after the revolution. The profile of the Freemasons who settled in Saint John reflects this Loyalist demographic. Of the first 41 men who joined Hiram Lodge between 1784 and 1786, 60 percent were in skilled and middling occupations. Although 10 members identified as merchants, they were undoubtedly modest shopkeepers. Only four members identified as gentlemen.[50] Many Freemasons lived in Lower Cove, a commercial neighborhood of Saint John along the waterfront, inhabited by shopkeepers, artisans, and seafarers, who had been denied commercial lots in the Upper Cove. Hiram Lodge met in Lower Cove, initially in the upper storey of Brother John Kirk's tavern on the north side of Britain Street, and then later at Brother Charles McPherson's Coffee House.[51] Upper Cove, situated on higher ground near Fort Howe, was comprised of professionals, officeholders, and other gentle folk. As Bell has noted, the "Lower Cove leaders were Freemasons; Upper Cove leaders were not."[52]

In this emotionally and politically charged environment, the first governor of New Brunswick, Thomas Carleton (brother of Commander-in-Chief Guy Carleton), attempted to manipulate the outcome of the first provincial election in New Brunswick in 1785. Upon being welcomed to New Brunswick in 1784, Carleton attempted to bring the genteel dream of the 55 to fruition. After establishing a "neo feudal oligarchy" comprised of officers and landowning Loyalists, he set about laying the foundations of a government and society that elite Loyalist Edward Winslow hoped would be the "most Gentlemanlike one on Earth." Carleton wrote to his superiors in London: "I think on all accounts it will be best that the American Spirit of innovation should not be nursed among the Loyal refugees." He was afraid of creating the same sort of fractious assembly dominated by New Englanders in Nova Scotia. Whitehall authorized Carleton to rule as long as he could without an elected assembly. But "[s]ooner or later, he would actually have to summon one." In October 1785, he finally issued the writs for an election.[53]

In the eighteenth-century British Atlantic World, governments typically awarded the franchise to males who met certain property qualifications. But because Loyalist settlers had arrived barely a year earlier and many still had land claims pending, Carleton extended the franchise to "all Males of full age who have been Inhabitants of the Province for not less than three months." He hoped this would ease the angst amongst the settlers, especially those with the "violent party spirit" in Saint John. The subsequent election, however, was marked by violence between Lower Covers and Upper Covers, including resident Freemasons. On 9 November 1785, after the poll had been moved to the Mallard House tavern, headquarters of the government candidates in Upper Cove, a crowd assembled at Peter McPherson's Coffee House in Lower Cove, the meeting place for Hiram Lodge. Elias Hardy was present and reported later that the men assembled were "very drunk." They descended on Mallard House, where approximately 30 government supporters were drinking. Sheriff William Oliver was in an awkward spot. He was a government supporter but had to keep the peace. He was also the only identifiable government supporter to be admitted as a Mason. An Upper Cover reportedly urged Hardy to appeal to the crowd, but he replied: "You are daring us to come on." A melee ensued, similar to the election riots that erupted throughout the British Atlantic World in the eighteenth century.[54]

Government corruption further enraged Saint John Loyalists, as the ruling oligarchy proposed allowing soldiers in the garrison to vote in an effort to drum up supporters for the government slate. Nonetheless, the Lower Covers won the day: the non-government slate won by a margin of more than 10 percent. Carleton's strategy of allowing a broader cross section of settlers to vote had backfired. It is revealing that four of the six challengers on the non-government slate were Freemasons, while none of the government candidates were members.[55]

Faced with electoral defeat, the colonial administration challenged the election results, held a recount, and disallowed almost 200 votes, enough to allow them to install only government candidates. After the *Saint John Gazette* ran a protest letter, the government charged printer and Freemason John Ryan and his colleague William Lewis with seditious libel and shut down the newspaper. Petitions against the election results circulated widely throughout the province, calling on the British monarch to dissolve the assembly and call a new election. Bell suggests that approximately 70 percent of the Freemasons in Saint John signed these petitions.[56] But Governor Carleton would not admit defeat. He responded, instead, by introducing legislation that essentially made petitioning illegal. When four citizens appealed to the legislature, they were arrested and sent to trial with detained election rioters and the newspaper printers, all of whom were "severally convicted and punished."[57]

Some of the detained men were Freemasons, including printer John Ryan. On 1 May 1786, on the eve of their trial, Hiram Lodge wrote to the Grand Lodge of Nova Scotia, noting that another brother, Joseph Montgomery, was confined under a military guard for nearly three months with three other citizens

> only for presenting a petition for redress of Grievances at the late Election, which was resented so highly that the Writ of Habeas Corpus has been refused. Tomorrow their Trial comes on, the Event of which will determine whether we are to have a British Constitution or not.[58]

Just as American Patriots had "invoked the British constitution in pleading for just representation," Saint John discontents, including the Freemasons who wrote to their provincial lodge, "protested recent events as a violation of their rights as British subjects."[59] After absorbing the results of the election, "Americanus" published a plea to his "distressed Countrymen" in the *Saint John Gazette*:

> Be firm in the protection of the Birth Right handed down to you, and supported by our happy Constitution [...] upon no account [...] lose sight of what you are. In Fine, let the world know, as you know, the Rights you are jealous of [as] Descendants of Britons.[60]

The largest opposition petition, signed by nearly one-third of the electors of Saint John including many Freemasons, detailed how they were not being treated properly as British subjects:

> we have publicly seen British Subjects confined in Irons [...] The Military introduced & unnecessarily & unlawfully patrolling the streets, during an Election [...] The freedom of Election violated [...] in the most public manner [...] We must positively affirm these Proceedings to be unjust, Injurious to the Freedom of Election, manifest Violations of the Rights of the People & Subversive of the first Privileges of the British Constitution.[61]

In what they envisioned to be the ultimate insult to Lower Cove Loyalists and Freemasons, Governor Carleton and his entourage labeled several of them as "rebels."[62] Moreover, a commentator referred to them in the *Royal Gazette* on 24 January 1786 as members of a "republican craft," whose principles "correspon[d] exactly with those of the rebels [...] they brought with them all that restless turbulence and leveling disposition, that characterized the enemies of loyalty." Bell has suggested that this government supporter intended the denunciation to apply not only to the election protestors, but to Freemasons more specifically. Is the allusion to "republican craft" also a backhanded swipe at the Masonic craft? Might the correspondent's critique of the inhabitants' "leveling disposition" also be an allusion to the Mason's level and to the Ancients' commitment to the involvement of the lower orders?[63] Regardless of the intent, there was a growing suspicion of Freemasonry in the British Atlantic World. Since the 1730s, some Roman Catholics and evangelical Protestants portrayed Freemasonry as a "rival, parallel or false religion." Conservatives also suspected "Whig affiliations" amongst British Freemasons and accused them of sporting a "form of republicanism" and participating in revolutionary conspiracies.[64]

A transition in Freemasonry

Opposition candidates in Hiram Lodge No. 17 survived this political unrest, but peace was to last for only 12 more years, as the lodge became rent by dissension among members and between the local lodge and the Nova Scotia Grand Lodge. The latter conflict would eventually force Hiram Lodge to surrender its warrant in 1796. These disputes, like the involvement of Freemasons in the United Irish Rebellion in 1798, are a further example of what Harland-Jacobs calls a "hinge event," an occurrence that both reveals the Freemasons' cosmopolitan legacy but also anticipates what the order would become in the nineteenth century: a loyal defender of the British state.[65]

The unrest in Hiram Lodge began with a falling out between two members: Samuel Hake, Commissary of Stores of War and Provisions at Fort Howe, and John Sinnot, a clerk in his office. Both men supported the earlier electoral unrest. Hake had served with Elias Hardy and two other Loyalists on the New York committee that prepared the counter-petition against the 55. He also wrote a political pamphlet accusing the 55 of planning to turn their fellow Loyalists into "tenants," much like the "Patroons" of New Netherland who set up feudal manors along the Hudson River. When Hake arrived in Saint John in 1786, 449 signed a welcome address as a "gesture of renewed defiance against those who just triumphed in the house [Carleton's government candidates]."[66] Sinnot, born and educated in Ireland, had migrated to Halifax and then to Saint John around the same time as the arrival of the Loyalists. He initially opened a school, but then took a job as a clerk in the Commissariat. He also supported the Lower Covers, having signed opposition petitions. Although Hake was older and seemingly more involved in political unrest, they seem to have been mutually aligned in the past, which makes their altercation that much more ironic and contentious. The members of Hiram Lodge had also respected Sinnot enough to choose him as secretary and then as master for two terms. According to Bunting, Sinnot was also the first candidate initiated into Freemasonry in New Brunswick and attained a Royal Arch degree in 1805.[67]

Problems between Hake and Sinnot began when a cooper in Hake's department reported that Hake had misappropriated stores and provisions. A Court of Enquiry subpoenaed Sinnot to provide evidence. Hake attempted to persuade Hiram Lodge to intervene and dissuade Sinnot from testifying. Sinnot agonized over testifying against his fellow Freemason, but decided that he had little choice because he could lose his job, be court-marshaled, or both for refusing to testify. After hearing the case, the Court of Enquiry found Hake guilty of fraud (making a false return) and embezzlement and dismissed him from the service. Significantly, this case was not the first time that Samuel Hake had been accused of duplicitous behavior. Bell describes the former New York merchant as a "brutal, scheming liar who made trouble everywhere he went." He was ejected from a group of Loyalists planning resettlement in the Bahamas, and later the Loyalist Claims Commission dismissed his petition due to his use of fraudulent information.[68]

The paper trail for this controversy begins on 24 July 1793, when Sinnot penned a letter to the Nova Scotia Grand Lodge informing them that he had been suspended as master. A few days later, on 1 August 1793, two past masters informed the Grand Secretary, John Selby, that they had been directed by Hiram Lodge to

> acquaint the Right Worshipful The Grand Lodge of the suspension of our Brother John Sinnot from the duties of his office as master and that he is excluded from the Benefits of Communication with any of the members of this or those of our Sister Lodges in this province – for the most vile and unprecedented violation of every masonic duty, which has not only been already fatal in its Consequences to an aged, infirm and deserving brother, but also tends in every possible degree to become more to the Craft in general.[69]

Sinnot followed with a memorial defending his actions, including a supporting testimonial from Captain Francis M. Dixon, President of the Military Court of Enquiry and Past Grand Master of the provincial lodge at Minorca.[70] The Grand Lodge subsequently authorized Past Deputy Master William Campbell to form a Grand Lodge Pro Tempore to investigate. Campbell had difficulties assembling a Grand Lodge Pro Tempore, so instead established an investigative committee consisting of two members nominated by Sinnot and two by Hiram Lodge. The committee met four times, the sessions lasting until midnight on a couple of occasions.[71]

Upon hearing the committee's report, the Nova Scotia Grand Lodge determined at their meeting on 8 August 1794 that there was "not sufficient grounds for passing so severe a Censure on said Brother." Although Sinnot's actions were "in some degree reprehensible," they thought that being "so long deprived of the benefits of Masonry to be a sufficient Atonement for the same." They resolved that Sinnot be "restored to the Rights and Privileges of Masonry."[72] The Saint John lodge, however, objected to this decision, noting that it was "not Consistent with the most distant Idea of Masonic Faith and Duty [to] admit the said late Bro: John Sinnitt [sic] to the Rights and privileges adverted to in the aforesaid Grand resolve." Moreover, they threatened that "If the Right Worshipful the Grand Lodge turn a Deaf ear" to the "Rights of a unanimous Body of Regular Ancient working Masons, They with all due submission to their Wisdom will resign the Warrant and pay all dues thereto."[73]

This entreaty failed to impress the provincial grand lodge, and on 4 March 1795, adopted the following resolution:

> That, unless No. 17 make ample apology to this Right W[orshipful]. Body, as may be to the entire satisfaction thereof, this warrant to continue no longer in force, and the same to be reported to all Grand Lodges who are in Communication with us.[74]

A committee from Hiram Lodge responded to the charge in a letter dated 27 July 1795, admitting that they had been surprised that the Grand Lodge would pass "so SEVERE a decision against the body." The committee members also noted that Hiram Lodge had ceased operations and had deposited the warrant in their Ark.[75]

Again, the Grand Lodge was not impressed by the behavior of their Masonic brothers in Saint John. At their meeting on 2 September 1795, they resolved that the committee appointed to transmit the resolutions of the Grand Lodge to Hiram Lodge No. 17 be authorized to inform them that the apology contained in their letter was "by no means satisfactory" and to point out the "most exceptional parts of their conduct."[76] The Grand Secretary addressed the members of Hiram Lodge, in a letter dated 18 January 1796, that

> instead of an ample apology which they expected to receive from Hiram Lodge for the impropriety of their former conduct, they had in further contempt proceeded to put into execution the threat mentioned in their letter [...] an act highly unconstitutional and in open violation of the laws of masonry; we mean the ceasing to work, and depositing their warrant etc., in the ark, without the sanction and approbation of the grand lodge.

Grand Secretary Selby "earnestly recommended to the lodge to meet and revoke their objectionable acts and words, and by an ample apology save themselves from the inevitable consequences." Just as a "sincere and penitent apology" was integral to the reintegration of Loyalists into post-revolutionary South Carolina society, so too was a sufficient apology deemed as necessary for the Grand Lodge to move on from this controversy.[77]

But the members of Hiram Lodge refused to budge. On 7 September 1796, the provincial grand lodge unanimously passed the following order: that the warrant of Hiram Lodge, No. 17 be

> forthwith recalled, and that the members thereof, agreeably to the last return transmitted, be expelled for apostasy, and the same be reported to all the private lodges in the jurisdiction of Nova Scotia, and likewise to all the grand lodges of Ancient York Masons throughout the known world.

The Grand Lodge then addressed a communication to all Masters, Wardens, and Members of the Most Ancient and Honorable Fraternity of Free and Accepted Masons stating that the 22 members noted in the last return of the lodge (who were listed by name) were

> all and every one of them expelled for apostasy, and in grand lodge, held the 7th day of September, 1796, unanimously declared unworthy of admittance into any regular lodge, or holding any masonic conversation with any of the free and accepted fraternity.[78] (For copy of communication, see Figure 2)

What was the substance of this dispute? In part, this was a test case over the relative weight to apply to different parts of the Masonic code when elements were in conflict. Although debating the most significant tenets of Freemasonry was not unique to this time and place, the diffusion of Freemasonry throughout the British Atlantic World to localities such as Saint John provides a good opportunity to assess the transmission of fraternal knowledge and values. Hake's most serious charge against Sinnot was "divulging his secrets."[79] This charge was serious, for remaining "constant in amity and faithful in secrecy," according to the *Ahiman Rezon*, was amongst the most significant qualities of a Freemason:

> One of the principal parts that makes a man to be deemed wise, is his intelligent strength and ability to cover and conceal such honest Secrets as are committed to him, or his own serious affairs [...] God himself is well pleased with secrecy.[80]

This passage is significant for it is extracted from a copy of the *Ahiman Rezon* published in Halifax in 1786 under direction of the Nova Scotia Grand Lodge, and thus was probably read by many of the Freemasons involved in this dispute. Perhaps it is not surprising, therefore, that Hiram Lodge ultimately endorsed Hale's position. A Standing Committee

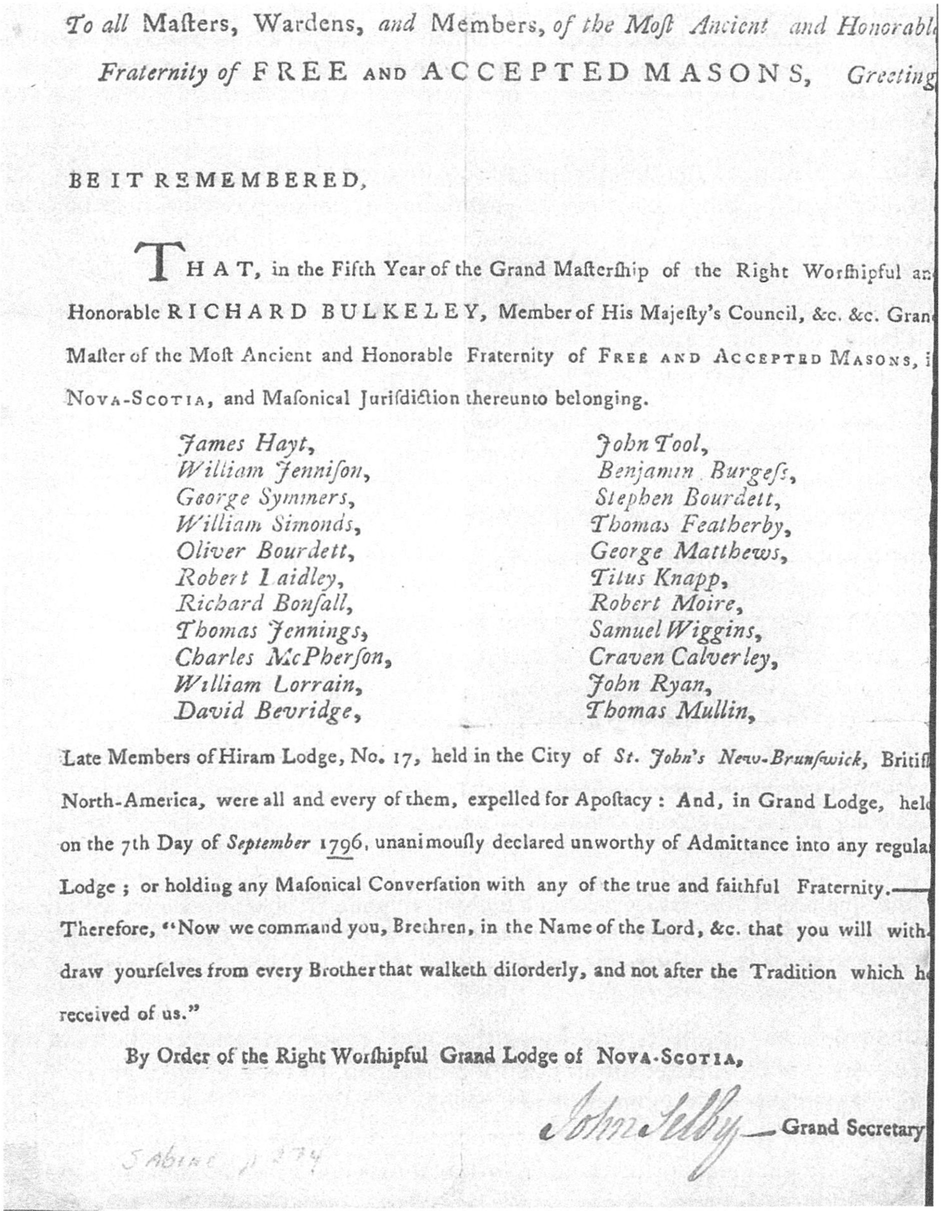

To all Masters, Wardens, *and* Members, *of the Most Ancient and Honorabl*

Fraternity of FREE AND ACCEPTED MASONS, *Greeting*

BE IT REMEMBERED,

THAT, in the Fifth Year of the Grand Mastership of the Right Worshipful an Honorable RICHARD BULKELEY, Member of His Majesty's Council, &c. &c. Gran Master of the Most Ancient and Honorable Fraternity of FREE AND ACCEPTED MASONS, i NOVA-SCOTIA, and Masonical Jurisdiction thereunto belonging.

James Hayt,	*John Tool,*
William Jennison,	*Benjamin Burgess,*
George Symmers,	*Stephen Bourdett,*
William Simonds,	*Thomas Featherby,*
Oliver Bourdett,	*George Matthews,*
Robert Laidley,	*Titus Knapp,*
Richard Bonsall,	*Robert Moire,*
Thomas Jennings,	*Samuel Wiggins,*
Charles McPherson,	*Craven Calverley,*
William Lorrain,	*John Ryan,*
David Bevridge,	*Thomas Mullin,*

Late Members of Hiram Lodge, No. 17, held in the City of *St. John's New-Brunswick,* Britis North-America, were all and every of them, expelled for Apostacy : And, in Grand Lodge, hel on the 7th Day of *September* 1796, unanimously declared unworthy of Admittance into any regula Lodge ; or holding any Masonical Conversation with any of the true and faithful Fraternity.— Therefore, "Now we command you, Brethren, in the Name of the Lord, &c. that you will with- draw yourselves from every Brother that walketh disorderly, and not after the Tradition which he received of us."

By Order of the Right Worshipful Grand Lodge of NOVA-SCOTIA,

*John Selby*___ Grand Secretary

Figure 2. Freemasonic Pamphlet. Used courtesy of Library and Archives Canada/To all masters, wardens, and members, … /AMICUS 7587729/e010765876.

of Hiram Lodge members was formed to look into the dispute between Hake and Sinnot, and they reputedly used "every Brotherly and reasonable argument" to reconcile the latter to Mr. Hake, but they found him "obstinate." Hiram Lodge also held up the seventh charge of the *Ahiman Rezon*:

> If a brother do you an injury, apply first to your own or his lodge, and if you are not satisfied, you may appeal to the Grand Lodge; but you must never take a legal course, till the cause cannot otherways be decided; for if the affair is only between masons, and about masonry, law suits ought to be prevented by the good advice of prudent brethren, who are the best referees of differences.[81]

Indeed, according to Bunting, Hiram Lodge members viewed the support of fellow members as a "binding obligation."[82] Freemasons were supposed to help each other and show benevolence – to be "humane of nature" – particularly toward elderly members like Hake. With ties stretching back to New York City, Hiram Lodge's Loyalist members probably respected Hake for his former actions as a political dissident on their behalf and thus supported him in this controversy.

Sinnot, on the other hand, emphasized the Masonic quality of honesty, arguing that

> Masonry requires our relieving the necessities & ministering to the wants of a Br[other] – but I confess I never thought so lightly of its institution, as to suppose that this Charity for a Br[other] required us to sacrifice the principles of truth and honesty to assist him in defending himself from the effects of his own unwarrantable acts.[83]

In identifying the essence of Freemasonry as the "Eternal & immutable Pillars of Religion, Truth, Justice & honesty," Sinnot believed that Freemasonry was, "next to the Christian Religion, the most perfect the World ever saw, a blessing to Mankind founded upon Religion, good Conscience and the soundest Policy." He could not comprehend how the lodge could "screen so guilty a Brother from Justice, as well as that a Brother could be capable of such Crimes." Indeed, the Grand Lodge had informed Hiram Lodge on 10 November 1788, over another matter, that no Freemasonic officer "would ever countenance any lodge in admitting a candidate who has been rejected by another Lodge for any capital case."[84] The *Ahiman Rezon* dictated that litigation between brothers should be avoided if possible, but if

> either impracticable or unsuccessful, and the affair must be brought into the courts of law or equity, yet still you must avoid all wrath, malice, and rancor in carrying on the suit; nor saying or doing anything that may hinder the continuance or renewal of brotherly love and friendship.[85]

In other words, law and order, truth and justice, and Christian values were the most significant elements of Freemasonry in this transitional period. This is the beginning of the transition to Freemasonry as an embodiment of loyalist values.

This test case also permitted lodge members to debate the parameters of acceptable behavior at their meetings. Grounded in the tenets of the Enlightenment and polite society, eighteenth-century lodges were "places that sought to instill decorum. Modifying the behavior of men helped them to internalize discipline and manners," which were required to establish a "new more commonplace sense of an inner self that took pride" in these qualities.[86] According to the Halifax version of the *Ahiman Rezon,* Freemasons "have ever been charged to avoid all manner of slandering and backbiting of true and faithful brethren, or talking disrespectfully of a brother's performance or person, and all malice or unjust resentment." And if others speak badly of a brother, a Mason is to "defend his character as far as is consistent with honour, safety and prudence." If a brother "curse, swear [...] or use any reproachful Language in Derogation of GOD's Name, or Corruption of good Manners, or interrupt any Officer while speaking, he shall be fined at the Discretion of the Master and Majority." Moreover, if a member "come disguised in Liquor" he would be "admonished" the first time, fined the second, and expelled the third time.[87] Despite these regulations, Sinnot contended that Hake had accused him in the lodge meeting "in the most vehement & passionate manner in Language very unbecoming a Mason, [and] charged me with the blackest & foulest Crimes." Sinnot also objected to the inebriated conduct of Brothers Hayt and Bourdett, who came into the lodge room as Hake and Sinnot were ending their altercation:

> with Spirits very much elated & their understandings as appeared to me somewhat clouded with Drinking, without having heard scarcely anything that passed, they came up to me apparently to take me by force out of the Room & Brother Hayt addressed himself to the Chair & said in a very vehement manner 'Say but the word Worshipful we will execute your Commands, we will take the Villain out, if he has Brass enough to stay, let us strike his name off the Books and Report him to the Grand Lodge, & have him forever deprived of the Benefits of Masonry' or words of similar heat & violence.[88]

The members subsequently decided to suspend Sinnot from the lodge and from his office as master. They considered the court testimony against Hake a betrayal of trust: they ended their letter of 18 February 1796 to the Grand Lodge, with the phrase "Since a Traitor was found among the Apostles."[89]

Perhaps the most significant source of tension in this incident was over the parameters of authority. Antagonism between Hake and Sinnot may be partially attributed to a clash between competing hierarchies in the lodge room versus the workplace. In the workplace, Sinnot, as a clerk, challenged Hake's authority as his superior when he agreed to testify, while at the lodge, Hake challenged Sinnot's suitability as lodge master when he pressed the lodge to investigate Sinnot's conduct. Sinnot viewed the subsequent behavior of lodge members as an assault, not only on his experience and reputation as a Mason, but on the hierarchy of the lodge.

Sinnot objected to his brethren holding a private meeting without his knowledge to discuss the case. This contravened the sixth charge: "You must not hold private committees, or separate conversation, without leave from the master."[90] Sinnot also refused to step down as master and chair of the proceedings, only acquiescing after members threatened to take a vote on the matter. Masons were expected to provide allegiance to elected lodge officers, beginning with the master, including respecting the master as chair of the meetings, which the members of Hiram Lodge clearly did not do.[91] In that sense they were contravening Masonic constitutionalism, which was predicated on "government by consent within the context of subordination to 'legitimate' authority."[92] Ironically, the other members of Hiram Lodge charged that Sinnot, by being obstinate and often repeating "unjustifiable threats" to Hake, was not being "grave in [providing] council and advice" as a master should.[93]

The provincial grand lodge argued that the Saint John Freemasons did not have the authority to suspend Sinnot, that the case should have been brought before them first, and that only the Grand Lodge could have made that determination. From earliest records of the London grand lodge, Freemasonic officers had taken steps to ensure that "its own authority was singularly upheld." All lodges were expected to respect Masonic hierarchy: to "give allegiance to the Grand Lodge of London, and hence to its Grand Master," to the officers of the provincial lodges, and then to the "elected officers of each lodge."[94] The Grand Lodge of Nova Scotia was supported by Charge No. XVIII of the Halifax version of the *Ahiman Rezon* which stipulated that:

> if a Dispute [...] should happen between Brethren out of the Lodge, which they cannot decide between themselves, such Dispute, Complaint or Controversy, shall be laid before this Lodge and here decided, if possible. But if the Disputants will not then agree, in order to prevent vexatious Lawsuits, &c, the Master shall order the Secretary to take proper Minutes of Such Complaint, Dispute, or Controversy, and lay the same before the next Grand Lodge, where such Disputants are to attend [...] and agree as the Grand Lodge shall order.

In cases of non-compliance, the British grand lodges expelled delinquents from enjoying the benefits of Freemasonry throughout the boundaries of its reach in Europe, Asia, Africa, and the Americas.[95]

The parent lodge interpreted the refusal of Hiram Lodge members to abide by the ruling to reinstate Sinnot as an act of insubordination. In demanding an apology, the Halifax Grand Lodge contended that Hiram Lodge was in "open violation of the Laws of Masonry" and "highly derogatory to the honor and dignity of this R.W. Gr. Lodge in particular, and the Craft in general." The Grand Lodge committee delegated to transmit the substance of the parent lodge's feelings to members of Hiram Lodge said "you must be sensible that the Sentiments contained in your Letter, is a direct attack upon their Authority as a Provincial Grand Lodge, and which has been Vested in them by the RW Mother Grand Lodge of England." The committee also informed Hiram Lodge that their queries about the decisions made by the parent lodge were an "attack upon their [the parent lodge's] Probity – as it accuses them of Partiality in their decision [...] They formed their opinion from the Evidence adduced to them, and that alone."[96] Hiram Lodge members responded that they never had

> the Idea of [...] having attacked the Probity or even the Authority of that Right Worshipful Body [...] We do most sincerely RENOUNCE that there ever was intended the most distant Reflection on the Right Worshipful the Grand Lodge either with regard to their probity or their Authority in their decision. We wished only to convey our sentiments in the language of our feelings, which we humbly conceived to have been both our duty as well as conducing to the General Good of Ancient Masonry.[97]

This is clearly a case of contested constitutionalism.[98] Hiram Lodge members and the Grand Lodge had different understandings of Masonic constitutionalism. Saint John Masons were probably accurate in their assessment that the parent body was imputing to them "the ungracious Charge of disaffection, and even a Revolt from their Constituted authority." Hiram members clarified that their actions were also bound by the "Constitutional Laws sent us by the Right Worshipful Grand Lodge for our regulation." They cited the 18th article of the *Ahiman Rezon* that called on "every good Mason" to "prevent any litigious controversies between Brethren if possible." With regard to Sinnot, they did admit to putting "confidence in him" until he "discovered a disposition to betray it."[99] The Nova Scotia Grand Lodge would have been within their rights to respond with a proviso from the 1723 constitution that a convicted brother (or brothers) "must and ought to disown his Rebellion."[100] Perhaps the ruling of the parent body can be viewed as a way to discountenance the rebellious actions of Hiram Lodge, since the members would not do so themselves.

Members of Hiram Lodge who identified as Loyalists also claimed a birthright to the British constitution, which they believed enabled them to dissent from constituted authority if warranted. The escape clause in the 1723 constitution had also allowed them to dissent without the threat of expulsion. Hiram Lodge members were victims of the transition in Freemasonry from an acceptance of cosmopolitanism to a narrower vision that championed the interests of the British state. The decision of the Grand Lodge to defend Sinnot reflected an officialdom that increasingly aligned itself with the state. As they argued, Sinnot had to testify against his brother or he risked losing his job or being court marshaled. In other words, Sinnot and the Grand Lodge risked defying the state. And this they would not condone.

A new era

The transition in British Freemasonry from a cosmopolitan to a loyalist fraternity was instigated in part by the intervention of the British state. A tense atmosphere permeated Britain in the 1790s, due to popular radicalism within the nation, sectarian problems in Ireland, and the French Revolution. Upon entering war against France in 1793, Britain passed repressive measures curtailing personal and associational freedoms: the Suspension of Habeas Corpus in 1794, the Treasonable and Seditious Practices Act in 1795, and the Seditious Assemblies Act in the same year. In the aftermath of rebellion in Ireland in 1798, the British state also passed the Unlawful Societies Act, which banned all societies whose members had "taken unlawful Oaths and Engagements of Fidelity and Secrecy, and Used Secret Signs, and appointed Committees, Secretaries, and other Officers, in a secret manner" for the purposes of undermining British government and society. As one of the largest secret fraternities, the Freemasons were an obvious target. Conspiracy theories abounded, some blaming Masons for instigating the French Revolution. This fear was not entirely manufactured, as Masonic lodges had developed ties with British Jacobins, Wilkites, American Patriots, and the Society of United Irishmen. After a series of meetings between grand masters and Prime Minister Pitt, mediated by support from influential MPs, the government introduced a revised bill that specifically exempted Freemasons from this ban. In return, the fraternity was informed that they would be surveilled: each lodge was to report annually to the local clerk of the peace and provide membership lists and meeting times.[101]

British Freemasons complied. What choice did they have? They even boasted of the "special treatment" they had received from the government. In the longer term, they consciously engaged in a rebranding exercise, which transformed Freemasonry from a cosmopolitan fraternity to a bulwark of the British state. How would they reconcile this shift from cosmopolitanism to loyalism? Their strategy was to posit that loyalty was not by definition "political." This argument, ironically, led to the "overt politicization of the brotherhood."[102] Loyalist Freemasonry reinforced its connection to the state by consolidating authority, adopting royal patrons, engaging in ceremonial performances of British and imperial power, and by bolstering Freemasonry's ties with Christianity, specifically Protestantism.

Masonic officials worked hard over the course of the late eighteenth and early nineteenth centuries to create a unified and patriotic institution. They consolidated authority by facilitating the union of the Ancients and Moderns in 1813, creating the United Grand Lodge of England. British Freemasons also improved and accelerated communication among and about the grand lodges throughout the empire. Indeed, the minutes of the Nova Scotia Grand Lodge indicate that it received frequent circulars from the grand lodges in the British Isles and read them aloud in their meetings.[103] Parent lodges, in this way, urged their members to stay on message. As Harland-Jacobs has noted, Freemasons of the Enlightenment had not "prescribed or proscribed" political affiliation or behavior. But now they were "telling members exactly how they should act vis-a-vis the British state."[104]

How should they act? The Nova Scotia Grand Lodge paved the way toward an explicitly loyalist fraternity. In their 1794 address to Prince Edward, Duke of Kent, when he arrived in Nova Scotia, they pledged their "firm adherence to that excellent form of Government which is the peculiar blessing of a British Subject," and their "unshaken loyalty to His Majesty, and our zealous attachment to every branch of the Royal Family."[105] In 1803 Reverend Thomas Shreve, Grand Chaplain of the Nova Scotia Grand Lodge, preached a sermon at St. Paul's Church in Halifax entitled "Love the Brotherhood; Fear God; Honor the King."[106] Concerned about the upheaval of the French Revolution and the Napoleonic Wars, Shreve linked support for the monarch with Freemasonry's longstanding support for British constitutionalism:

> when the blast of War is again found in our ears [...] when it is thought consistent with the rights of man, to deny the existence of God [...] and to substitute in the stead, a ridiculous equality, totally inconsistent with the present imperfect state of man,

then it is time to honor the king, "who, in union with the Lords and Commons of the nation, forms such a constitution, as with all its excellencies is not to be found in all the world besides."[107]

The accommodation of political cosmopolitanism officially ended in 1815, when the escape clause protecting members who rebelled was "conspicuously absent" in the charges. Instead, the 1815 constitution read as follows: "A Mason is a peaceable subject to the civil powers wherever he resides or works, and is never to be concerned in plots and consequences against the peace and welfare of the nation."[108] Indeed, it is fair to say that Hiram Lodge dissenters who were expelled for apostasy saw the writing on the wall: in the aftermath of their expulsion, almost all of them wrote to the Grand Lodge of Nova Scotia, either explaining or apologizing for their actions, and seeking readmission as Freemasons.[109] Fortunately the provincial lodge provided them with an escape clause of a different sort: on 25 September 1796, the Grand Lodge anticipated that some of the expelled persons "may not have coincided in sentiment with those who proceeded to those rash and unjustifiable measures which has caused this severe sentence," and as it is "hard that the innocent should be punished with the guilty," they were willing "upon application made, and testifying their disapprobation of said conduct, to take off the censure of any brother or brothers who shall require it."[110] The Grand Lodge subsequently received so many petitions from former Hiram Lodge members seeking readmission that it formed a special committee to consider them all.[111] Former Hiram Lodge member Robert Laidley, for example, explained in his 1797 petition that

> I am moved from principles of good faith and do therefore after serious and deliberate considerations think it my indispensable duty hereby to declare that I am heartily sorry, and sincerely repent to have given my signature to a paper, which I was not apprised would cause offense and wrong-doings.

The Nova Scotia Grand Lodge resolved that since he had acknowledged the "great Impropriety of his Conduct" and was "penitent for the Error he had unguarded fallen into," he was restored and permitted to join the Annapolis Royal lodge.[112]

Hiram Lodge was not resuscitated after surrendering its warrant. Instead a new lodge was formed in 1802: the Free and Accepted York Masons Saint John Lodge No 29.[113] This new loyalist lodge was keen to show its royalist credentials. Lodge members mourned the deaths of the Duke of Kent in 1820 and his brother, the Duke of Sussex, in 1843; both were royal patrons and had been instrumental in uniting the Ancients and Moderns.[114] Moreover, the toasts offered up at the celebration of the anniversary of St. John the Evangelist on 27 December 1836 reflect an explicitly loyalist orientation. After toasting their patron saint, the members of Lodge No. 29 drank to the king, who by this time was "grand patron" of the society, to the Duke of Sussex, to "other members of the royal family who are members of the craft," and then to the Queen and the "female branches of the royal family." After toasting the United Grand Lodge of England and the grand lodges in Ireland and Scotland, the celebrants then recognized the clergy, "all workmen at the same temple," suggesting that Freemasons and clergy were united in their desire to promote Christianity.[115] In 1840, the Masons of No. 29 also organized a ball in honor of the nuptials of Queen Victoria and Prince Albert. Dancing ended at midnight when the brethren formed a circle and toasted "The Queen and Prince Albert." A "Queen's cake" was then wheeled into the ballroom, cut up, and distributed. According to Bunting, this was a "mammoth affair supported on a platform on wheels." He asserted that "At that date such an affair was in advance of the usual ceremonials at balls."[116]

Freemasons in Saint John and Halifax also participated in cornerstone rituals, which involved laying cornerstones for a number of prominent institutions. Although the ceremonies themselves began as occasional rituals in Scotland and England, and then became more popular in the United States, the objects of the rituals were symbols of British economic and cultural superiority. Saint John Masons laid the foundations for the Commercial Bank (1837), the Provincial Lunatic Asylum (1847), Saint John's city hall (1878), and the St. Croix Cotton Mills at Milltown (1882). Freemasons from Lodge No 29 were also present at the turning of the sod of the European and North American Railway, and the laying of the first electric telegraph cable across the Atlantic Ocean.[117] Haligonian Freemasons participated in the cornerstone ceremonies for Province House (the governor's residence) in 1811, Dalhousie College (the embryo of Dalhousie University) in 1820, and the Shubenacadie Canal (a canal that linked Halifax Harbour to the Bay of Fundy) in 1826.[118] Provincial and municipal elites attended most of these ceremonies. The laying of the cornerstone of Province House was attended by the Lieutenant Governor, the Chief Justice, and other provincial politicians. The Grand Master noted in his address: "May the Building that shall rise from this foundation perpetuate the loyalty and Liberality of the Province of Nova Scotia."[119] By dedicating these institutions, Freemasons were quite literally participating in the "building of empire."[120]

By the 1820s, Freemasonry was entering a period of decline, particularly in the United States, precipitated by the alleged murder of Mason William Morgan in Batavia New York in 1826 after he promised to expose Masonic secrets. However, as Hannah M. Lane argues, this decline also reflected "broader anxieties" about secret societies and the perceived threat that Freemasonry posed to Protestant churches, particularly in siphoning off potential male attendees. Antimasonry was strong enough to shutter many Masonic lodges in the United States. Even in New Brunswick, all but two Masonic lodges formed before 1830 were shut down, part of the virtual "eclipse of freemasonry in the northeast."[121] Lodge No. 29 was one of the two to survive. Perhaps the appeal of Freemasonry as a loyalist institution was strong enough in Saint John to protect the lodge or at least distract its critics. In any case, Freemasons experienced a revival by mid-century, as they reinvented themselves as a respectable institution by establishing women's auxiliaries, embracing temperance and abolitionism, and attracting a more respectable middle-class clientele by imposing higher fees.[122] In Saint John, Freemasons continued to celebrate the imperial and royal connection by participating in Queen Victoria's Jubilees. Another interesting development after mid-century was the overlapping of imperial and Anglo-American sentiment, as Masons from the neighboring state of Maine participated in the ceremony for the turning of the sod of the European and North American Railway in 1854 and again during the laying of the foundation stone of St. Croix Cotton Mill in June 1881.[123] Although British Freemasonry continued to champion loyalism to the British state, they retained enough of their former elasticity to realize the benefits of borderlands fraternalism.

Notes

1. Harland-Jacobs, *Builders of Empire*, 5, 99–100, 130–131.
2. Harland-Jacobs, "Worlds of Brothers," 10.
3. Armitage, "Three Concepts of Atlantic History," 21. 'Cis' is a Latin prefix which means "on this side [of]": http://www.class.uidaho.edu/luschnig/EWO/24.htm.
4. Jansen, "In Search of Atlantic Sociability," 98.
5. The phrase "prospects and potentials" is borrowed from Ibid., 76.
6. Harland-Jacobs, "'Hands Across the Sea'," 237.
7. Jansen, "In Search of Atlantic Sociability," 80.
8. Eamon, *Imprinting Britain*, 113–138; Lane, "Evangelical Churches and Freemasonry," 60–78.
9. Raible, "'The threat of being Morganized'," 3–25; Klages, "Freemasonic and Orange Order Membership," 192–214.
10. Kenney, *Brought to Light*.
11. Hackett, *The Religion in Which All Men Agree*, 60.
12. Bullock, "'A Pure and Sublime System'," 359–373; Bullock, *Revolutionary Brotherhood*; Bullock, "The Revolutionary Transformation of American Freemasonry," 347–369.
13. Harland-Jacobs, *Builders of Empire*, 116.
14. York, "Freemasons and the American Revolution," 231.
15. Study of Shelburne lodge: Huskins, "'Ancient' Tensions and Local Circumstances," 47–72.
16. Bell, *Loyalist Rebellion in New Brunswick*, 151–152; Bell, "Sedition Among the Loyalists," 163–178; Bell, *Early Loyalist Saint John*; Bell, "The Republican Craft and the Politics of Loyalist Saint John."
17. Milbourne, "Loyalist Masons in the Maritimes," 1955–1995; "History of Freemasonry in Nova Scotia," chapters 1–2; MacDonald, *History of Hiram Lodge No. 17*, 1, Library and Museum of Freemasonry (hereafter cited as LMF).
18. Hackett, *The Religion On Which All Men Agree*, 29.
19. Jacob, *The Origins of Freemasonry*, 87, 99.
20. Hackett, *The Religion In Which All Men Agree*, 33.
21. Harland-Jacobs, *Builders of Empire*, 66.
22. Jansen, "In Search of Atlantic Sociability," 80.
23. Jacob, *Living the Enlightenment*, 60–61; Tabbert, *American Freemasons*, 26–27.

24. Harland-Jacobs, *Builders of Empire*, 31.
25. Ibid., 37.
26. Ibid., 112.
27. Bullock, "'A Pure and Sublime System'," 368–369; Bullock, *Revolutionary Brotherhood*, 9; Bullock, "According to their Rank," 492; York, "Freemasons and the American Revolution," 231.
28. Bullock, *Revolutionary Brotherhood*, 109–114; Bullock, "According to their Rank," 490.
29. Harland-Jacobs, *Builders of Empire*, 35.
30. "History of Freemasonry in Nova Scotia," chapters 1–2.
31. Huskins, "'Ancient' Tensions and Local Circumstances," 52.
32. MacDonald, *History of Hiram Lodge No. 17*, 7–8, LMF.
33. Harland-Jacobs, *Builders of Empire*, 118.
34. MacDonald, *History of Hiram Lodge No. 17*, 7, LMF.
35. Bullock, "According to their Rank," 494.
36. MacDonald, *History of Hiram Lodge No. 17*, 7, LMF; Milbourne, "Loyalist Masons," estimates that there were 13 members of Hiram Lodge who had belonged to No. 210.
37. Ross, *A Standard History of Freemasonry*, chapter 5.
38. Bunting, *History of the St. John's Lodge*, 10; Milbourne, "Loyalist Masons in the Maritimes," 1957–1960.
39. Bunting, *History of the St. John's Lodge*, 310–311.
40. Bell, *Loyalist Rebellion in New Brunswick*, 151.
41. *Anderson's Constitutions of 1723*.
42. *Charges and Regulations*, 6, 12.
43. *Anderson's Constitutions of 1723*.
44. Harland-Jacobs, *Builders of Empire*, 99, 113.
45. Bell, *Loyalist Rebellion in New Brunswick*, 77, 166 n.4.
46. Ibid., 77.
47. Ibid., 74; Jasanoff, *Liberty's Exiles*, 55–81.
48. For works on the Loyalist myth, see Marquis, "Commemorating the Loyalists in the Loyalist City," 24–33; Barkley, "The Loyalist Tradition in New Brunswick," 3–45; Richard et al., "Markers of Collective Identity."
49. Huskins, "Shelburnian Manners," 157.
50. Bell, "The Republican Craft," 13–14.
51. Bunting, *History of the St. John's Lodge*, 17.
52. Bell, *Loyalist Rebellion in New Brunswick*, 151.
53. Jasanoff, *Liberty's Exiles*, 182–184.
54. Bell, *Loyalist Rebellion in New Brunswick*, 112–114.
55. Ibid., 151.
56. Bell, "The Republican Craft," 6.
57. Jasanoff, *Liberty's Exiles*, 187.
58. Richard Bonsall et al. to Joseph Peters, Saint John, 1 May 1786. Nova Scotia Archives, Halifax (hereafter cited as NSA), Grand Lodge of Ancient Free & Accepted Masons of Nova Scotia fonds (hereafter cited as Halifax fonds), MG 20 Vol. 2001 #10.
59. Jasanoff, *Liberty's Exiles*, 197.
60. Bell, *Loyalist Rebellion in New Brunswick*, 87.
61. Ibid.
62. Ibid., 122.
63. Bell, "A Republican Craft," 6.
64. Tabbert, *American Freemasons*, 11–12, 29–30; Jacob, *Origins of Freemasonry*, 18, 70.
65. Harland-Jacobs, *Builders of Empire*, 120–127.
66. Bell, *Loyalist Rebellion in New Brunswick*, 124, 141
67. Bunting, *History of the St. John's Lodge*, 221.
68. Bell, *Loyalist Rebellion in New Brunswick*, 174; MacDonald, *History of Hiram Lodge No. 17*, 13.
69. Oliver Bourdett et al. to John Selby, Saint John, 1 August 1793. NSA, GLNS fonds, MG 20 Vol. 2001, #10.

70. MacDonald, *History of Hiram Lodge No. 17*, 15.
71. GLNS, Minute Book, 20 November 1793, and 5 March 1794. NSA, GLNS fonds, MG 20 Vol. 2133 #1, 218, 231.
72. GLNS, Minute Book, 8 August 1794. NSA, GLNS fonds, MG 20 Vol. 2133 #1, 242.
73. James Hayt et. al. to John Selby, Saint John, 23 October 1794. NSA, GLNS fonds, MG 20 Vol. 2001 #10 (emphasis in original).
74. GLNS, Minute Book, 4 March 1795. NSA, GLNS fonds, MG 20 Vol. 2133 #1, 256–257; Bunting, *History of the St. John's Lodge*, 14.
75. Richard Hayt et al. to John Selby. Saint John, 27 July 1795. NSA, GLNS fonds, MG 20 Vol. 2001 #10.
76. GLNS, Minute Book, 2 September 1795. NSA, GLNS fonds, MG 20 Vol. 2133 #1, 265.
77. Ibid. For South Carolina, see Brannon, *From Revolution to Reunion*, 73.
78. GLNS Minute Book, 7 September 1796. NSA, GLNS fonds, MG 20 Vol. 2133 #2, 19–20.
79. John Sinnot to William Campbell, Saint. John, 10 April 1794. NSA, GLNS fonds, MG 20 Vol. 2001, #10.
80. *Charges and Regulations*, 1.
81. *Ibid.*, 10.
82. Bunting, *History of the St. John's Lodge*, 15.
83. John Sinnot to Grand Master, Grand Wardens & Brethren of the GLNS. Saint. John, 15 August 1793. NSA, GLNS fonds, MG 20 Vol. 2002, #10, 39.
84. Sinnot also insisted that several lawsuits had been brought against Hake in the past: Ibid; John Sinnot to William Campbell. Saint. John, 10 April 1794. NSA, GLNS fonds, MG 20 Vol. 2001, #10.
85. *Charges and Regulations*, 11.
86. Jacob, *Origins of Freemasonry*, 20.
87. *Charges and Regulations*, 10, 42.
88. John Sinnot to William Campbell et al. Saint John, 5 April 1794. NSA, GLNS fonds, MG 20 Vol. 2001 #10, 46.
89. James Hayt et al. to Duncan Clark et al. Saint John, 8 February 1796. NSA, GLNS fonds, MG 20 Vol. 2001 #10, 64.
90. *Charges and Regulations*, 9.
91. Jacob, *Living the Enlightenment*, 46.
92. Ibid., 40.
93. John Sinnot to William Campbell et al. 5 April 1794. NSA, GLNS fonds, MG 20 Vol. 2001 #10, 46.
94. Jacob, *Origins of Freemasonry*, 57; Jacob, *Living the Enlightenment*, 46.
95. *Charges and Regulations*, 43.
96. John Selby to Hiram Lodge #17. Halifax, 20 July 1795. NSA, GLNS fonds,, MG 20 Vol. 2001 #10, 61.
97. James Hayt et al. to John Selby. Saint John, 27 July 1795. NSA, GLNS fonds,, MG 20 Vol. 2001 #10.
98. I am indebted to Elizabeth Mancke for this phrase, although we are using it quite differently.
99. James Hayt et al. to Duncan Clark et. al., Saint John, 8 February 1796. NSA, GLNS fonds, MG 20 Vol. 2001 #10, 64.
100. *Anderson's Constitutions of 1723*.
101. Harland-Jacobs, *Builders of Empire*, 137–38.
102. Ibid., 139.
103. On 20 May 1795 the Grand Stewards began their meeting by reading the circular from the Grand Lodge of England: GLNS, Minute Book, 20 May 1795. NSA, GLNS fonds, MG 20 Vol. 2133 #1, 258–59. The fonds of the Nova Scotia Grand Lodge includes a file of circulars from the grand lodges in Britain; also see Harland-Jacobs, *Builders of Empire*, 30, 50, 143.
104. Harland-Jacobs, *Builders of Empire*, 102.
105. GLNS, Minute Book, Halifax, 27 May 1794. NSA, GLNS fonds, MG 20 Vol. 2133 #1, 237; Harland Jacobs, *Builders of Empire*, 160–161.
106. GLNS, Minute Book, 24 June 1803. NSA, GLNS fonds, MG 20 Vol 2133 #2, 164.
107. Shreve, *Sermon, Preached at St. Paul's Church*, 15–16.

108. Harland-Jacobs, *Builders of Empire*, 99.
109. Thomas Jennings: GLNS, Minute Book, 15 February 1797. NSA, GLNS fonds, MG 20 Vol 2133 #2, 34; John Tool & Robert Moir: 6 September 1797, 46, and 28 September 1797, 48 in Ibid; Oliver Bourdett & David Beveridge: 15 November 1797, 52 in Ibid.; William Jennison, Symons, Charles McPherson, George Matthews, Richard Bonsall, John Ryan, Claven Calverly, William Lorrain, Thomas Featherby, William Symonds, Samuel Wiggins, & Stephen Bourdett: 7 March 1798, 57 in Ibid.; Charles McPherson: 23 Aug 1815, 337 in Ibid..
110. Bunting, *History of the St. John's Lodge*, 15–16.
111. GLNS, Minute Book, 28 September 1797. NSA, GLNS fonds, MG 20 Vol. 2133 #2, 49.
112. Robert Laidley to GLNS. 27 February 1797, Annapolis Royal, in GLNS, Minute Book, 7 June 1797. NSA, GLNS fonds, MG 20 Vol 2133 #2, 40.
113. GLNS, Minute Book, 2 June 1802. NSA, GLNS fonds, MG 20 Vol 2133 #2, 139.
114. Harland Jacobs, *Builders of Empire*, 68, 124.
115. Ibid., 108–109.
116. Bunting, *History of the St. John's Lodge*, 121
117. Ibid., 445, 149, 182, 188.
118. Province House: GLNS, Minute Book, 7 August 1811. NSA, GLNS fonds, MG 20 Vol 2133 #2, 274-75; College: 8 May 1820, 416 in Ibid.; Canal: GLNS, Minute Book, 25 July 1826. NSA, GLNS fonds, MG 20 Vol. 2142 #4.
119. GLNS, Minute Book, 12 August 1811. NSA, GLNS fonds, MG 20 Vol. 2133 #2, 276 (emphasis added by author).
120. Harland-Jacobs, *Builders of Empire*, 14, 56, 201.
121. Lane, "Evangelical Churches and Freemasonry," 63–64.
122. Ibid., 75–78.
123. Bunting, *History of the St. John's Lodge*, 133, 188.

Acknowledgements

I would like to thank the participants of the workshop *Atlantic Brotherhoods* for their collegiality in welcoming a scholar new to the field. I also acknowledge the contributions of Elizabeth Mancke and the anonymous readers who pressed me to clarify my arguments, and the Grand Lodge of Nova Scotia, who granted me permission to access their amazing collection at the Nova Scotia Archives. The staff at the archives were helpful as always, especially now-retired Philip Hartling. And of course, I offer my sincere thanks to Michael Boudreau for his unflagging support in all things.

Disclosure statement

No potential conflict of interest was reported by the author.

Bibliography

Anderson's Constitutions of 1723, *Freemason Information: A Web Magazine About Freemasonry*. http://freemasoninformation.com/masonic-education/books/andersons-constitutions-of-1723.
Armitage, David. "Three Concepts of Atlantic History." In *The British Atlantic World, 1500–1800*, edited David Armitage and Michael J. Braddick, 11–30. New York: Palgrave Macmillan, 2002.

Barkley, Murray. "The Loyalist Tradition in New Brunswick: The Growth and Evolution of an Historical Myth, 1825–1914." *Acadiensis* 4, no. 2 (Spring 1975): 3–45.

Bell, David G. *Early Loyalist Saint John: The Origin of New Brunswick Politics, 1783–1786*. Fredericton, NB: New Ireland Press, 1983.

Bell, David G. *Loyalist Rebellion in New Brunswick Loyalist Rebellion in New Brunswick: A Defining Conflict for Canada's Political Culture*. Halifax, NS: Formac, 2013.

Bell, David G. "The Republican Craft and the Politics of Loyalist Saint John." Paper presented at the Atlantic Canada Studies Conference, University of New Brunswick at Saint John, May 5, 2012.

Bell, David G. "Sedition Among the Loyalists: The Case of Saint John, 1784–86." *University of New Brunswick Law Journal/Revue de droit de l'Universite de Nouveau-Brunswick* 36 (1987): 146–162.

Brannon, Rebecca. *From Revolution to Reunion: The Reintegration of the South Carolina Loyalists*. Columbia: University of South Carolina Press, 2016.

Bullock, Stephen C. "According to their Rank: Masonry and the Revolution. 1775–1792." In *Freemasonry on Both Sides of the Atlantic: Essays Concerning the Craft in the British Isles, Europe, the United States, and Mexico*, edited by R. William Weisberger, Wallace McLeod, and S. Brent Morris, 489–523. New York: East European Monographs, 2002.

Bullock, Stephen C. "'A Pure and Sublime System': The Appeal of Post-Revolutionary Freemasonry." *Journal of the Early Republic* 9, no. 3 (1989): 359–373. http://doi.org/10.2307/3123594.

Bullock, Stephen C. *Revolutionary Brotherhood: Freemasonry and the Transformation of the American Social Order, 1730–1840*. Chapel Hill: University of North Carolina Press, 1998.

Bunting, William F. *History of the St. John's Lodge, F & AM of Saint John, Together with Sketches of All Masonic Bodies in New Brunswick from A.D. 1784 to A.D. 1894*. Saint John, NB: J & A MacMillan, 1895.

Charges and Regulations of the Ancient and Honourable Society of Free and Accepted Masons, Extracted from Ahiman Rezon, &c. Together With A Concise Account of the Rise and Progress of Free Masonry in Nova-Scotia, from the first Settlement of it to this Time; And A Charge given by the Revd. Brother Weeks, at the Installation of His Excellency John Parr Esq; Grand Master. Designed For the Use of the Brethren, and published by the Consent and Direction of the Grand Lodge of this Province. Halifax, NS: John Howe, 1786.

Edwards, J. Plimsoll. "The History of Freemasonry." *Transactions of the Nova Scotia Lodge of Research* 1, no. 2 (13 January 1916), 14–19.

Fairbairn, James. "Masons who Made America: Interesting Story – the Boston Tea Party." *The Masonic World* (8 September 1974).

Hackett, David G. *That Religion in Which All Men Agree: Freemasonry in American Culture*. Berkeley: University of California Press, 2015.

Harland-Jacobs, Jessica. *Builders of Empire: Freemasons and British Imperialism, 1717–1927*. Chapel Hill: University of North Carolina Press, 2007.

Harland-Jacobs, Jessica. "'Hands Across the Sea': The Masonic Network, British Imperialism, and the North Atlantic World." *Geographical Review* 89, no. 2 (April 1999): 237–254.

Harland-Jacobs, Jessica. "Worlds of Brothers." *Journal for Research into Freemasonry and Fraternalism* 2, no. 1 (2011): 10–37. http://doi.org/10.1558/jrff.v2i1.10.

"History of Freemasonry in Nova Scotia," chapter 1: Beginnings. https://www.kingsolomonlodge54.com/history/freemasonry-nova-scotia/history-of-freemasonry-in-nova-scotia-chapter-1-beginnings/.

"History of Freemasonry in Nova Scotia," chapter 2: The First Provincial Grand Lodge. https://www.kingsolomonlodge54.com/history/freemasonry-nova-scotia/history-of-freemasonry-in-nova-scotia-chapter-2-the-first-provincial-grand-lodge/.

Huskins, Bonnie. "'Ancient' Tensions and Local Circumstances: Loyalist Freemasons in Shelburne Nova Scotia." *Journal for Research into Freemasonry and Fraternalism* 5, no. 1 (2015): 47–72. http://doi.org/10.1558/jrff.v5i1.22786.

Huskins, Bonnie. "'Shelburnian Manners': Gentility and the Loyalists of Shelburne Nova Scotia." *Early American Studies: An Interdisciplinary Journal* 13, no. 1 (Winter 2015): 151–188.

Jacob, Margaret C. *Living the Enlightenment: Freemasonry and Politics in Eighteenth-Century Europe*. New York: Oxford University Press, 1991.

Jacob, Margaret C. *The Origins of Freemasonry: Facts and Fictions*. Philadelphia: University of Pennsylvania, 2006.

Jansen, Jan C. "In Search of Atlantic Sociability: Freemasons, Empires, and Atlantic History." *Bulletin of the German Historical Institute* 57 (Fall 2015): 75–99.

Jasanoff, Maya. *Liberty's Exiles: American Loyalists in the Revolutionary World*. New York: Alfred A. Knopf, 2011.

Kenney, J. Scott. *Brought to Light: Contemporary Freemasonry, Meaning, and Society*. Waterloo, ON: Wilfred Laurier University, 2016.

Klages, Gregory. "Freemasonic and Orange Order Membership in Rural Ontario during the Late 19th Century." *Ontario History* CIII, no. 2 (Autumn 2011): 192–214.

Lane, Hannah M. "Evangelical Churches and Freemasonry in Mid-Nineteenth-Century Calais, Maine and St. Stephen, New Brunswick." *Journal of Research Into Fraternalism and Freemasonry* 2, no. 1 (2011): 60–78.

Logan, Jackie. "The Sheet Harbour Loyalist of 1784 and Hiram's Lodge No. 8." *Nova Scotia Historical Review* 15, no. 1 (1995): 118–126.

MacDonald, Stuart. *History of Hiram Lodge No. 1, Saint John, New Brunswick*. Nova Scotia: np, 2004, Library and Museum of Freemasonry.

Marquis, Greg. "Commemorating the Loyalists in the Loyalist City: Saint John, New Brunswick, 1883–1934." *Urban History Review* 33, no. 1 (Fall 2004): 24–33.

Milbourne, A. J. B. "Loyalist Masons in the Maritimes." *Canadian Masonic Research Association* 3. Cambridge: Heritage Lodge No. 730, 1986: 1955–95.

Raible, Chris. "'The Threat of Being Morganized Will not Deter Us': William Lyon Mackenzie, Freemasonry and the Morgan Affair." *Ontario History* 100, no. 1 (Spring 2008): 3–25.

Richard, Chantal, Anne Brown, Margaret Conrad, Gwendolyn Davies, Bonnie Huskins, and Sylvia Kasparian. "Markers of Collective Identity in Loyalist and Acadian Speeches of the 1880s: A Comparative Analysis." *Journal of New Brunswick Studies* 4 (2013): 13–30. http://journals.hil.unb.ca/index.php/JNBS/article/view/21160.

Ross, Peter. *A Standard History of Freemasonry in the State of New York*. Vol. 1. New York: Lewis Publishing Company, 1899.

Shreve, Reverend Thomas. *Sermon. Preached at St. Paul's Church in Halifax Before the Provincial Grand Lodge of Free and Accepted Masons, June 24th, 1803. On the Celebration of St. John the Baptist*. Halifax, NS: A Gay, 1803.

Tabbert, Mark A. *American Freemasons: Three Centuries of Building Communities*. Lexington, KY: National Heritage Museum, 2005.

York, Neil L. "Freemasons and the American Revolution." *The Historian* 55, no. 3 (Winter 1993): 315–330. http://doi.org/10.1111/j.1540-6563.1993.tb00899.x.

Brothers in exile: Masonic lodges and the refugees of the Haitian Revolution, 1790s–1820

Jan C. Jansen

ABSTRACT
In the wake of the Haitian Revolution (1791–1804), tens of thousands of people – white colonists, free people of color, and slaves – left the French colony of Saint-Domingue for neighboring Caribbean colonies and North America. Scattered and diverse as they were, these refugees maintained diasporic bonds, constituting a community with distinct social, cultural, linguistic, and religious traits. Fraternalism, and Masonic lodges in particular, played a pivotal role in shaping these connections. Based on new empirical evidence from the major centers of the refugee community (the US, Louisiana, Cuba, Jamaica), this paper examines the emergence of these refugee lodges. Placing them in their social contexts and analyzing their membership practices, it argues that Freemasonry provided an important social infrastructure for a segment of the refugee population – an infrastructure that was used to cultivate diasporic connections, to (re)enhance internal hierarchies, and to build networks in the host societies.

The experience of exile made some of the best observers of life in the early national United States. A Martinique-born white Creole, civil servant both in France and in its most important colony, Saint-Domingue, and member of the National Constituent Assembly, Médéric Louis Elie Moreau de Saint-Méry (1750–1819) escaped from France and arrived on the shores of Virginia in early March 1794.[1] Moreau quickly became a central figure among the thousands of émigrés and refugees of the French and Haitian Revolutions. As the intellectual spearhead of the colonial branch in the French Enlightenment, he was also an astute observer and diarist during his four-and-a half years in American exile. His diary from this period contains details from his everyday life and everything he considered noteworthy about the early US Republic and the lives of the thousands of revolutionary-era exiles living there.[2]

Among the aspects that caught Moreau's attention early on was the public role of Freemasonry. Already during his first weeks in exile, he commented on the high density of Masonic lodges in Norfolk, his first base.[3] Later on, after moving to Philadelphia and during his extensive travels, he continued to note the importance of Masonic lodges and their processions.[4] Moreau was no stranger to this milieu. He had been an active member of several lodges operating in Saint-Domingue and Paris, and he was also said to have participated in a French-speaking lodge in Philadelphia.[5] In his reporting on Freemasonry, Moreau applied a similar approach to his American diary as to his masterpiece, the multi-volume *Description* of the Spanish and French parts of the island of Hispaniola, more commonly known as Santo Domingo and Saint-Domingue, in which he described Masonic lodges as an integral part of white French colonial society.[6] Likewise, later in his life, when back in Europe, he continued to play a prominent role in Freemasonry and to reflect on its development on both sides of the Atlantic.[7]

Yet the prominence of Freemasonry in Moreau's diary is more than a mere reflection of its author's personal interests. In fact, Masonic lodges constituted a widespread phenomenon among Saint-Domingue refugees throughout the Americas. Private papers left by some of the roughly 20,000 to 30,000 refugees include Masonic certificates and other documents attesting to membership in Freemasonry.[8] Some of the refugees – such as Pierre Antoine Lambert, a planter from Saint-Domingue's southern province, who first went to Santiago de Cuba and then ended up in New Orleans – made sure to carry these documents between their different places of refuge.[9] From a bird's-eye view, we see that almost everywhere large numbers of Saint-Domingue refugees settled, Masonic lodges composed of refugees appeared. Between 1793 and 1820, more than thirty such lodges were founded throughout the United States, the British West Indies, Louisiana (even before it was purchased in 1803 by the United States), and the Spanish colonies of Santo Domingo and Cuba.

These numbers suggest that the period of revolutionary turmoil and displacement, which is often described as a period of deep crisis for Freemasonry, was, at least in the case of the Saint-Domingue diaspora, a time of high demand for Masonic sociability and fellowship.[10] Masonic lodges were among the most widespread social organizations embraced by refugees of the Haitian Revolution. This article sets out to explore and explain this phenomenon. Why, in a situation of personal distress, did a large segment of Saint-Domingue refugees devote considerable time and resources to an organization aimed at promoting moral and civic improvement through friendly social intercourse between like-minded men? Were there specific uses they made of the organization, maybe even as a sort of "refugee Freemasonry"? And, more broadly, what were the connections between exile and fraternal sociability?

The article seeks to shed new light on a still largely understudied aspect of the history of the Saint-Domingue refugees. To be sure, today's scholarship has repeatedly pointed to the importance of Masonic lodges among them.[11] Most scholars have attributed it to the thriving Masonic culture in late-colonial Saint-Domingue. Understood as such, Masonic affiliations do not account for more than a cultural quirk and "influence," baggage the refugees carried with them. This article argues that it does not suffice to rely on the time before the refugees' flight when it comes to understanding the role of Freemasonry among certain segments of the refugee population. Instead, we need to focus more on the moment of flight and exile and to examine the factors that may have attracted a considerable portion of refugees to this organization at that very moment.

This approach ties in with recent scholarship in Atlantic revolutionary history. Historians have become increasingly interested in the different strategies and means historical actors employed in finding their way through the turbulence and confusion of the age of revolutions. I argue that Masonic certificates were not essentially different from other paper documents historians have recognized as vital resources for refugees at this time, such as "freedom papers," that is, real or fabricated documents showing the legal status of a person, or letters of introduction, that they carried with them to their destinations.[12] A Masonic certificate provided access to a universe of informal social networks that shaped the eighteenth-century Atlantic world, thereby helping people communicate and move about during a time of uncertainty.[13] This article thus also speaks to recent attempts at delineating cultural practices shared across the revolutionary Atlantic, from Western Europe to North, Central, and South America and the Caribbean.[14] With its claims to universal fraternalism and – political as well as religious – non-partisanship, Freemasonry proved to involve a particularly elastic set of practices and organizational forms across the Atlantic that could be appropriated by a myriad of groups, who, in turn, charged it with particular meanings.[15] While it was pervasive among revolutionists and often claimed to be one of their main organizations, we see that Freemasonry was also widespread among people escaping and often fiercely opposed to revolutionary change. A study of the uses of Freemasonry among Saint-Domingue refugees questions and complicates the very idea of clear-cut boundaries between revolutionary and non- (or even counter-) revolutionary social and cultural practices.

Seen from this broader Atlantic angle, an analysis of the system of refugee lodges can help advance a new transregional approach for the study of the Saint-Domingue refugees, which tends to be dominated by local studies. The lodges enable us to describe the different local refugee communities as part of a diaspora stretching across several state and imperial borders. As will be shown, Masonic lodges were an important element of this diaspora's cross-regional integration. Along with Catholicism, Freemasonry constituted the most important social infrastructure of Saint-Domingue refugees across borders. It allowed them to communicate and move across their places of refuge and provided means of creating social structures and hierarchies within the diaspora. At the same time, it was a significant field of interactions with their respective host societies and other groups of migrants and exiles, such as the émigrés from revolutionary France in the United States. This cross-regional integration through Freemasonry was only open to a certain subset of refugees. While mobilizing a universalist discourse, the lodges operated – and entrenched – exclusions within the diaspora, along social, gender and racial lines.

Examining Saint-Domingue refugee lodges can also benefit research into Atlantic Freemasonry and, more broadly, the social history of sociability and fraternalism. Social and cultural historians have analyzed Freemasonry, which was the most widespread voluntary organization in many eighteenth-century Western European countries, as a major element of the "associational revolution" in Enlightenment Europe.[16] The same holds true for the United States, where Freemasonry has been described as a bedrock of political and civic culture during the first decades after the American Revolution.[17] Notwithstanding the organization's cosmopolitan ideology and global reach, most scholarship on Freemasonry has remained encased in a local or national framework. Only recently have researchers started to flesh out more thoroughly its transnational and cross-border dimensions. Thus, some scholars have made a strong case for using larger units of analysis – such as the British Empire, Europe, or the Atlantic world – for the study of Freemasonry or fraternalism in general.[18] Research on the connection between migration and Freemasonry, however, still remains scant. There is no American equivalent to French historian Pierre-Yves Beaurepaire's pioneering studies on the role of Masonic sociability among European migrants, which also call attention to the importance of forced migrants such as refugees, exiles, and prisoners of war.[19] Apart from a short foray by a Masonic scholar in 1939, no academic interest is evident concerning the prominent place of refugees in early US Freemasonry.[20] In line with broader directions in early American history, this study of Saint-Domingue refugee lodges can help advance a more Atlantic framework for scholarship on American Freemasonry and civil society.

In short, as this article seeks to demonstrate, the study of refugee lodges can provide new elements for a cross-border, Atlantic perspective on both the refugees of the Haitian Revolution and Masonic sociability. I will first retrace the emergence and features of Masonic lodges among Saint-Domingue refugees across the Americas, before discussing Freemasonry's place within transatlantic sociable networks of the late eighteenth and early nineteenth centuries. The major part of my analysis will focus on the specific uses Saint-Domingue refugees made of Freemasonry and show how Freemasonry became a means for them to establish and maintain diasporic links across various state and imperial borders.

Refugees and refugee lodges in the Americas, 1790s–1820

The revolutionary period in the Atlantic world, stretching from the American Revolution of the 1770s–1780s to the revolutionary independence movements in Spanish America in the 1810s–1820s, was not just a succession of military exploits, popular uprisings, or the dawn of a new age of liberty and virtue. As much as it had its winners and heroes, the age of revolutions created losers and victims too. Among the latter were the tens of thousands of political exiles and refugees crisscrossing the Atlantic world in the wake of successful and failed revolutions in North and South America, France, Ireland, and the French Caribbean.[21] Americans who remained loyal to the British crown ("loyalists") and émigrés from revolutionary France constituted the two largest and best known of these Atlantic exile diasporas, not least because they had several well-known public figures in their midst.[22]

Less prominent were the refugees of the Haitian Revolution.[23] The 20,000 to 30,000 individuals leaving the colony of Saint-Domingue between the outbreak of the slave rebellion in 1791 and the independence of Haiti in 1804 formed a heterogeneous group. They comprised men and women of all ages, white and black, free and unfree, propertied and destitute, pro-revolutionary and monarchist. Several waves brought them to different places across the Americas: the eastern United States, the British West Indies, Santo Domingo and Cuba, Louisiana and the Gulf region. Despite state and imperial borders between them, these refugees upheld important family, social, political, and economic ties. Mobility remained high among these places. While Philadelphia and Santiago de Cuba stood out as centers of the Saint-Domingue diaspora in the first two decades, New Orleans became their major hub from 1810 on. More than 10,000 refugees eventually settled there. As heterogeneous and scattered as they were, Saint-Domingue refugees nonetheless constituted a coherent Atlantic diaspora.

The arrival of thousands of refugees had sweeping consequences for the demographic, political, social, and economic structure of their places of settlement. They swelled the ranks of local Catholic parishes, invested in land and plantation ventures, required charity and housing, set up political organizations and newspapers – and quickly founded Masonic lodges. Between the early 1790s and 1820, at least 30 lodges were established or run by Saint-Domingue refugees in North America, Cuba, Santo Domingo, Jamaica, and Trinidad. Urban centers on the US East Coast quickly became centers of refugee lodges, with Philadelphia and New York being major hubs (with three lodges founded between 1792 and 1805 in each city). Still more lodges emerged in Charleston, Baltimore, Savannah, and Portsmouth, Virginia. From the early 1800s on, New Orleans became the single most important location for Masonic activity related to Saint-Domingue, with at least eight lodges founded between the mid-1790s and 1811. While the great number of refugee lodges along the US East Coast may be explained by the general thriving of Freemasonry in the early national United States, a comparative look at other places complicates the picture. In Jamaica's Kingston, also a major hub of Anglo-British Atlantic Freemasonry and where all British governors throughout the 1790s were also prominent Freemasons, refugee lodges were in a more difficult situation; evidence for lodges established by Saint-Domingue refugees is fragmentary and only applies to the 1810s.[24] By contrast, in several places with less sympathetic authorities – pre-US Louisiana, Santo Domingo and Cuba, above all – numerous lodges appeared. In these places, the refugee lodges were the first local Masonic organizations to be established. Santiago de Cuba, with at least four French-speaking lodges founded between 1805 and 1820, stands out as the major Masonic hub at that time in the Spanish Caribbean.

If we take a closer look at the circumstances of their establishment, we may distinguish roughly three types of refugee lodges: (1) pre-existing lodges that the refugees took over; in the current sample there is only one such case, the lodge La Sagesse (Wisdom) in Portsmouth, Virginia, which had been founded by French migrants in the early 1780s and then taken over by Saint-Domingue refugees in the 1790s; (2) lodges that had already existed in Saint-Domingue and were then "temporarily" transferred to another place; examples may be the lodge La Réunion des cœurs (Union of Hearts), founded in the mid-1780s in Jérémie and moved to Santiago de Cuba sometime during the 1790s, where it was officially reestablished in 1805, or La Vérité (Truth), one of Le Cap's longest-lasting lodges, founded in 1767 and refounded in Baltimore in the 1790s;[25] these lodges constitute roughly a third of the sample; and (3) lodges that were newly established, in most cases with the help of regional Masonic authorities; these lodges make up the remaining two-thirds of the sample.

Beyond these differences, lodges of all three types shared several distinguishing traits. They operated in French and, most often, with French ritual systems, and they were largely composed of white (male) refugees from Saint-Domingue – a group from which most of the officers that oversaw the lodge activities came. In cases for which reliable numbers exist, Saint-Domingue refugees made up more than nine out of ten members; the rest came from the local population and, wherever available, from French or other foreign expatriate communities. We do not have full membership records for all these lodges, but from the existing archival evidence we can estimate that well over a thousand individuals were members in these lodges between 1790 and 1820. To these numbers we have to add Saint-Domingue refugees who joined lodges other than those run by their co-nationals, and we have to take into account the proliferation of unauthorized lodges among Saint-Domingue refugees, which was reported in several places. By 1805, for example, Santiago de Cuba had become a hotbed of clandestine Masonic activities.

Along with the high number of officially recognized lodges, such "frequent private committees and clandestine makings to scandal and abuses of all kinds," as a group of outraged Freemasons in Cuba put it, show us the considerable demand for Masonic sociability among Saint-Domingue refugees.[26] In that sense, Freemasonry had a lot in common with other sociable organizations at this time. It did not stop at imperial or state borders but constituted an important, if often overlooked, element of border-crossing in the late eighteenth-century Atlantic.

Sociability and exile

Recent scholarship has pointed to the pivotal role of certain centers and sites of sociability and social gathering within the community of Saint-Domingue refugees. Depending on the local conditions and the degree of freedom on the ground, the refugees rapidly organized their social life around certain spaces: cafés, taverns, hotels, and bookstores quickly became known as meeting places for exiles. Local refugee communities gravitated to these sites. They used them to gather news and information from France and the French West Indies; to establish contacts or find jobs; to organize political activities and receive material and emotional support; and to socialize with their comrades in misfortune, cultivate nostalgic memories, and overcome widespread feelings of solitude. Moreau de Saint-Méry's Philadelphia bookstore or the Café des réfugiés in New Orleans are just two well-known examples of a much larger phenomenon.[27]

The Masonic lodges were among the hubs of sociability around which certain segments of the refugee population organized. As we will see, the lodges fulfilled various functions at the local level, as they served as a source for relief or personal contacts. But there was more to them. In his study on French émigré life in Philadelphia, historian François Furstenberg pointed to the transatlantic dimensions of certain modes of sociability. According to him, a "well-integrated transatlantic salon culture"[28] united the highest circles of Philadelphia's merchant elite and French expatriates. The Philadelphia mansion built by William and Anne Bingham served as a venue for splendid soirées and was probably the most elaborate local expression of this shared salon culture. While their exclusive social gatherings were particularly open toward French noble émigrés like François Alexandre Frédéric, duc de la Rochefoucauld-Liancourt (1747–1827) or Charles-Maurice de Talleyrand-Périgord (1754–1838), among the most renowned individuals of Ancien Régime courtly society, Saint-Domingue refugees were also eager to mingle with the most affluent and sophisticated circles of Philadelphia. Alexandre de Laujon, for example, a young colonial administrator from Saint-Domingue, sought access to such soirées immediately after his arrival in Philadelphia in 1793: "For, who knows where a ball can bring you?"[29] Philadelphia's salon culture enabled certain groups of refugees to interact with influential members of the host society and to become involved in the social, political, and economic life of the early US republic, which was still shaped in and emerging from rather informal circles and settings to a large extent.

The idea of a shared transatlantic salon culture fits into a broader argument about the prominent role that the informal, semi-private world of association and sociability played in the Atlantic world. Both Philadelphia's salons and its refugee lodges can be seen as elements of multifaceted and complex transatlantic systems of sociability. Compared to salon culture, Freemasonry was a more recent eighteenth-century innovation in the sphere of polite manners and society. Even more than salons, Masonic lodges were an institution of cross-border sociability. They served to facilitate bonds and male friendship across political, religious, social, and national boundaries among men who would have otherwise remained strangers. A lodge was always embedded simultaneously in several contexts of different scale: It was an essential feature of local polite society, and it was part of a cross-regional, often national or imperial, institutional system organized around a grand lodge, and it was part of an intercontinental, if not global, movement based on an ideology of cosmopolitan fraternalism.[30]

At the time of the Haitian Revolution, Freemasonry was already a well-established organization in the Atlantic world. Masonic lodges were not only a central element of the political culture of the post-revolutionary United States and in Western European civil society; they also permeated social life in the Caribbean colonies, including in Saint-Domingue, where a considerable number of lodges had developed.[31] At the same time that they shaped local social and public life, Saint-Domingue's lodges were also integrated into a multi-layered system of Atlantic relations.[32] Not surprisingly, they maintained close ties with lodges in metropolitan France, even if their focus was not necessarily Paris and the Masonic authorities at the Grand Orient de France, which had asserted its authority in France and the French colonies from the 1770s on. Thus, St. Jean de Jérusalem, one of the oldest and most prestigious lodges in Cap-Français, cultivated a vast correspondence network with lodges primarily in Atlantic port cities in France and the French West Indies.[33] Deeply entrenched in an overseas milieu of merchants, colonial administrators, sailors, and planters, these French Atlantic Masonic connections revealed a degree of intensity and a life of their own that was hardly controllable by Parisian Masonic authorities.[34]

Yet, Saint-Domingue's lodges also cultivated relations across the Americas, far beyond the boundaries of the French colonial empire. Those connections across imperial borders left few traces in the official archives. Still, some documents offer a glimpse of what happened, often unbeknownst to Masonic authorities in Europe. A member of Cap-Français's La Vérité, for example, maintained an unauthorized lodge in North Carolina – and stood in contact with Bordeaux Freemasons.[35] Jérémie's La Réunion des cœurs lodge was even created by a Jamaica-based English or Irish military lodge in the mid-1780s and only later sought official recognition from Masonic authorities in Paris.[36] After attaining such recognition, this lodge continued to maintain and diversify its connections outside the French imperial sphere. Before moving to Santiago de Cuba later during the Haitian Revolution, it cultivated relations with Saint Thomas, at that time a Danish colony.[37] In the mid-1780s, a group of Freemasons in Cap-Français sent a petition to "Grand Master" George Washington as they sought permission to form a lodge under the authority of the Grand Lodge of Pennsylvania, in order to see "brotherhood cement a union which the interest of both nations has already formed" – a connection that would prove decisive in the course of the events to come.[38]

Refugee lodges in action

Saint-Domingue refugees used a variety of social institutions and networks to move to and then get organized in their places of refuge. Many of them drew on preexisting relationships, based on family, kinship, and professional connections, most of which were highly personalized, small-scale, and informal.[39] With its transatlantic lodge network, Freemasonry was slightly different. It involved larger numbers and broader ranges of individuals and built on an established set of institutionalized practices. Together with the Roman Catholic Church – one of its arch-enemies – Freemasonry was perhaps the most important framework for social infrastructure; it integrated, shaped, and structured the Saint-Domingue diaspora across its different places of refuge, and at the same time provided channels into and networks within the host society.[40]

With the outbreak of the Haitian Revolution, French white colonial Freemasonry, of which Cap-Français had been the major hub, unraveled. The refugees rebuilt the lodge infrastructure and adapted it to the new situation with great haste, reflecting, as argued, the importance of Freemasonry in transatlantic society at that time. This process of rebuilding was shaped by individual initiatives as well as by institutional support. Both came together most forcefully in one place, Philadelphia, which by the late 1790s had become the new major hub of Atlantic French Freemasonry within only a few years' time. In fact, the revolution in Saint-Domingue catalyzed developments, both internal and external to Freemasonry, from the previous decade. First, the breakdown of US trade relations with the British West Indies in the wake of American independence and a relative opening in French colonial trade policies in the mid-1780s intensified commercial relations between Philadelphia and the French West Indies, in particular, Saint-Domingue. These trends were supported by the rise of more France-oriented consumer tastes and of a number of French and American merchant houses in Philadelphia specializing in this trade.[41] Trade between Philadelphia and Saint-Domingue soared further in the 1790s as France further lifted restrictions and supplies from the USA became vital to the struggling colony. Second, American lodges emancipated themselves from British colonial Freemasonry; the Pennsylvania Grand Lodge declared its independence in the 1780s and started to broaden its scope of action, becoming an actor in international Freemasonry.[42] By 1789, building on a contact established in the mid-1780s, the Grand Lodge of Pennsylvania had already founded a lodge in Port-au-Prince run by French and American merchants involved in the trade between Philadelphia and Saint-Domingue.[43] After the outbreak of the Haitian Revolution, these cross-border activities of Philadelphia Freemasonry continued. The Grand Lodge of Pennsylvania chartered no less than seven new lodges in Saint-Domingue during the revolution and more than a dozen refugee lodges in Cuba, Trinidad, and Louisiana.[44]

The doyenne of these refugee lodges was L'Aménité, a French-speaking lodge founded in Philadelphia in 1797 by a group of Saint-Domingue refugees, some French émigrés, and Philadelphia-based French and American merchants involved in the West Indies trade.[45] L'Aménité provided a model for many other refugee lodges. It served as a point of contact for Freemasons among the refugees and as an entry point for refugees seeking to become members. Citing the refugees' extraordinary circumstances, the lodge provided a fast-track admission procedure designed for its highly mobile constituency.[46] This procedure allowed newly admitted members to become Master Masons – that is, the highest of the three basic degrees in Freemasonry – within a few days after their initiation. According to the rules, achieving this status would normally require several months. A rapid rise in the Masonic hierarchy entitled these members to a Masonic certificate, thus enabling them to display their Masonic identity to fellow Freemasons while traveling, to initiate new Freemasons, and to found new lodges in other places.

L'Aménité's admission policy resulted in a considerable membership of nearly 300 by the early 1820s. Many of the newly admitted members, however, left Philadelphia and the lodge after a short period of time.[47] L'Aménité's membership fluctuation, which was appreciably higher than that of Philadelphia's other lodges, shows that we cannot understand this lodge outside of the system of refugee lodges that it had helped to build up. During most of the Haitian Revolution, the lodge was Philadelphia's bridge to lodges in Saint-Domingue. L'Aménité maintained a correspondence network, through which it exchanged important news and information about their members and officers with lodges in France and the French West Indies, as well as with most French-speaking lodges in the United States, Cuba, and Trinidad. Several deputies, honorary members, and special affiliations further facilitated the exchange of information and people among many of these lodges.[48]

L'Aménité and the other refugee lodges used the infrastructure and means provided by Freemasonry for the purpose of integrating, shaping, and structuring the Saint-Domingue diaspora across imperial and national borders. The diasporic dimension is evident in several features of these lodges. Most obvious, perhaps, was their involvement in identity politics. They struggled to maintain French as their working language and, in some cases, French rites, against pressures to adapt to the English-speaking Masonic landscape around them, reflecting the refugees' particular resistance to Anglicization.[49] Lodges that had already existed before the revolution cultivated an exile identity and the myth of return, refusing to update their seals or to accept their new location as anything other than temporary.[50] Lodge speeches referred to pre-revolutionary Saint-Domingue (and France, at times) as "the beautiful country," as "the most fortunate country in the world" and recalled "the horrible torrent of all kinds of evils" that destroyed it.[51] By L'Aménité members' own account, their meetings "naturally brought us back to the memory of our shared mother, France" and provided a space for "the moving tears of the orphan chased away from his motherland."[52] Freemasonry thus became a repository of identity and a way for them to keep up the way of life from the lost homeland. More than once, L'Aménité made clear to Philadelphia's Grand Lodge that a true Freemason was driven not only by cosmopolitanism but also by "that holy sentiment, the *Amor Patria*, the source of so many sublime actions and paramount to every other sentiment."[53]

In the fierce struggles around French revolutionary politics in the 1790s, especially the massive opposition among (mainly white) Saint-Domingue refugees to emancipatory policy in the Caribbean, such "patriotic" Saint-Domingue credentials could also reveal a political bent. Thus, numerous prominent and outspoken critics of slave emancipation counted among L'Aménité's founding members. These included Pierre Gauvain, the main organizer of refugee relief and spokesperson in front of the American Congress; Charles Nicholas Donatien Gervais, a leading opponent of emancipation, deported by French authorities; and L'Aménité's first master Claude-Corentin Tangui de la Boissière, a publisher, political organizer and particularly unruly critic of emancipation.[54] With people regarded as leading "counter-revolutionists" at its helm, L'Aménité also functioned as a counterpart to the French Embassy and Jacobin-friendly local clubs in Philadelphia's associational landscape. L'Aménité's members' involvement in exile politics shone through in some of the organization's usually measured public statements. Thus, in 1800 the lodge mentioned "false ideas of freedom" as the reason for its members' exile, a barely veiled reference to slave emancipation.[55] This statement came, however, at a time when France was swiftly moving away from its emancipatory policy.

At times, the French and Saint-Dominguan identity (and politics) professed by the refugee lodges were in danger of backfiring. Some lodges were pulled into the maelstrom of xenophobic or specifically anti-French movements and policies taking shape in most places where refugees were arriving, making the reception of refugee lodges an overlooked chapter in the transatlantic history of anti-Masonry. In Cuba, French Freemasons expressed their alarm over the "great partialities" and widespread "unfair prejudices" against Masonic activities.[56] These concerns were not completely unfounded. A prominent Freemason, for example, was denounced and expelled from Cuba in 1806; similar denunciations continued to reach Spanish authorities in Havana, while the administration in Santiago appeared to tolerate and cover up the existence of French lodges.[57]

The situation also proved difficult in territories generally more favorably disposed toward Freemasonry. This even applied to the United States in the late 1790s, when relations with France deteriorated into an undeclared naval war. Thus, a Baltimore-based refugee lodge in 1798 thought it prudent to interrupt its activities, "considering that the unfortunate circumstances that trouble this country can expose the French Masons to unjust and dangerous suspicions on the part of those who do not know their rules."[58] Another refugee lodge, La Sagesse in Portsmouth, Virginia, soon realized how well-founded such precaution was. In spring 1799, this lodge found itself at the center of a frantic public argument, when Massachusetts pastor Jedidiah Morse, the leading voice of the anti-Illuminati panic in the United States, cited a membership list of this lodge as ultimate evidence for his assertions of widespread French conspiratorial activities.[59] And even after the high tide of anti-French opinion, stories about refugee Freemasons' subversive dealings lingered on. In the midst of major refugee movements to New Orleans in 1809, for example, US newspapers spread the rumor that one of the city's leading refugees, Louis Moreau de Lislet, had been "head of a free-mason lodge composed of negroes" in Saint-Domingue – adding a racial dimension to these negative stereotypes.[60]

The refugee lodges' diasporic dimensions were not just about French, Creole, or exile identity. In many ways, lodge membership provided access to certain material and symbolic resources – charity, information, contacts, respectability – and had an impact on their distribution within the diaspora. Charity was a case in point. Historians have emphasized the importance of charity to (mainly white) Saint-Domingue refugees, provided by a broad range of actors: local public subscriptions and government authorities, French consular representatives, and benevolent societies set up by more affluent French expatriates, such as Philadelphia's Société française de bienfaisance, established in 1793.[61] The refugees also relied heavily on aid from Masonic lodges. Early on, Freemasonry had developed elements of mutual aid and charity. Assistance, including financial support, for a Masonic "brother" or his relatives in need was considered a central part of the fraternal obligations between the members. Masonic institutions became, in fact, one of the most widespread non-religious providers of charity within the eighteenth-century Atlantic world.[62] While reflecting the general movement of solidarity among white Americans towards white Saint-Domingue refugees, grand lodge authorities in Pennsylvania, for example, saw themselves overwhelmed by an ever-growing number of requests.[63]

In this situation, the refugee lodges established themselves as the main contact and authority when it came to the distribution of charity to Freemasons or their relatives from Saint-Domingue. Thus, shortly after its foundation, L'Aménité made clear that it was to be the sole distributor of Masonic charity to French refugees in Philadelphia. It set up its own charity fund distinct from the common charity fund of all Pennsylvania lodges, directed at "our unfortunate countrymen flying [sic] from the dagger of their murderers."

> When men destituted of every comfort, pennyless residues, orphans in rags, escaped from the bloody thirst of the tygers of St. Domingue, came at the door of our temple, and made a solemn appeal to the mercy, to the benevolence of Masons, was not such an affecting, such a tearing spectacle, fit to strike to the heart of the man of feelings?[64]

This self-imposed commitment, funded through members' contributions, brought the lodge to the brink of insolvency several times in the late 1790s and early 1800s.

The network of refugee lodges also provided important means to those moving on and navigating between different places of the reshaped French Atlantic: material assistance, information, and personal contacts. When setting up his bookstore and printing business in Philadelphia, for instance, Moreau de Saint-Méry surrounded himself with Saint-Domingue refugees holding Masonic credentials. His closest business partners, the clerk at his office Gabriel Descombaz, and his agent Gauvain were founding members of L'Aménité.[65] The case of Descombaz also shows that Saint-Domingue refugees were intent on using the sprawling network of newly warranted lodges in revolutionary Saint-Domingue with a view to a potential return to the island. Initiated by a refugee lodge upon his arrival in New York, Descombaz transferred his membership to Philadelphia, soon becoming also a member of La Vérité, as it was reestablished in Cap-Français.[66]

The development of Freemasonry in Louisiana was also driven by refugees' networking needs. First controlled by the Spanish and later the French, it became an important regional hub for Saint-Domingue refugees. Lacking a Masonic infrastructure, the new arrivals soon started to build it from scratch, putting emphasis on its importance for mobile constituencies. In 1800 a group of refugees pressed Pennsylvania Grand Lodge authorities to broaden the lodge infrastructure in New Orleans, specifically in view of "the quantity of Masonic brothers from the United States that trade brings daily to New Orleans."[67] Fifteen years later, New Orleans had replaced Philadelphia as the major center of French Atlantic Freemasonry with wide-ranging Atlantic relations. A member of L'Etoile Polaire, one of the leading French lodges, was able to rely on this network when he fell seriously ill during a longer stay in Cuba. With his lodge far away, another refugee lodge based in Havana came to help. Thereafter, L'Etoile Polaire sought to deepen its relations to Havana, expressing the hope that Freemasonry would spread "in all regions of America, so that there will be everywhere societies guarding moral and social virtues."[68] In a similar fashion, other refugee lodges emphasized the need to secure the mobility of their constituents. In August 1800, L'Aménité singled out Philadelphia-based captain Matthias Ford for praise on account of his "human generous and truly Masonic conduct [...] towards two worthy members of this lodge and other persons who went to St. Domingo as passengers on board the Vessel whereof the said Brother Ford was Captain." The incident the lodge had heard

THE FRATERNAL ATLANTIC, 1770–1930   53

of from "our sister-lodges of Port-au-Prince" was not further explained but may have involved the attack on Ford's vessel by a privateer. As a token of "gratitude and admiration," L'Aménité declared Ford, who was already a member of another lodge in Pennsylvania, an honorary member.[69]

Yet, the most important resource Saint-Domingue refugees sought from Freemasonry seems to have been something less tangible than charity or assistance: respectability. In the words of L'Aménité:

> a Free Mason is possessed of something more valuable than Life, and his brethren are bound to cooperate in preserving this treasure in proportion of the high price he sets upon it. This treasure [...] is his Honor and his Reputation.[70]

The Masonic lodges thus strove to structure the refugee community by insisting on the principle of respectability and the solid reputations of its members. This led to tight monitoring of members' conduct and the way they were perceived within the larger community. This became clear, for example, in an affair involving Gabriel Descombaz of Philadelphia, a former clerk of Moreau de Saint-Méry's bookstore and printing business. After parting ways with Moreau, Descombaz entered a rival venture with a flamboyant figure in Philadelphia's émigré circles, Frank de la Roche, who was not a Freemason. In 1797 the business failed and Descombaz found himself in considerable debt. Since Descombaz was also a founding member of L'Aménité, the lodge set up a committee that produced "minutes and enquiry about the mercantile affairs of Brother Decombaz" and weighed their brother's responsibility in the affair. Once the committee concluded that their member had been honest and innocent in the affair, the lodge demanded from its members "that every one of you will by all means within his power, endeavor to dispel in the profane world, the clouds which malice or credulity may attempt to spread over [his] character."[71] A few years later, the lodge concluded that it had succeeded, "by a swift and successful use of our Masonic correspondence" in reestablishing Descombaz's good public reputation.[72]

The questions debated in such internal Masonic surveys and trials were of the utmost importance to the individuals concerned, especially as a bad reputation could easily spread within the highly mobile diaspora of Saint-Domingue refugees. Thus, when refugee Joseph Marcadier became embroiled in a series of conflicts among French refugee lodges in New York, he insisted that his reputation be repaired by the grand lodge. For him, the affair was even more pressing as

> I am about to leave this country and some brethren who were present at the lodge and particularly one brother who then required that the matter should be properly discussed and a regular vote taken, also intend soon to depart from this state.[73]

One important rationale for the intense communication between the lodges was in fact the control of the "respectable" segment of the refugee population. Regularly, the lodges informed one another about traveling swindlers who tried to gain access to lodges or about individuals who had been excluded for "un-Masonic" behavior.[74]

Moreover, the lodges did not refrain from defending their authority to assess their own refugees' qualifications against grand lodge officials. When, for instance, the Grand Lodge of New York decided to overturn the exclusion of a French member from the most influential refugee lodge in New York, the lodge asked, in no uncertain terms, how [it had] been possible for them to decide so peremptorily upon facts, voluminous proofs of which were written in a language they do not understand, they, who are perfect Strangers to our manners, our habits and to both parties' character.[75]

The politics of respectability were also instrumental in another central element of the lodges' diasporic existence. In fact, these institutions not only worked at integrating and controlling a segment of the diaspora but also served to incorporate refugees into broader circles of their surrounding host societies. In the United States and the British West Indies, the refugee lodges became part of the existing fabric of Freemasonry, in which important segments of the local elites and notables participated. Despite their clear links to the Saint-Domingue communities, most lodges had members from the local population, and in the United States also from existing French merchant communities and émigré groups from France. Whereas, in their delicate situation, the lodges in Cuba were wary of "making proselytes," they sought to teach the local population "that mason and honest are almost synonyms; that the Masons, one cannot repeat this enough, are the example of all the civil and religious virtues."[76]

In some contexts, especially in the United States, the refugee lodges also engaged in displays of loyalty, especially in times of public pressure. Thus, in January 1800, L'Aménité organized and sponsored a huge public memorial service for their deceased "brother," George Washington, centered on a sarcophagus. In their translated and published homage to Washington, they described themselves – along with the deceased president – as "apostles of humanity," as members of an "empire of virtue, whose only limits are the boundaries of the universe." On a slightly different note, they also emphasized the close bonds between the United States and France, and stated that "to no nation after his own was he [Washington] so dear as he was to France."[77] The ceremony involved various other local lodges and American public figures and earned them praise from US government officials, including President John Adams, Vice-President Thomas Jefferson, and Pennsylvania Governor Thomas McKean.[78] Events like these were part of L'Aménité's long-standing effort to be included in Philadelphia's Masonic establishment. Less glamorous than Anne Bingham's salon in Philadelphia, Masonic lodges nevertheless served a similar purpose: to establish polite Franco-American networks and spaces of interaction.

These integrating forces of refugee Freemasonry cannot be separated from several modes of exclusion that were constitutive of Masonic sociability. In fact, the cross-border incorporation of a segment of the Saint-Domingue diaspora based on "respectability" operated, to a certain degree, to the exclusion of several categories of refugees. First, while some currents in continental European Freemasonry began lifting the ban on active female participation, there is no evidence that any of the refugee lodges did so. On the contrary, conformity with the dominant gender norms and the male character of Freemasonry seems to have represented a way of increasing their members' respectability. In this regard, they clearly contrasted with the glamorous salons of Philadelphia's high society, which often centered on certain elite women. Second, while they tended to be more socially open than these fashionable circles, the refugee lodges' membership was primarily upper middle class.[79] In their moderate social elitism, they were clearly distinct from the Roman Catholic Church, another important cross-border integrating force within the diaspora, comprised of all social classes and races.

Third, the refugee lodges remained bound to a colonial type of Freemasonry that had been practiced in Saint-Domingue and other Caribbean colonies and for which whiteness was a central criterion for admission.[80] In the decades before the revolution, and under the pressure of an aspiring class of free people of color, racial exclusion in Saint-Domingue's Freemasonry had become dogma. In the United States and Jamaica, where arriving black refugees and refugees of color were met with suspicion and rejection, this Masonic link to whiteness certainly strengthened the bonds of solidarity toward white refugees.

However, there are hints that this may be only half of the story. By the time of the Haitian Revolution, an African American counterpart to white Freemasonry had emerged. Established in Boston in the 1780s and spreading across the United States from the mid-1790s on, so-called Prince Hall lodges formed a powerful network of communication and mobility within the revolutionary Black Atlantic. Likewise, the racial profile of Saint-Dominguan colonial Freemasonry got blurred in the turmoil of the Haitian Revolution, when some free men of color were admitted to lodges, including people from black general Toussaint Louverture's inner circle. In exile, a few Saint-Domingue refugees of color appear to have found their way into Prince Hall lodges in the United States, building on interactions that had begun in the 1780s.[81] His Masonic credentials clearly shaped the short captivity of Jean-Pierre Boyer, a black officer in the French army and later Haitian president, in Connecticut in 1800–1801.[82] Others seem to have founded their own, unauthorized lodges. According to a 1798 report by a refugee to the governor of Jamaica, for instance, mulatto leader André Rigaud was said to have established a clandestine lodge in Danish Saint Thomas as part of his broader schemes to organize rebellion across the region.[83] A quarter century later, colonial authorities in Jamaica cited alleged Masonic correspondence and conspiratorial activities with Haiti as their reason to deport several prominent descendants of free-colored Saint-Domingue refugees from the island.[84] With Haiti turning into another Atlantic pole of black Freemasonry, in the 1810s and 1820s, Masonic networks more clearly became an integral part of border-crossing within the Black Atlantic.[85] In this way, refugee Freemasonry, despite its racial animus, helped set the stage for a very different kind of diasporic networking.

Conclusions

Moreau de Saint-Méry experienced only a trickle of French refugee Freemasonry first hand that was spreading across the Americas during the Haitian Revolution. In contrast to the majority of Saint-Dominguans, Moreau's American exile did not last long. He left Philadelphia in 1798 and returned to France – at the very moment when groups of Saint-Dominguans had begun to establish a vibrant network of Masonic lodges across the United States, Louisiana, and the Spanish and British Caribbean. Two decades later – when Moreau died in Paris in early 1819 – most refugee lodges had disappeared. Only a few of them managed to remain active, and some have even persisted up to today – such as New York's L'Union française or L'Etoile Polaire in New Orleans – by opening their doors to other segments of the local population. The fact that they left only a few lasting marks, however, should not diminish their significance. For the period from the mid-1790s until well into the 1810s, many of these lodges stood out as relatively stable in generally volatile local Masonic landscapes, where most lodges – due to internal rivalries or lack of resources or members – only existed for a few years.

Both their stability and their sudden disappearance highlight how closely these lodges were connected with the diasporic situation of the Saint-Domingue refugees. Already in the decades before the Haitian Revolution, Freemasonry had been a major element of cross-border sociability and fraternal networking across the Atlantic world. Pre-revolutionary Saint-Domingue, replete with dozens of Masonic lodges, was well integrated into this system of Atlantic Masonic relations. In the late eighteenth century, the colony and especially its commercial center, Cap-Français, arguably constituted the major hub of French Atlantic Freemasonry, while at the same time maintaining a web of external relations well beyond the French imperial sphere. With the Haitian Revolution, colonial Freemasonry in Saint-Domingue unraveled, but the lodge network was quickly rebuilt and adjusted to the new situation. For several decades, the centers of French Atlantic Freemasonry in the Americas would be outside of French-controlled territory: in Philadelphia and later New Orleans.

Freemasonry's high degree of elasticity, or "plasticity," as some historians have termed it,[86] revealed itself in this moment of revolutionary turmoil and displacement. The lodge infrastructure, of which Saint-Domingue had been part, did not simply disappear but took on new forms and meanings. Tailored to their specific needs, it morphed into a crucial social infrastructure and integrating force of the Saint-Domingue diaspora across their different places of refuge. A certain segment of Saint-Dominguan refugees used the means and resources provided by Freemasonry to move and to get organized in exile. Their lodges turned into refugee lodges as they responded to the specific needs of the diaspora. Thus, they functioned as a repository of French exile identity, culture, and even politics. They were a central provider of charity to destitute Saint-Domingue refugees and their relatives. They offered assistance and contacts to those on the move and provided a communication infrastructure between the major places of refuge. Most importantly, the lodges worked at structuring the diaspora by serving as a repository of respectability for their male, white, middle-class membership. Through the various forms of exclusion, the diasporic integration they fostered was primarily geographic, after all. While strengthening the diasporic ties across state and imperial borders, the lodges also built interpersonal links to the host societies. Despite Freemasonry's exclusive character, the universalist claims and organizational forms it provided could also be appropriated by groups that were excluded from "official" refugee lodges. Thus, early Masonic interactions between the United States and Saint-Domingue, later Haiti, foreshadowed the more widespread black Atlantic brothering that would come in the following decades.

The vibrant Masonic life many Saint-Dominguan refugees engaged in where they settled – with lodge meetings, formulaic correspondence, ceremonies, and processions in peculiar costumes – were not just a mere cultural quirk. Nor were they an expression of escapism from their real fate. They were a quintessential feature of how these refugees coped with and shaped their situation. In this, the refugee lodges illustrated the power of the discrete and semi-private spheres of fraternalism and sociable gathering in Atlantic border-crossings. They formed the core of a network of places of sociability and association – boarding houses and informal salons, academies and societies, stores, cafés and taverns – geared to facilitate mobility, enable interactions, provide contacts, and foster the exchange of information across borders in a time of radical transformation and uncertainty.

Notes

1. On Moreau's life, see Elicona, *Un colonial sous la révolution*; on various aspects of his life and thinking, see Taffin, *Moreau de Saint-Méry*. Creole here means person born in the colonies.
2. Moreau de Saint-Méry, *Voyage aux Etats-Unis*. On the broader context of Francophone refugee literature about the United States, see Faÿ, *Bibliographie*; Echeverria, *Mirage in the West*.
3. Moreau de Saint-Méry, *Voyage aux Etats-Unis*, 61.
4. Ibid., 125, 202.
5. Furstenberg, *When the United States Spoke French*. The book provides an excellent account of Moreau's time in the United States. See also Harsanyi, *Lessons from America*.
6. Moreau de Saint-Méry, *Description*, Vol. 1, 434, 554; Vol. 2, 408, 577, 700–1.
7. See, for example, his extensive notes about the Ancient and Accepted Scottish rite and its Supreme Council in Charleston, SC, Archives nationales d'outre-mer (Aix-en-Provence), Fonds Moreau de Saint-Méry, F3/112, fs. 379–395.
8. See the cases cited in Debien, "Réfugiés de Saint-Domingue," esp. 1–3; Dessens, *From Saint-Domingue*, 146.
9. See Lambert's certificate issued by the lodge La Réunion des cœurs (Union of Hearts) in Santiago de Cuba, 1807, Tulane University, Louisiana Research Collection (hereafter LaRC), Lambert Family Papers, 244, Box 1.
10. On the revolutionary period as a moment of crisis, see, for example, Harland-Jacobs, *Builders of Empire*, 130–143.
11. Among the earlier studies that pointed to this were Childs, *French Refugee Life*, 107–108; Babb, "French Refugees," 363–366; more recently, Dessens, *From Saint-Domingue*, 145–147; Debien, "Saint-Domingue Refugees," 105–106; Renault, *D'une île rebelle*, 304–317; Renault, "L'influence de la franc-maçonnerie."
12. For freedom papers, see Scott and Hébrard, *Freedom Papers*; Dun, *Dangerous Neighbors*, 137–139; for letters of introduction, see Furstenberg, *When the United States Spoke French*, 137–154.
13. The pioneering study in this line of scholarship is Scott III, "The Common Wind." For the case of the Saint-Domingue refugees, see Meadows, "Engineering Exile."
14. Perl-Rosenthal, "Atlantic Cultures."
15. Excellent case studies of this elasticity and the tension between universalism and particularism are Hoffmann, *Politics of Sociability*; Harland-Jacobs, *Builders of Empire*, 112–119.
16. Clark, *British Clubs and Societies*, 471.
17. The pathbreaking survey on this is Bullock, *Revolutionary Brotherhood*.
18. For discussions of these historiographic strands, see Harland-Jacobs, "Worlds of Brothers."
19. Beaurepaire, *L'Autre et le Frère*, 95–152; Beaurepaire, "Universal Republic."
20. Wright, "Refugee Lodges."
21. Attempts at putting these refugee communities in the larger historical context are Jasanoff, "Revolutionary Exiles" and Jansen "Flucht und Exil."
22. Good recent overviews are Jasanoff, *Liberty's Exiles*; Pestel, *Kosmopoliten wider Willen*.
23. There is no integrated history of these different communities. On different places, see White, *Encountering Revolution*; Debien and Wright, "Colons de Saint-Domingue," as well as the references in note 11. On the estimates of the total size, see Babb, "French Refugees," 370–384; Meadows "The Planters of Saint-Domingue," 1–2.
24. At least two lodges, Les Frères réunis and La Benignité, seem to have been established locally in 1812 and 1818 but were never recognized by grand lodge authorities in London. See "List of lodges refused warrants due to insufficient information," Provincial Grand Lodge of Jamaica, c. 1820. Library of the United Grand Lodge of England, London (LUGLE), HC 22/D/9; *Jamaica Almanac, for the Year 1818*, 91. See also Seal-Coon, *Jamaican Freemasonry*, 83, 86; Escalle and Gouyon Guillaume, *Francs-maçons des loges françaises*, 178–179. On the Masonic credentials of British governors, see Ranston, *Masonic Jamaica*, 104–110, 124.
25. On these two lodges, see Fondeviolle, député de La Réunion des cœurs, to Grand Orient de France (hereafter GODF), 22 October, 1807. Bibliothèque nationale de France, Paris (hereafter BnF), Fonds maçonnique (hereafter FM), FM2/545, Dossier "Saint Domingue, La Réunion des

cœurs"; Vérité séante à l'Orient de Baltimore to GODF, s.d. [1808]. BnF, FM, FM2/543, Dossier 1 "Saint-Domingue, La Vérité"; *Tableau de La Vérité du Cap François, no. 42*. Information on many other Saint-Domingue lodges in exile can be found in Escalle and Gouyon Guillaume, *Francs-maçons des loges françaises*; Combes, "La Franc-Maçonnerie aux Antilles."

26. "Report of Committee of Correspondence to whom were referred sundry communications from the RW Provincial Grand Master of St. Domingo and Cuba, from the lodges no. 88, 98," 15 September 1806. Archives of the Grand Lodge of Pennsylvania, Philadelphia (hereafter AGLPA), File Y.

27. On Moreau's bookstore, see Rosengarten, "Moreau de Saint Méry"; Childs, *French Refugee Life*, 109. On refugee cafés in New Orleans, see Dessens, *From Saint-Domingue*, 145.

28. Furstenberg, *When the United States Spoke French*, 177. Further accounts of the social and intellectual life of French emigrants in the United States include Kennedy, *Orders From France*; Harsanyi, *Lessons from America*; Childs, *French Refugee Life*; Spaeth, "Purgatory or Promised Land?"; Faÿ, *L'esprit révolutionnaire*; Rosengarten, *French Colonists*.

29. Laujon de Latouche, *Souvenirs*, Vol. 2, 109–123, quoted on 110.

30. On Freemasonry's transnational dimensions, see Beaurepaire, *République universelle*; Harland-Jacobs, *Builders of Empire*, esp. chapter 2; Hoffmann, *Civil Society*.

31. Le Bihan, "La Franc-Maçonnerie"; Combes, "Franc-Maçonnerie aux Antilles"; Cauna, "Quelques aperçus"; Escalle and Gouyon Guillaume, *Francs-maçons des loges françaises*; Fouchard, *Les plaisirs de Saint-Domingue*, 96–97; Regourd, "Lumière coloniale," esp. 198; McClellan III, *Colonialism and Science*, 105–106, 187.

32. Jansen, "Atlantic Sociability," esp. 93.

33. "Tableau des loges avec lesquelles correspond celle de St. Jean de Jérusalem écossaise à l'orient du Cap [c. 1777]." BnF, FM, FM2/543, Dossier "St. Jean de Jérusalem écossaise, Orient du Cap."

34. Saunier, "L'espace caribéen," esp. 49–52. On Masonic membership as a marker of the slave traders' milieu, see Pétré-Grenouilleau, *L'argent de la traite*, 107–109.

35. L'Anglaise, Bordeaux, to GODF, 5 January 1779. Archives de la Grande Loge de France, Paris, Archives russes, Opis 4 Boîte no. 9.

36. Copy of warrant by Saint James' Lodge no. 1, Kingston, 1 July 1785. BnF, FM, FM2/545, Dossier "Saint Domingue, La Réunion des cœurs." Saint James' Lodge, created in 1765 in Gibraltar, seems to have never been officially recognized by one of the grand lodges in England. It appears, however, in local almanacs, e.g., *Douglass and Aikman's Alamanck*, 81.

37. La Réunion des cœurs, Jérémie, to La Réunion des Etrangers, St. Thomas, 20 March 1800. Jamaica Archives, Spanish Town, VAS, "John" to H.M.S. "York," 28 August, 1800.

38. J.L. Galbert Baron, Master of St. Jean d'Ecosse, Cap-Français, to George Washington, s.d. [July 1785]. AGLPA, BL Cape François 47 St John of Scotland at St Domingo.

39. The most important scholarship in this direction is by Meadows, "The Planters of Saint-Domingue"; Meadows, "Engineering Exile."

40. On the role of Catholicism, see Babb, "French Refugees," 250–265; Dessens, *From Saint-Domigue*, 100–103; Debien and Wright, "Colons de Saint-Domingue," 107–111.

41. On Philadelphia's trade with the French Caribbean, see Coatsworth, "American Trade," 245–6; Doerflinger, *A Vigorous Spirit*, 242–250, 335–356; Dun, "Philadelphia's Vantage"; for consumption, see Branson, *Fiery Frenchified Dames*.

42. Barrat and Sachse, *Freemasonry in Pennsylvania*, Vol. 2, 103–180; Huss, *Master Builders*, Vol. 1, 55–83.

43. "Copy of the Warrant of Lodge no. 47, La Réunion des cœurs franco-américains, Port-au-Prince, 18 December 1789." AGLPA, File 47e.

44. For the lodges in Saint-Domingue, see AGLPA, Warrant Book, A, 81–82, 85–86, 95–96, 105–106, 119, 124–125; for the other refugee lodges, see *Minutes of the Grand Lodge of of Pennsylvania*, Vol. 1, 331–332, 471–472; Vol. 2, 33, 135, 211–213, 331–333, 354–356, 393, 477–478; Vol. 3, 46–47; Vol. 4, 274.

45. *Minutes of the Grand Lodge of Pennsylvania*, Vol. 1, 269–270; *Tableau des frères, L'Aménité no. 73* (1797). L'Aménité was the most successful out of a cluster of French refugee lodges in

THE FRATERNAL ATLANTIC, 1770–1930   59

Philadelphia. Other lodges created at the same time were Saint-Louis (1792–94) and Parfaite Union (founded in 1798 by the GODF); *Minutes of the Grand Lodge*, Vol. 1, 187–8; *Tableau des membres, La Parfaite Union*.

46. See, e.g., "Return of the members of lodge no. 73 [L'Aménité]," 1797–1798. AGLPA, BL PA 73. See also Huss, "Pennsylvania Freemasonry," 160.

47. See the nearly complete returns of members for the years 1797–1820. AGLPA, BL PA 73.

48. Lists provided in *Tableau des frères, L'Aménité no. 73* (1811), 11–15. See also *Tableau des frères, L'Aménité No. 73* (1803), 7–8; *Correspondance entre la R. Lo. Française l'Aménité No. 73*.

49. See, e.g., Minutes of meeting of La Persévérance no. 4, New Orleans, 12 February 1832. Tulane University, LaRC, 895 Freemason lodges in Louisiana, Series 1: La Persévérance no. 4, Vol. 15: Minutes of La Persévérance no. 4, 1829–1839, 93r. On resistance against Anglicization, see Dessens, *From Saint-Domingue*, 162–165.

50. As late as 1810, for example, the lodge La Persévérance, transferred to New Orleans via Santiago de Cuba, still used a seal referring to its Saint-Dominguan hometown, Les Abricots (La Persévérance, New Orleans, to Parfaite Union, New Orleans, 29 February 1810. Tulane University, LaRC, 895 Freemason lodges in Louisiana, Series 1: La Persévérance, Box 1, 895-1-1).

51. *Oraison funèbre des FF. Tanguy de la Boissière, Gauvain et Décombaz*, 27.

52. *Extrait des registres de la loge française L'Aménité no. 73*, quotes on 1 and 4. The exact date of the January 1800 session is not mentioned.

53. L'Aménité no. 73 to Grand Lodge of Pennsylvania, 22 June 1809. AGLPA, BL PA 73. Emphasis in the original document.

54. *Tableau des frères, L'Aménité no. 73* (1797); *Oraison funèbre des FF. Tanguy de la Boissière, Gauvain et Décombaz*. On the broader political context, see Childs, *French Refugee Life*, 141–85; Marino, "French Refugee Newspapers"; Pierce, *Discourses of the Dispossessed*, 140–210; Dun, *Dangerous Neighbors*, 87–120.

55. *Extrait des registres de la loge française L'Aménité no. 73*, 3–4. On the debates surrounding freedom and philanthropy, see White, *Encountering Revolution*, 51–86.

56. Quotes are from "Extrait du livre d'architecture de la Grande Loge Provinciale de Saint-Domingue," Baracoa, 6 April 1805; and Grande Loge Provinciale de Saint-Domingue, Baracoa, to Morel de Guiramant, Santiago de Cuba, s.d. [1805]. AGLPA, File Y.

57. *Minutes of the Grand Lodge of Pennsylvania*, Vol. 2, 243–244; Renault, *D'une île rebelle*, 315.

58. "Extrait de la délibération de la loge La Vérité, Cap-Français, accidentellement à l'orient de Baltimore," 1 March 1798. Archives of the Grand Lodge of Maryland, Scrapbook of Curiosities, Maryland's Masonic Veterans Association.

59. *Sermon exhibiting the Present Dangers*. On conspiracy theories about the Illuminati and anti-Jacobinism in the United States, see Lienesch, "Illusion of the Illuminati"; Stauffer, *New England*; Cleves, *Reign of Terror*.

60. *Federal Republican & Commercial Gazette* (Baltimore), 14 August 1809; *The Evening Post* (New York), 16 August 1809.

61. Childs, *French Refugee Life*, 84–90; White, *Encountering Revolution*, 51–86; Debien and Wright, "Colons de Saint-Domingue," 85–97; Meadows, "Planters of Saint-Domingue."

62. Bullock, *Revolutionary Brotherhood*, 186–198; Harland-Jacobs, *Builders of Empire*, 51–63.

63. E.g., Petitions from M. Chédal, 16 April 1804 and S.M. Mareck, 16 July 1804. AGLPA, Vol. 8, 47 and 51a.

64. "Address delivered by the master of L'Aménité no. 73 to the Grand Master and Grand Officers," 25 June 1805. AGLPA, BL PA 73. The "tigers of St. Domingue" was a trope in white planters' accounts of the Haitian Revolution.

65. Saint-Méry, *Voyage aux Etats-Unis*, 191, 209–210; Childs, *French Refugee Life*, 122–125. His initial financier, Frank de la Roche, with whom Moreau soon broke, was not a Freemason.

66. Maydieu to Grand Lodge of New York, 7 August 1794. Archives of the Grand Lodge of New York (hereafter AGLNY), Scrapbook Vol. 62, L'Unité américaine.

67. La Candeur, New Orleans, to Grand Lodge of Pennsylvania, 3 August 1800. AGLPA, BL 90.

68. Etoile Polaire, New Orleans, to Las Virtudes teologales, Havana, 14 July 1814. Historic New Orleans Collection (hereafter HNOC), T100818.9720 Etoile Polaire #1, Letter Book (3 March 1814–20 July 1815).
69. L'Aménité no. 73, state meeting of 6 August 1800. AGLPA, BL PA 73.
70. "Representation from Lodge no. 73 respecting Bro. Decombaz," 4 May 1797. AGLPA, BL PA 73.
71. All quotes from ibid. On the characters involved in this affair, see also Childs, *French Refugee Life*, 122–123, 125. The bankruptcy is also documented in *Courrier français* (Philadelphia), 23 August 1797.
72. *Oraison funèbre des FF. Tanguy de la Boissière, Gauvain et Décombaz*, 34.
73. Petition of Joseph Marcadier, read in Grand Lodge, 15 June 1797. AGLNY, Scrapbook Vol. 57, L'Union française.
74. E.g., L'Union française, New York, to La Candeur, Charleston, and Etoile Polaire, New Orleans, 3 August 1819. AGLNY, Scrapbook Vol. 57, L'Union française.
75. L'Union française, New York, to Grand Lodge of New York, 8 August 1797. AGLNY, Scrapbook Vol. 57, L'Union française.
76. Grande Loge Provinciale de Saint-Domingue, Baracoa, to Morel de Guiramant, Santiago de Cuba, s.d. [1805]. AGLPA, File Y.
77. *Funeral Oration on Brother George Washington*, quotes on 3–4; *Extrait des registres de la loge française L'Aménité no. 73*, quote on 22. An account of the event also in *Minutes of the Grand Lodge of Philadelphia*, Vol. 1, 402–404.
78. *Lettres écrites à la loge L'Aménité no. 73*.
79. Huss, "Pennsylvania Freemasonry," 159, 170, 181–186; Renault, *D'une île rebelle*, 313.
80. Combes, "Franc-Maçonnerie aux Antilles;" Beaurepaire, *L'Autre et le Frère*, 576–585; Harland-Jacobs, *Builders of Empire*, 215–220; Révauger, "Freemasonry in Barbados," 85–86.
81. On Prince Hall Freemasonry as a cross-border network, see Scott, "The Common Wind," 293; Kantrowitz, "African American Freemasonry," 1005; on Saint-Dominguan membership, Davies, "Class, Culture, and Color," 84, 92–93. A reason for the small number of colored Saint-Dominguans in these lodges may have been the close relationship between Prince Hall Freemasonry and African American Protestant churches; see Hackett, *Religion*, 151–174. On the contentious question of Black Freemasonry in revolutionary Saint-Domingue, see Garrigus, *Before Haiti*, 291–296; Garrigus, "Secret Brotherhood"; Cauna, "Thèse du complot."
82. Hinks, "Perfectly Proper and Conciliating."
83. See, for example, the report by Marquis de La Jaille to Lord Balcarres, Governor of Jamaica, 31 October 1798. National Library of Scotland, Muniments of the Earls of Crawford and Balcarres, Papers of the 6th Earl of Balcarres, Acc. 9769/23/12/24.
84. Testimony by James Stewart Innes, 21 November 1823, Minutes of the Secret Committee of the House of Assembly. The National Archives, Kew, Colonial Office, CO 137/174, fs. 13–15. The deportation of Louis Lecesne and John Escoffery turned into a major legal battle and scandal.
85. On these developments, see Hinks, "To Commence a New Era."
86. Chevallier, *Première profanation*, 34; Saunier, *Révolution et sociabilité*, 78, 161; Beaurepaire, *République universelle*, 24, 76, 167, 170.

Acknowledgements

I would like to thank the anonymous readers, as well as Jessica Harland-Jacobs, Peter Hinks, and Elizabeth Mancke, for their brilliant suggestions and comments on earlier drafts of the article. I owe a deep gratitude to the archivists and librarians at the following institutions for providing me access and guiding me through their rich collections: Archives de la Grande Loge de France, Paris; Archives nationales d'outre-mer, Aix-en-Provence; Bibliothèque nationale de France, Paris; Etoile Polaire #1 Lodge, New Orleans; Grand Lodge of Maryland, Baltimore; Grand Lodge of New York, New York City; Grand Lodge of Pennsylvania, Philadelphia; Historic New Orleans Collection, New Orleans; Jamaica Archives, Spanish Town; Louisiana Research Collection, Tulane University, New Orleans;

National Library of Scotland, Edinburgh; and United Grand Lodge of England, London. I am grateful to GHI editors Casey Sutcliffe and Mark Stoneman for copy-editing, and GHI interns Cora Schmidt-Ott, Alina Weishäupl, and Johanna Strunge for research assistance.

Disclosure statement

No potential conflict of interest was reported by the author.

Bibliography

Babb, Winston C. "French Refugees from Saint-Domingue to the Southern United States: 1791–1810." PhD diss., University of Virginia, 1954.

Barrat, Norris S., and Julius F. Sachse. *Freemasonry in Pennsylvania, 1727–1907*. Philadelphia: New Era Printing Company, 1909.

Beaurepaire, Pierre-Yves. *L'Autre et le Frère: L'étranger et la franc-maçonnerie en France au XVIIIe siècle*. Paris: Champion, 1998.

Beaurepaire, Pierre-Yves. *La République universelle des francs-maçons: De Newton à Metternich*. Rennes: Éd. Ouest-France, 1999.

Beaurepaire, Pierre-Yves. "The Universal Republic of the Freemasons and the Culture of Mobility in the Enlightenment." *French Historical Studies* 29, no. 3 (2006): 407–431.

Branson, Susan. *These Fiery Frenchified Dames: Women and Political Culture in Early National Philadelphia*. Philadelphia: University of Philadelphia Press, 2001.

Bullock, Stephen C. *Revolutionary Brotherhood: Freemasonry and the Transformation of the American Social Order, 1730–1840*. Chapel Hill: University of North Carolina Press, 1996.

Cauna, Jacques de. "Quelques aperçus sur l'histoire de la franc-maçonnerie en Haïti." *Revue de la Société d'Histoire et de Géographie d'Haïti* 189–190 (1996): 20–34.

Cauna, Jacques de. "Autour de la thèse du complot: franc-maçonnerie, révolution et contre-révolution à Saint-Domingue, 1789–1791." In *Franc-maçonnerie et politique au siècle des lumières: Europe-Amériques*, edited by Cécile Révauger, 289–310. Pessac: Presses Universitaires de Bordeaux, 2006.

Chevallier, Pierre. *La première profanation du temple maçonnique: Ou Louis XV et la fraternité 1737–1755*. Paris: J. Vrin, 1968.

Childs, Frances S. *French Refugee Life in the United States, 1790–1800: An American Chapter of the French Revolution*. Baltimore: The Johns Hopkins University Press, 1940.

Clark, Peter. *British Clubs and Societies 1580–1800: The Origins of an Associational World*. Oxford: Oxford University Press, 2000.

Cleves, Rachel Hope. *The Reign of Terror in America: Visions of Violence from Anti-Jacobinism to Antislavery*. Cambridge: Cambridge University Press, 2009.

Coatsworth, John H. "American Trade with European Colonies in the Caribbean and South America, 1790–1812." *The William and Mary Quarterly* 24, no. 2 (1967): 243–266.

Combes, André. "La Franc-Maçonnerie aux Antilles et en Guyane française de 1789 à 1848." In *La période révolutionnaire aux Antilles: Images et résonnances*. Schœlcher: Université des Antilles et de la Guyane, c. 1989.

Correspondance entre la R. Lo. Française l'Aménité No. 73, séante á l'orient de Philadelphie, et sa sœur affiliée, la T. R. Lo. Française Le Choix des Vrais Amis, séante à l'O. de Marseille. Philadelphia: T. & W. Bradford, 1802.

Davies, John. "Class, Culture, and Color: Black Saint-Dominguan Refugees and African-American Communities in the Early Republic." PhD diss., University of Delaware, 2008.

Debien, Gabriel. "Réfugiés de Saint-Domingue aux Etats-Unis." *Revue de la Société d'Histoire et de Géographie d'Haïti* 20 (January 1949): 1–20.

Debien, Gabriel. "The Saint-Domingue Refugees in Cuba, 1793–1815." In *The Road to Louisiana: The Saint-Domingue Refugees, 1792–1809*, edited by Carl E. Brasseaux and Glenn R. Conrad, 31–112. Lafayette, LA: Center for Louisiana Studies, 1992.

Debien, Gabriel, and Philip Wright. "Les colons de Saint-Domingue passés à la Jamaïque." *Bulletin de la Société d'Histoire de la Guadeloupe* 26, no. 4 (1975): 3–217.

Dessens, Nathalie. *From Saint-Domingue to New Orleans: Migration and Influences.* Gainesville: University Press of Florida, 2007.

Doerflinger, Thomas M. *A Vigorous Spirit: Merchants and Economic Development in Revolutionary Philadelphia.* Chapel Hill: University of North Carolina Press, 1986.

Douglass and Aikman's Alamanck and Register for the Island of Jamaica. Kingston: Douglass & Aikman, 1784.

Dun, James Alexander. "'What Avenues of Commerce Will You, Americans, Not Explore!': Commercial Philadelphia's Vantage Onto the Early Haitian Revolution." *The William and Mary Quarterly* 62, no. 3 (2005): 473–504.

Dun, James Alexander. *Dangerous Neighbors: Making the Haitian Revolution in Early America.* Philadelphia: University of Pennsylvania Press, 2016.

Echeverria, Durand. *Mirage in the West: A History of the French Image of American Society to 1815.* Princeton, NJ: Princeton University Press, 1957.

Elicona, Anthony Louis. *Un colonial sous la révolution en France et en Amérique: Moreau de Saint-Méry.* Paris: Jouve et Cie, 1934.

Escalle, Elisabeth, and Mariel Gouyon Guillaume. *Francs-maçons des loges françaises "aux Amériques" 1770–1850: Contribution à l'étude de la société créole.* Paris: Escalle, 1993.

Extrait des registres de la loge française L'Aménité no. 73, séante à Philadelphie. Philadelphia: Jacques Carey, 1800.

Faÿ, Bernard. *Bibliographie critique des ouvrages français relatifs aux Etats-Unis (1770–1800).* Paris: Champion, 1925a.

Faÿ, Bernard. *L'esprit révolutionnaire en France et aux Etats-Unis.* Paris: Champion, 1925b.

Fouchard, Jean. *Les plaisirs de Saint-Domingue: Notes sur la vie sociale, littéraire et artistiques.* Port-au-Prince: Editions Henri Deschamps, 1988.

Funeral Oration on Brother George Washington, Delivered January 1st, 1800, Before the French Lodge L'Aménité, by Brother Simon Chaudron. Philadelphia: John Ormrod, 1800.

Furstenberg, François. *When the United States Spoke French: Five Refugees Who Shaped a Nation.* New York: Penguin, 2014.

Garrigus, John D. *Before Haiti: Race and Citizenship in French Saint-Domingue.* New York: Palgrave-Macmillan, 2006.

Garrigus, John D. "A Secret Brotherhood? The Question of Black Freemasonry Before and After the Haitian Revolution." *Atlantic Studies: Global Currents*, forthcoming.

Hackett, David. *That Religion in Which all Men Agree: Freemasonry in American Culture.* Berkeley: University of California Press, 2014.

Harland-Jacobs, Jessica. *Builders of Empire: Freemasons and British Imperialism, 1717–1927.* Chapel Hill: University of North Carolina Press, 2007.

Harland-Jacobs, Jessica. "Worlds of Brothers." *Journal for Research Into Freemasonry and Fraternalism* 2, no. 1 (2011): 10–37.

Harsanyi, Doina Pasca. *Lessons from America: Liberal French Nobles in Exile, 1793–1798.* University Park: Pennsylvania State University Press, 2010.

Hinks, Peter P. "'To Commence a New Era in the Moral World': John Telemachus Hilton, Abolitionism, and the Expansion of Black Freemasonry, 1784–1860." In *All Men Free and Brethren: Essays on the*

History of African American Freemasonry, edited by Peter P. Hinks and Stephen Kantrowitz, 40–62. Ithaca, NY: Cornell University Press, 2013.

Hinks, Peter P. "'Perfectly Proper and Conciliating': Jean-Pierre Boyer, Freemasonry, and the Revolutionary Atlantic in Eastern Connecticut, 1800–1801." *Atlantic Studies: Global Currents*, forthcoming.

Hoffmann, Stefan-Ludwig. *Civil Society, 1750–1914*. Basingstoke: Palgrave-Macmillan, 2006.

Hoffmann, Stefan-Ludwig. *The Politics of Sociability: Freemasonry and German Civil Society, 1840–1919*. Ann Arbor: University of Michigan Press, 2007.

Huss, Wayne A. "Pennsylvania Freemasonry: An Intellectual and Social Analysis, 1727–1826." PhD diss., Temple University, 1984.

Huss, Wayne A. *The Master Builders: A History of the Grand Lodge of Free and Accepted Masons of Pennsylvania*. Philadelphia: The Grand Lodge, 1986.

Jamaica Almanac, for the Year 1818. Kingston: Alex. Aikman, Jr., 1818.

Jansen, Jan C. "In Search of Atlantic Sociability: Freemasons, Empires, and Atlantic History." *Bulletin of the German Historical Institute* 57 (2015): 75–99.

Jansen, Jan C. "Flucht und Exil im Zeitalter der Revolutionen (1770er–1820er Jahre): Perspektiven einer atlantischen Flüchtlingsgeschichte." *Geschichte und Gesellschaft* 44, no. 4 (2018).

Jasanoff, Maya. "Revolutionary Exiles: The American Loyalist and French Émigré Diasporas." In *The Age of Revolutions in Global Context, c. 1760–1840*, edited by David Armitage and Sanjay Subrahmanyam, 37–58. Basingstoke: Palgrave Macmillan, 2010.

Jasanoff, Maya. *Liberty's Exiles: American Loyalists in the Revolutionary World*. New York: Knopf, 2011.

Kantrowitz, Stephen. "'Intended for the Better Government of Man': The Political History of African American Freemasonry in the Era of Emancipation." *The Journal of American History* 96, no. 4 (2010): 1001–1026.

Kennedy, Roger G. *Orders from France: The Americans and the French in a Revolutionary World 1780–1820*. New York: Knopf, 1989.

Laujon de Latouche, Alexandre de. *Souvenirs de trente années de voyages, à Saint-Domingue, dans plusieurs colonies étrangères, et au continent d'Amérique*. Paris: Schwartz & Gagnot, 1835.

Le Bihan, Alain. "La Franc-Maçonnerie dans les colonies françaises du XVIIIᵉ siècle." *Annales historiques de la Révolution française* 46 (1974): 39–62.

Lettres écrites à la loge L'Aménité no. 73, à l'occasion de l'oraison funèbre du Frère George Washington. Philadelphia: Thomas & William Bradford, 1801.

Lienesch, Michael. "The Illusion of the Illuminati: The Counterconspiratorial Origins of Post-Revolutionary Conservatism." In *Revolutionary Histories: Transatlantic Cultural Nationalism, 1775–1815*, edited by W. M. Verhoeven, 152–165. Basingstoke: Palgrave-Macmillan, 2002.

Marino, Samuel L. "French Refugee Newspapers and Periodicals in the United States, 1789–1825." PhD diss., University of Michigan, 1962.

McClellan, III, James E. *Colonialism and Science: Saint Domingue in the Old Regime*. Baltimore: The Johns Hopkins University Press, 1992.

Meadows, R. Darrell. "Engineering Exile: Social Networks and the French Atlantic Community, 1789–1809." *French Historical Studies* 23, no. 1 (2000): 67–102.

Meadows, R. Darrell. "The Planters of Saint-Domingue, 1750–1804: Migration and Exile in the French Revolutionary Atlantic." PhD diss., Carnegie Mellon University, 2004.

Minutes of the Grand Lodge of Free and Accepted Masons of Pennsylvania. Philadelphia: The Grand Lodge, 1895ff.

Moreau de Saint-Méry, Médéric Louis Elie. *Description topographique, physique, civile, politique et historique de la partie française de l'île Saint-Domingue*. Philadelphia: Moreau de Saint-Méry, 1797–1798.

Moreau de Saint-Méry, Médéric Louis Elie. *Voyage aux Etats-Unis, 1793–1798*, edited with an introduction and notes by Stewart L. Mims. New Haven, CT: Yale University Press, 1913.

Oraison funèbre des FF. Tanguy de la Boissière, Gauvain et Décombaz, prononcée par le V. de la Grange, dans la loge française L'Aménité, no. 73, séance du 8 du dixième mois 1799. Philadelphia: John Ormrod, 1800.

Perl-Rosenthal, Nathan. "Atlantic Cultures and the Age of Revolution." *The William and Mary Quarterly* 74, no. 4 (2017): 667–696.

Pestel, Friedemann. *Kosmopoliten wider Willen: Die "monarchiens" als Revolutionsemigranten*. Berlin: De Gruyter Oldenbourg, 2015.

Pétré-Grenouilleau, Olivier. *L'argent de la traite: Milieu négrier, capitalisme et développement, un modèle*. Paris: Aubier, 1996.

Pierce, Jennifer J. "Discourses of the Dispossessed: Saint-Domingue Colonists on Race, Revolution and Empire, 1789–1825." PhD diss., State University of New York, 2005.

Ranston, Jackie. *Masonic Jamaica and the Cayman Islands. Vol. 1*. London: Lewis Masonic, 2017.

Regourd, François. "Lumières coloniales: Les Antilles françaises dans la République des lettres." *Dix-huitième siècle* 33 (2001): 183–199.

Renault, Agnès. "L'influence de la franc-maçonnerie française dans le Département Oriental de Cuba dans les années 1820: Les apports de la prosopographie." *Revista de Estudios Históricos de la Masonería Latinoamericana y Caribeña* 1 (2009): 75–93.

Renault, Agnès. *D'une île rebelle à une île fidèle: Les Français de Santiago de Cuba*. Mont-Saint-Aignan: Publications des universités de Rouen et du Havre, 2012.

Révauger, Cécile. "Freemasonry in Barbados, Trinidad and Grenada: British or Homemade?" *Journal for Research Into Freemasonry and Fraternalism* 1 (2010): 79–91.

Rosengarten, Joseph G. *French Colonists and Exiles in the United States*. Philadelphia: Lippincott, 1907.

Rosengarten, Joseph G. "Moreau de Saint Méry and his French Friends in the American Philosophical Society." *Proceedings of the French Historical Society* 50, no. 199 (1911): 168–178.

Saunier, Eric. "L'espace caribéen: Un enjeu de pouvoir pour la franc-maçonnerie française." *Revista de Estudios Históricos de la Masonería Latinoamericana y Caribeña* 1 (2009): 42–56.

Saunier, Eric. *Révolution et sociabilité en Normandie au tournant des XVIIIe et XIXe siècles: 6000 francs-maçons de 1740 à 1830*. Rouen: Publications des Université de Rouen et du Havre, 1998.

Scott III, Julius S. "The Common Wind: Currents of Afro-American Communication in the Era of the Haitian Revolution." PhD diss., Duke University, 1986.

Scott, Rebecca J., and Jean M. Hébrard. *Freedom Papers: An Atlantic Odyssey in the Age of Emancipation*. Cambridge, MA: Harvard University Press, 2012.

Seal-Coon, Frederick William. *An Historical Account of Jamaican Freemasonry*. Kingston: Golding Printing Service Ltd, 1976.

Sermon Exhibiting the Present Dangers, and Consequent Duties of the Citizens of the United States of America, Delivered at Charlestown, April 25, 1799, the day of the National Fast, by Jedidiah Morse. Charlestown: Hartford, 1799.

Spaeth, Catherine T.C. "Purgatory or Promised Land? French Emigrés in Philadelphia and Their Perceptions of America during the 1790s." PhD diss., University of Minnesota, 1992.

Stauffer, Vernon. *New England and the Bavarian Illuminati*. New York: Columbia University Press, 1918.

Tableau des frères qui composent la r.l. française de S.-J. de J., sous le titre distinctif, L'Aménité no. 73. Philadelphia: Parent, 1797.

Tableau des membres qui composent la r.l. française de Saint-Jean de Jérusalem, sous le titre distinctif, La Parfaite Union. Philadelphia: Parent, 1798.

Tableau des frères composant la T. R. Loge Française L'Aménité No. 73. Philadelphia: Thomas & William Bradford, 1803.

Tableau des frères qui composent la r.l. française de S.-J. de J., sous le titre distinctif, L'Aménité no. 73. Philadelphia: Blocquerst, 1811.

Tableau de La Vérité du Cap François, no. 42, régulièrement assemblée à l'orient de Baltimore. Baltimore: G. Gobbin & Murphy, 1807.

Taffin, Dominique, ed. *Moreau de Saint-Méry ou les ambiguïtés d'un créole des Lumières*. Fort-de-France: Société des amis des archives et de la recherche sur le patrimoine culturel des Antilles, 2006.

White, Ashli. *Encountering Revolution: Haiti and the Making of the Early Republic*. Baltimore: The Johns Hopkins University Press, 2010.

Wright, Richardson. "Refugee Lodges." *Transactions of the American Lodge of Research, Free and Accepted Masons* 3, no. 1 (1938–39): 81–96.

Part II

Race

A secret brotherhood? The question of black Freemasonry before and after the Haitian Revolution

John D. Garrigus

ABSTRACT

Late eighteenth-century Saint-Domingue produced both a thriving Masonic movement and the most successful slave uprising in modern world history. Scholars have suggested but never proven that these two movements were linked. One biographer hypothesizes that white planters who knew the future Toussaint Louverture from colonial Masonic circles helped him organize the slave uprising of August 1791. This speculation is inspired by the fact that in the late 1790s Louverture signed his name with a distinctive pattern of dots. Many colonists and free men of color used similar symbols, which have been described as Masonic signatures.

This article examines whether the approximately 300 men of all races who made such signatures in the 1780s and early 1790s were Masons. It finds little or no evidence that they were. It hypothesizes that men used these symbols to suggest their membership in secret societies that did not, in fact, exist.

Introduction

Was Freemasonry involved in the Haitian Revolution (1791–1804)? Did Masonic brotherhood unite some whites and men of color during these epochal events, either across the Atlantic or within the colony? A 2008 biography of Toussaint Louverture and a 2009 study of Hegel's awareness of the Haitian Revolution both suggest this possibility.[1] By 1790, Saint-Domingue, as Haiti was known under French colonial rule, was perhaps the most "masonized" society in the Atlantic world.[2] Many prominent figures in the Age of Atlantic Revolutions were Freemasons,[3] including men who worked closely with Saint-Domingue's free men of color. In Paris the Marquis de Lafayette and Etienne de Joly collaborated with wealthy free men of color who were trying to get full citizenship from the Revolution. One-quarter of the anti-slavery *Amis des Noirs* were Freemasons. Etienne Polverel, one of the two Revolutionary commissioners who proclaimed the end of slavery in Saint-Domingue in 1793, was a Freemason.[4] Toussaint Louverture and his secretaries routinely placed three points after his signature, making a sign that has been described as a masonic symbol (Figure 1).[5] A handful of Louverture's close associates were Freemasons in the late 1790s. Finally, after defeating Napoleon's troops, Haiti rapidly established its own Masonic system. Just two years after independence, Haiti had its first national lodges.

Figure 1. Signature of Toussaint Louverture (ca. 1743–1803), with so-called "masonic" points on a document dated in Port-au-Prince on 27 prairial, Year 9 [16 June 1801], appended to a notarized document dated 1 messidor Year 9 [20 June 1801]. Photo by author, 2007.

One key to this mystery is whether Toussaint Louverture's signature indicates he was a Freemason, as Madison Smartt Bell proposes. Bell suggests he was in order to flesh out a conspiracy scenario advanced by contemporaries and by prominent nineteenth-century Haitian historians.[6] According to this view Louverture's white employer François Bayon de Libertat and other royalists convinced the ex-slave to mount a slave rebellion in August 1791, believing that a black uprising would dissuade pro-Revolutionary whites from their plans to restructure colonial society.[7] Twentieth-century historians largely dismissed the idea of a white royalist plot for lack of evidence, and because its proponents believed that blacks could not have organized an uprising without white leadership. Bell's Freemasonic hypothesis suggests that the royalists intended the rebellion to be a sham, but that Louverture made it into the very successful insurrection that launched the Haitian Revolution. Building on research by Jacques de Cauna, Bell extends the conspiracy scenario by hypothesizing that the plot came together because Bayon and two other moderate royalists belonged to the same the unspecified Masonic lodge in Cap Français, where Toussaint, still hypothetically, worked as a "servant-brother."[8]

Bell acknowledges the "sheer preposterousness" of his Masonic hypothesis. In fact there is no evidence that Toussaint was involved in the slave revolt until December 1791. But Bell is not the only scholar tantalized by the possibility that Masonic bonds crossed the colonial color-line and influenced the Haitian Revolution. In a 2006 book, I used signature evidence to conclude that a number of free men of color in the parish of Aquin probably belonged to a hidden lodge that showed their allegiance to the civic ideals of the French Revolution. Susan Buck-Morss believes that "freemasonry was a crucial factor in the uprisings in Saint-Domingue." Basing this statement, like Bell's conspiracy, on the speculations of other, often anti-Masonic historians, Buck-Morss correctly observes: "We know far too little of freemasonry in the black/brown/white Atlantic, a major chapter in the history of hybridity and transculturation."[9]

This article examines the evidence for multi-racial Freemasonry in Saint-Domingue, before and during the Haitian Revolution. The involvement of men of color in transatlantic fraternalism would confirm that the Haitian Revolution was more than a reaction to political chaos in France, that it was influenced by the concepts and institutions of enlightenment universalism.[10] To set the stage, the article reviews the scholarship on Freemasonry

THE FRATERNAL ATLANTIC, 1770–1930

and race in Saint-Domingue before and after 1791. Then it considers the phenomenon of "Masonic signatures," the distinctive combinations of dots and lines that some men made as they signed their names on public documents. It addresses the question of whether these marks were a sign of Masonic affiliation in Saint-Domingue in the 1790s. After discussing the scholarly literature on these marks in metropolitan France, the article examines signatures on hundreds of notarized contracts in the early 1790s, from the town of Bainet, about 15 miles west of Jacmel, on Saint-Domingue's southern coast.

Freemasonry in Saint-Domingue

The main sources for the history of French colonial Freemasonry are the records of metropolitan grand lodges. Most of these records stem from the 1770s, when French Freemasonry was re-organizing itself around a central Grand Orient de France, located in Paris. While helpful, these records obscure the messy colonial reality. French Freemasonry began in Paris in 1726 and lodges appeared in Bordeaux in 1732, established by English and Irish merchants.[11] Not long after, around 1738, English merchants, in this case smugglers from Jamaica, established Saint-Domingue's first lodge, in the southern city of Les Cayes. In 1748, Freemasons from Bordeaux established the St. Jean de Jérusalem Ecossais lodge in Cap Français, the colony's main port city.[12]

We know of those early beginnings from letters and memoranda written twenty and thirty years later. The English lodge of Les Cayes applied for a constitution from the Grand Orient de France in 1774 and reported its history at that time. All in all there were approximately 20 colonial lodges that established relations with French sponsor organizations. But some historians conclude there were as many as 40 lodges in the colony, some of which left little trace. Surviving documents reveal a striking variety of Masonic organizations and ideas, and hint at still greater diversity among the lodges that did not feel the need to receive charters and constitutions from Paris. By the early nineteenth century, Saint-Domingue had, or had once had, half a dozen lodges affiliated with Grande Loge de France, and ten lodges constituted – and six re-constituted – by the Grand Orient also in Paris. But there were also lodges affiliated with the Contrat Social de Paris and the Grand Lodge of Pennsylvania. Still other lodges had affiliated with Bordeaux. There were three purely local lodges, the Frères Choisis du Fond des Nègres; Concorde of Saint Marc; and Saint-Esprit de Léogane, with no external affiliations. In 1776 a Grande Loge Provinciale was started in the isolated town of Fond des Nègres, and eventually moved to the slightly larger port town of Petit Goave. Moreover British Freemasonry made an imprint on the colony. The Saint Jean de Jérusalem of Cap Français and the Frères Réunis lodge of Les Cayes each claimed to have been started on the English system. By the end of the 1790s, after a failed British occupation, there were lodges corresponding with their "mother lodge" in Kingston, Jamaica, as well as at least one "high degree" lodge based in the Môle St Nicolas in 1798.[13]

The membership rolls and letters generated by these lodges hint at the existence of a number of lodges that would otherwise be invisible to historians. In 1799, as many whites returned to Saint-Domingue, the list of members of the La Vérité lodge of Cap Français included men who had once been members of two undocumented lodges in that city, Sion and Coeurs Sans Fard, as well members of collapsed lodges from outlying towns, like Intimité of Port-de-Paix or La Céleste Amitié of Dondon. A re-copied mid-eighteenth-century ritual book sent to New Orleans from revolutionary Saint-Domingue is all that remains from a lodge that was apparently founded in Port-de-Paix in the 1760s. Although these lodges, with almost no documentation, appear quite ephemeral in the archives, they were not necessarily obscure organizations. La Solitude in Terrier Rouge, a plantation parish far enough from Cap Français as to make for an inconvenient trip, had a number of prominent members, including some who sat on the Superior Conseil of Cap Français and high-ranking members of the provincial militia organization. Yet we only know this lodge existed because these men signed a single surviving certificate in 1788. Such "irregular" lodges – which were not authorized by metropolitan bodies – were in rich sugar zones but they also existed in more far-flung regions. The minor colonial town of Petit Trou had a lodge, Raison Perfectionnée, and its meetings were attended by a representative from an even more rural and isolated lodge in the canton of Gris-Gris.[14]

One reason why lodges proliferated in Saint-Domingue, especially in rural zones, was the difficulty of transportation, and some planters' reluctance to be gone too long or too regularly from their estates. But another reason – one that may shed light on the question of Masonic signatures – was that Freemasonry in Saint-Domingue appears to have fulfilled a variety of cultural needs.

In France and Saint-Domingue, lodges provided a setting for elite sociability, much as they did in the British Atlantic. By the 1770s Saint-Domingue's larger cities offered a number of Enlightened social and cultural institutions: theatres, bookstores, and coffee-houses. In 1784 a scientific academy was founded in Cap Français.[15] Masonic ideas dove-tailed with enlightenment ideologies of politeness, progress, and cosmopolitanism, but Masonic institutions and networks were particularly suited for the rootlessness of colonial life. Saint-Domingue's towns were full of men who came to make their fortune, or who were tied to merchant houses in France. As Martin Foäche informed a young friend due to arrive in Cap Français in 1760, "There is little or no custom [here] of going to eat [with colleagues] at the inn, even those with whom one is doing business. When mid-day strikes, everyone goes in his own direction."[16] He told his friend to seek out guest tables instead of eating at his inn during his first six months in the city. This would allow him to meet people and gain information about the colony. Meeting like-minded people was especially important, as travelers to Saint-Domingue stressed the lack of connection that many colonists felt to any country. In his 1754 *Essai sur les colonies françaises* Pierre-Louis de Saintard wrote, "The Europeans who live in the colonies, having become by voluntary transplantations outsiders everywhere, no longer pretend to have a fatherland."[17]

These conditions made Masonry especially attractive in the Caribbean. A network of correspondence joined lodges on a national or geographic basis. Masons developed what have been called "management tools of mobility": initiation certificates, inter-lodge affiliations, passwords, and maps of lodge locations, all designed to insure that a traveling Mason could find a friendly lodge in a new city.[18] In Caribbean and French port cities merchants primarily used lodges for commercial networking. In many port cities, like Le Havre, Freemasons also belonged to Catholic confraternities.[19]

Saint-Domingue's whites had no church organizations of this kind. The colony's priests were notoriously dissolute, and colonial society rewarded material success more than piety. Without a strong church, Frenchmen may have turned to Freemasonry to create a social identity in this Caribbean society where materialism, individualism, and racism were so much more prominent than they were in Europe. The great popularity in Saint-Domingue of Scottish Rite Freemasonry, with its elaborate hierarchy of over two dozen degrees, may owe something to a desire for alternative values. Some colonists sought spiritual direction in Freemasonry. One of the leading figures of French esoteric Freemasonry, Martinès Pasqually, died in Saint-Domingue, which had at least two lodges based on the Elus de Cohen order he founded. In France and in Saint-Domingue, these lodges combined Christian mysticism and the Jewish kabbala tradition with Scottish Rite Freemasonry. Martinès claimed his complex rites could bring forward angels or other spiritual beings who could guide men towards a reintegration with the Deity. Martinès's theosophy has similarities with Haitian Vodou, yet in the eighteenth century Martinism attracted white colonists, including prominent ones.[20] One of Martinès's disciples, Jean-Jacques Bacon de la Chevalerie, spent much of his military career in Saint-Domingue and in 1790 helped lead a failed movement for colonial autonomy.[21]

Other colonists criticized Freemasonry's increasingly elaborate rituals. One of those critics was Louis-Narcisse Baudry de Lozières, a planter and the district judge of Cap Français. Related by marriage to Charles Arthaud, the founder of the Cercle des Philadelphes, Baudry was one of the charter members of that scientific academy, founded in 1784. Arthaud, the founder of the Cercle, was a freemason as were many of its members and foreign correspondents. The Cercle had fraternal dinners and ceremonies that some scholars have described as inspired by freemasonry.[22] Baudry had been a member of the Verité lodge of Cap Français in 1777 (Escalle, 248) but at an early meeting of the Cercle he nevertheless appealed to its members to avoid "'those rituals that obscure reason and cannot fail to tire sensible people [...] those childish affectations that in themselves have toppled many of the masonic temples.'"[23]

Aspects of Freemasonry in Saint-Domingue differed strikingly from those found in other French – or even British– colonies. It was far more organizationally diverse than in Martinique and Guadeloupe, and more shaped by rivalry and controversy, both within lodges and among them.[24] Unlike British colonies, in Saint-Domingue the press said little about lodges' public activities. Saint-Domingue's commercial broadsheet, the *Affiches américaines*, did not mention local Freemasonry from its founding in 1763 until 1775 when a subscriber reported the loss of pocket watch with Masonic symbols. Although the *Affiches* did report on government persecution of Freemasons in Naples and Bavaria, local Freemasons were almost invisible in its pages.[25] Moreau de Saint-Méry, a Dominguan Mason, confirmed this lack of interest in publicity when he described Freemasonry as "a society that reminds men of their equality and inspires confidence by the secrecy that surrounds it."[26]

Free men of color and Freemasonry in Saint-Domingue

Over the past 30 years, research on French colonial Freemasonry has gradually focused on the question of racism within the lodges. In 1974, Alain LeBihan's overview of Freemasonry in France's eighteenth-century colonies made it clear that racial prejudice closed lodges in Guadeloupe to men of color, but said nothing specifically about racial issues in Saint-Domingue's lodges.[27] Writing in the 1980s, André Combes maintained that some free men of color were initiated into Freemasonry, remaining at the lowest two of Masonry's three basic degrees, those of "apprenti" and "compagnon." Without citing specific documents,

Combes claimed these men fit into colonial lodge life much like the working-class men who worked as "frères servants" in metropolitan lodges, setting up furniture and props for lodge meetings. He also noted that free colored Masons initiated in European lodges were refused entry to lodges in Saint-Domingue.[28]

In 1993, Elisabeth Escalle and Mariel Gouyon-Guillaume identified several free men of color on a lodge list from Basse-Terre, Guadeloupe in the 1780s and a single man of color listed on a 1785 membership list of a lodge in Port-au-Prince. The same lodge also listed two more men whose family origins were described as "unknown" and who may have been considered men of color.[29] Nevertheless, in 1997, Pierre-Yves Beaurepaire clarified how much Freemasons in Saint-Domingue and elsewhere had adopted the racial prejudices of colonial society.[30] In late eighteenth-century Martinique and Guadeloupe, where interracial marriage was illegal, Beaurepaire documented an "obsession with keeping men of color at a distance." Saint-Domingue never outlawed these marriages, but after the Seven Years' War, new laws and attitudes stressed the importance of white purity.[31] In 1770, after Freemasons learned that the Venerable of the Vérité lodge of Cap Français was married to a free woman of color, one member, François Lamarque, wrote to Masonic authorities in France, urging them convince the lodge "'to keep a strict watch over the admission of brothers who may be convicted of mixed blood marriage.'" The lodge did accept this strict policy of racial exclusion and promised "'to admit in our order only intact men.'"[32] On two occasions when Le Havre's lodges sent Masonic representatives to Cap Français, Lamarque successfully recruited them to his campaign to exclude men of color from lodges in port cities on both sides of the Atlantic.[33]

Other Masons shared this heightened scorn for biracial colonists. In a 1774 letter Martinès de Pasqually described the lodges of Port-au-Prince as full of "bastards and men of mixed blood."[34] Surviving Port-au-Prince records do not illustrate this but in 1788 Mme des Rouaudières in the Plaine des Cayes wrote her daughter that "Your papa is not a free mason though he is very convinced of the goodness of that respectable order; but all sorts of people are admitted there; this has distanced many people." However, as in Port-au-Prince surviving membership lists from Les Cayes do not reveal any men known to be of African descent, so Rouaudières may have been objecting to the presence of whites from a lower social class than his own.[35]

A few free men of color do appear in Saint-Domingue's surviving membership rolls during the Haitian Revolution. But it took colonial lodges years to accept the fact that freeborn men of color were equal to whites, under the French revolutionary law. In an initial stage from 1791 to 1794 many lodges dissolved as colonists fled the slave insurrection. No lodges from this period accepted free colored members. Émigré Freemasons sometimes reconstituted their lodges in North America or elsewhere in the Caribbean. Then, starting in 1797, colonists began to return to Saint-Domingue. In this second stage they formed or reconstituted roughly a dozen lodges in the colony and some of these had black and biracial members.

Their numbers were small. The 1800 tableau of the Réunion Désirée lodge in Port-au-Prince included many prominent white colonists among its 53 members. This was the most integrated lodge whose records have survived, and only three of its members were men of color. They were Louverture'sbrother Paul, Louverture's trusted aide Charles Belair, and Joseph-Balthazar Inginac, a wealthy merchant who would later serve as Secretary of State under the Haitian presidents Alexandre Pétion and Jean-Pierre

Boyer. A fourth member of Réunion Désirée, Jacques Hérard, may have been a member of an established free colored planter family.[36] The presence of these men proves that Toussaint Louverture, by that time Saint-Domingue's governor, approved of the lodge. During the Revolution, Freemasonry became more racially open. But even in the late colonial period, at the height of black power, only a few other lodges had even a single member of color.[37]

In addition to the three Freemasons of color in Port-au-Prince, the black army officer Louis Dieudonné was listed as a Freemason in the town of Jacmel in 1804 while another Port-au-Prince lodge in 1799 described one member, François Belair, as a plantation field supervisor or "commandeur," a role usually given to men of African descent.[38] None of the other surviving membership rolls from the late 1790s mentions men who can be identified as being of African descent. The historian Thomas Madiou, a Freemason himself in the 1840s, claimed that the biracial general Guy-Joseph Bonnet was initiated into Freemasonry in 1794.[39]

There is evidence that Masonic connections helped some men escape the violence of the Haitian Revolution. In 1801, Toussaint Louverture ordered his troops to invade territory controlled by his rival, the biracial general André Rigaud. Louverture's forces deliberately sank prison barges in the port of Les Cayes, hoping these mass drownings would eliminate Rigaud's resistance. A white colonist named Desclaux, the head of a masonic lodge in Les Cayes, contacted the French officer Pieret, who led the drownings in the harbor there. Pieret was a freemason himself and Desclaux asked him to safeguard the life of Jérôme Maximilien Borgella, a biracial officer in the resistance army, imprisoned on a ship at Les Cayes. Pieret transferred Borgella from the prison ship into Pieret's own quarters. Borgella lived there until one of his supporters convinced General Laplume, a black freemason who commanded the city for Louverture, to authorize his release.[40] Jean-Pierre Boyer, Haiti's future president, was another Freemason and officer in Rigaud's army. Captured while fleeing Saint-Domingue in 1800, Boyer was given refuge by Freemasons in Norwich, Connecticut after he showed them his Masonic regalia, though Masons from other towns treated him harshly.[41] The rapid growth of Masonic lodges after Haiti became independent in 1804 shows how strongly Freemasonry appealed to men of color.[42] The first Haitian lodge was started in 1806 at Les Cayes, about the time of the assassination of Emperor Jean-Jacques Dessalines, who was hostile to Freemasonry. By the 1810s, there were at least four lodges operating in the Republic of Haiti under Alexandre Pétion, eventually receiving constitutions from British grand lodges. Boyer succeeded Pétion in 1818, and in 1824 Haiti established its own Masonic system.[43] While little is known of Freemasonry in Henry Christophe's northern Kingdom of Haiti, it is perhaps more than a coincidence that he chose as his emblem a common Masonic device, the phoenix rising from its ashes, and named his palace, Sans Souci, after the country house of Prussia's Frederick II, the European monarch most closely identified with Freemasonry.[44] From 1816 until Christophe's death in 1820 the American black Freemason Prince Saunders worked with English abolitionists to set up schools and medical programs in Christophe's kingdom, but Christophe's suspicion of Saunders makes it unlikely that Saunders established lodges in the Kingdom. After Christophe's death, Saunders became Boyer's attorney general and died in Haiti in 1839.[45]

The unusual prominence of Freemasonry in colonial Saint-Domingue and in independent Haiti makes it tempting to assume, despite the lack of solid evidence, that free men of color like Toussaint Louverture and other future revolutionaries were Freemasons before the revolution began. This idea is supported by the fact that surviving membership rolls do not contain the full story of Saint-Domingue's lodges. Additionally, many whites and a number of free men of color – including Louverture – appended to their signatures distinctive symbols that some scholars have identified as Masonic marks.

The mystery of the Masonic signature

One of those scholars was the Frenchman Gustave Bord. Born in 1852, Bord was a monarchist who was fascinated by the Abbé Barruel's theory, already discredited by mid-century, that French Freemasons and German Illuminati had used secret codes and special signs to plot and carry out the French Revolution.[46] In the first volume of his 1908 history of French Freemasonry, Bord claimed to have accumulated 60,000 cards containing the names of about half of all late eighteenth-century French Freemasons. He maintained that 83 percent of the men who drew points and other symbols after their signatures were individuals he had identified as Freemasons. Bord analyzed five main types of Masonic signature and categorized those he believed came out of different Masonic traditions. He reproduced the elaborate signatures of key figures including that of Martinès de Pasqually, said to be the most elaborate of all. Bord claimed the earliest such signature on a French Masonic certificate dated from 1760, but said the oldest he had seen was from England before 1745, consisting of three points in a line or the same three points between two parallel lines. In 1774 the Grand Orient de France began using three points in a triangle to indicate abbreviations in its publications.

Although he believed these marks were secret Masonic signs, Bord pointed out that they were never required and that about only about half of Masons used them. He described them himself as "phantasmagorias designed to satisfy the vanity of initiates and to excite the curiosity of *profanes* [with] [...] a mysterious and cabalistic air."[47]

In 1968 the historian Maurice Agulhon, in a study of eighteenth-century Provence, provided a very different perspective on these signatures. Agulhon noted that many men who were members of religious confraternities drew such "Masonic" symbols after their signatures. Suggesting that three points referred to the Christian Trinity or the Holy Family, he wrote,

> There is therefore a habit based in mysticism that at the end of the old regime cannot be used to definitively identify either confraternity members or Freemasons but which is found among both and constitutes one more proof of their kinship or mutual influence.[48]

Agulhon's findings were amplified in a 1992 article by the genealogist Pierre Guillaume. Guillaume examined 500 signatures on Masonic documents in the northern French city of Reims from 1787 to 1875. Guillaume agreed that these signs were a stylistic choice that originated with religious confraternities and migrated into the Masonic lodges more or less unconsciously. Masons in Reims were most likely to sign this way in the late 1700s, and they gradually abandoned this practice in the 1800s. Of Guillaume's 500 signatures by Reims' Freemasons, but only 77 were "Masonic." Nor could he find any significant reason why 31 of these men used points between parallel lines and 46 drew only points or dots. Significantly, Guillaume found a number of Reims city officers in the revolutionary period who were not known to be Freemasons but did use these marks in their signatures. Guillaume found that upper class signers were more likely to use these signs than working class signers but no group used them consistently. He concluded that because so many non-masons signed this way, a signature with points and parallel lines could not be used to suggest that the signer was a Mason. For him this was merely a scribal fashion loosely identified with membership in religious and Masonic organizations. Most Masons did not sign this way.[49]

Signatures from the parish of Bainet

Late eighteenth-century documents generated in the parish of Bainet, on Saint-Domingue's southern coast, provide an opportunity to replicate Guillaume's study. If so-called Masonic signatures in Saint-Domingue can be correlated to lodge membership, then there is proof that many more men of color were Freemasons than scholars have believed. It seems possible that Freemasons in Bainet and nearby Jacmel might well have accepted free men of color into their ranks, because racial prejudice among free people was relatively weak in this region. Free blacks and whites had long intermarried in Bainet. In 1731 a visiting royal official noted there were few "whites of pure blood" in Bainet because so many had formed households with propertied women of color.[50]

Julien Raimond, the most important free colored political figure in the French Revolution, was the son of a southern French immigrant who moved to Bainet in the 1720s and married a free woman of half-African ancestry from a propertied family. Some members of the Raimond family still lived in Bainet parish in the 1790s, though most lived in neighboring Aquin or in France. Julien Raimond worked with many Freemasons in Paris, including Hector de Joly, who introduced him to Revolutionary politics.[51]

No members of the Raimond family signed with "Masonic signatures." But their neighbor and friend Jean Louis Depas Medina, who was related to a powerful Bordeaux Jewish merchant family, did. His father, Michel Depas Medina, did an apprenticeship in the 1760s in that port city. Though he lived in Aquin, Jean-Louis wrote his name and followed it with three points between two parallel lines in least three notarial documents in Bainet in the 1790s (Figure 2).[52]

André Rigaud, the biracial general defeated by Louverture's forces in 1801, has been described as a Freemason.[53] Born in the Saint-Domingue's southern peninsula, Rigaud, like Depas Medina's father, trained in Bordeaux as a young boy. During the Revolutionary era he rose through French army ranks in the revolution to rule this region., Like Jean-Louis Depas Medina, he signed documents that appeared among a notary's papers at Bainet, following his name with the same sign that Depas Medina and Toussaint Louverture used (Figure 3).

Bainet was close to Saint-Domingue's Masonic roots. The city of Les Cayes, where merchants from Jamaica established the colony's first lodge in 1738, was about 30 miles down the southern coast. Just 15 miles in the other direction was Jacmel, a smaller port where the Bordeaux merchant Etienne Morin landed in 1763. A traveling salesman, Morin was a Masonic entrepreneur, deeply involved with the emerging Scottish Rite form of Freemasonry, which he had helped to establish in Bordeaux in 1743. This was a more mystical form that by 1762 had 25 degrees, compared to the three fundamental degrees of "apprentice," "journeyman," and "master" that Freemasonry inherited from the medieval guilds.[54]

Figure 2. Signatures of Jean Louis Depas Medina, a wealthy free man of color, and the notary Funel De Séranon; from a notarized document dated 13 Janvier 1790. Photo by author, 2007.

Some historians believe Morin visited Saint-Domingue in the 1740s, perhaps making multiple trips to establish lodges. In 1762 he sailed from France to the Caribbean. The Scottish Rite had just formed a national organization in France, and its officers had given Morin credentials to found new colonial lodges. Captured by the British en route to Saint-Domingue, Morin eventually entered the colony at Jacmel, an entry port that suggests he was coming from Jamaica. Morin began to establish new "Scottish" lodges in Saint-Domingue, but by 1766 he had lost the support of French Masonic authorities. They accused him of exceeding his authority to grant higher degrees and criticized him for deputizing others to do the same. Although Bordeaux sent an inspector to Saint-Domingue to investigate, Morin continued to found lodges in Saint-Domingue, and eventually went on (or returned) to Jamaica, where he died around 1772.[55]

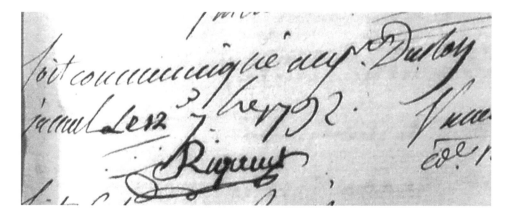

Figure 3. Signature of the André Rigaud, a free born man of color and eventually the commander of French revolutionary forces in Saint-Domingue's southern peninsula, on a letter to the district judge of Jacmel, dated 12 September 1792. Photo by author, 2007.

Morin's controversial career makes it quite possible that he organized lodges in Jacmel or Bainet that did not correspond with France. For example, Morin helped establish a lodge in Port-de-Paix that is known only because a copy of its ritual book, mentioned above, eventually turned up in New Orleans.[56] Although Jacmel had strong smuggling connections to Jamaica, the records of the Grand Orient indicate that its oldest known lodge, the Choix des Hommes, was not founded until 1783. However it is likely that Morin founded a lodge there earlier. In 1800 the U.S. navy captured a ship from Jacmel carrying officers of color who had evacuated after Jean-Jacques Dessalines invaded the region. One of the evacuees was Jean-Pierre Boyer, Haiti's future president. In New London County, representatives of a local Knights Templar lodge seized Masonic regalia and lodge documents from Boyer that reportedly included a 1774 charter for the Choix des Hommes at Jacmel, signed by "S. Morin". If this report is true, Etienne Morin (Stephen Morin, in English) may have established a lodge in Jacmel, which subsequently moved or died out.[57] The town's other lodge was Parfaite Harmonie, a military lodge founded in 1802. It was in Jacmel in 1803 that the black officer Louis Dieudonné, then commanding the town, became a Freemason.[58] Bainet's Masonic lodge is even briefer, for there is no evidence that the town ever had its own lodge. It is possible that records were lost, or that the town had an unaffiliated lodge like those in Léogane or Fond des Nègres. Bainet's Freemasons may have attended meetings in nearby Jacmel.

All the documents studied here were from the practice of one Bainet notary, Pierre-Joseph-Jean-Baptiste-Antoine Funel de Séranon, sometimes spelled Funel de Séranou. The French evacuated Bainet's notarial archives at the end of the Haitian Revolution, so many more legal documents survived from there than from other regions of the colony.[59] Funel's registers were chosen for three reasons. He himself signed with a "Masonic" sign. His handwriting was the most legible of any of the notaries in this region. And his registers of notarial deeds stretch from 1783 to 1809. This study focused on the documents he drafted from January 1789 to the end of March 1793. In these four years and three months he drafted 466 contracts.

On nearly every one of the more 1,400 documents that he drafted or which were deposited with him from 1789 to 1804, Funel signed his name and then made a horizontal row of points between two horizontal parallel lines. Over time his signature and the accompanying signs changed. His flourishes varied and for a while he made a small flower-like shape above his name. He switched from "B: Funel" to "Funel de Séranon,"adopting this more noble-sounding name like a number of other commoners during the early French Revolution. Then he reverted to "B: Funel." For a brief period he made three points forming a triangle around that B. However he mostly drew two horizontal lines after his signature and inscribed dots horizontally between them. He usually made three points but this number rose to five, six, and even seven, and then returned to three. This genre of mark was by far the most common among Funel's fellow signers. It was the mark that Toussaint Louverture and André Rigaud drew under their signatures.[60]

Not counting Funel's marks, approximately 20 percent (293/1441) of the signatures left by his clients, witnesses, and other officials included these mysterious marks. Men left these marks in all but three cases, where the signers were women. Many of the markers were part of a group of a dozen individuals, perhaps neighbors or friends of the notary, who witnessed multiple contracts. There were many habitual witnesses who did not make a mark with their signature. But the on-going participation of these witnesses means that 20 percent is an overestimation of how common it was to sign with these marks at Bainet.

None of Funel's clients who left "Masonic" signatures was on the Masonic lists published by Escalle. Some were possibly related to known Masons. In January 1792 Bernard Guionnet DuPeyrat was leaving the colony and gave two men legal powers to manage his Bainet properties. DuPeyrat left a "Masonic" signature. In 1804 and 1807, Pierre Adrien Dupeyrat, perhaps a relative of Bernard, was listed as a member of Jacmel's Choix des Hommes lodge, in exile in Santo Domingo. A merchant based in Bordeaux, Pierre DuPeyrat was also a member of the Les Cayes lodge in 1801, which suggests he had returned to the colony like many whites, hoping the worst violence was over.[61] One of the men Bernard DuPeyrat charged with caring for his Bainet lands was a Jacques Runifort, a free colored neighbor known as "Point-de-jour" or "Day Break." He too signed with a Masonic sign. Were the two men connected by Freemasonry, as well as by location?

As the most frequent maker of these marks, the notary Funel de Séranon provides the best evidence about what they might mean. No existing list of colonial Freemasons includes his name. Before coming to Saint-Domingue Funel was a lawyer (*avocat*) at the Parlement of Aix-en-Provence in southern France, near Marseilles. He married a creole, Marie Marguerite Margest, but their son was born in France, which suggests the couple met and lived in the metropole for several years before moving to Saint-Domingue.[62]

In France, the Funel family was active in pious organizations and in the legal professions. In 1782, just about the time that Funel de Séranon, the lawyer, took his creole wife and their son and left for Saint-Domingue, Pierre Théodore de Funel-Séranon died, and was remembered for founding the Black Penitent confraternity of Marseilles. While there is no evidence in colonial archives of their parentage, the two men were lawyers originally from the same small Provençal town.[63] This connection with confraternities in particular calls to mind Agulhon's observation that so-called "Masonic signatures" may have had their origin in religious confraternities.

Only seven of the men who left these signs in Funel's register from 1789 through March 1793 were described as being of African descent. However free people of color were a typical proportion of Funel's overall clientele, compared to other notaries in the region in the 1780s. Roughly 85 of the 466 deeds involved at least one client whose African descent was acknowledged. By 1793, notaries were beginning to drop the specific racial labels that pre-revolutionary law had required, as well the mandatory description of the freedom papers African-descended clients had to show notaries since the early 1770s . But up to 1793, Funel still applied racial labels to all African-descended people who signed or participated in their documents.

Funel described all seven of these Masonic-signing clients of color as biracial, using terms like mulatto or quadroon. His most common label for these men was the vague term *sang mêlé*, meaning he knew his client had African ancestors but they were genealogically remote. Social class influenced such racial judgments, so these men's wealth and/or mastery of metropolitan French culture probably shaped Funel's descriptive terms. None of these seven free men of color appears on surviving lodge records.

The notarial deeds that the men signed in Funel's study suggest a reason, a common profile, which might explain their use of these mysterious symbols. All of seven signed their names in a way that indicates a certain scribal confidence. Many free colored notarial clients – and many working class whites – could not sign at all. A number of those who could sign wrote as if this were something they did once or twice a year. Judging by their signatures, the free colored "markers" were clearly comfortable with a quill. Yet none of them – with exception of Depas Medina who was visiting Bainet from neighboring Aquin – was wealthy. All were men on the borderline between respectability and acceptance among propertied whites; they were all light-skinned and educated, but not wealthy enough to assert themselves in local society.

Two men who changed their signatures over time confirm this idea that these mysterious marks were a way for signers to affirm their identity as members of respectable society. Funel identified Pierre Louis Cangé as a "free mulatto" in May 1790 when he witnessed a marriage contract in Funel's study. Cangé was farmer or planter, living in a rural part of the parish. The marriage involved a free colored family at the edge of slavery and freedom. Pierre Louis Petit, the groom, was a free quadroon who was marrying Marie Jeanne, a 20 year-old enslaved creole woman he had purchased from another free man of color. Petit himself was not yet 25, so he signed the marriage contract under the authority of his mother, a widowed free *mulâtresse*. Petit's white father was dead. Neither the groom, nor his mother nor the bride, released from slavery by this marriage contract, could sign his or her name. In this setting, Cangé, the witness, made a hastily drawn Masonic sign next to his name (Figure 4).[64]

Such contracts with un-lettered friends and family were common for most free people in Saint-Domingue. But an upwardly mobile man of color like Cangé may have wanted to differentiate himself from these friends or clients. Cangé seems to have felt the need to do more than demonstrate his status as an educated man who could write his name. So he appended this mark – three points between two parallel lines – to his signature, perhaps as unsure about what it meant as we are.

The next time he appeared before Funel, Cangé did not make this mark. In January 1791 he came to the notary's study to accept a three-year lease of a well-developed cotton plantation with 64 enslaved workers. He would pay the significant sum of 15,000 livres per year to Barthelemy Barreau, another free of man of color. At this date, Revolutionary politics had not yet erased the law requiring notaries to describe racial categories. But Funel did not

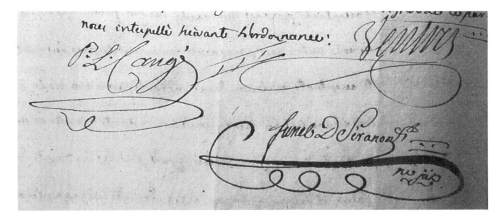

Figure 4. Signatures of Pierre Louis Cangé, a free man of color and future revolutionary officer, and the notary Funel De Séranon on a formal marriage contract between a free man of color and an enslaved woman, dated 25 May 1790. Photo by author, 2007.

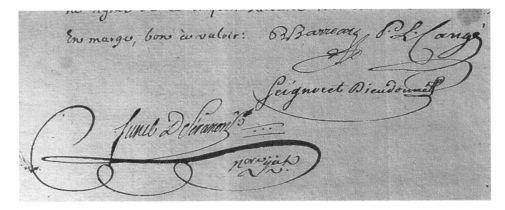

Figure 5. Signatures of Pierre Louis Cangé and the notary Funel De Séranon, on a contract in which Cangé leased a plantation from Barthelemy Barreau; dated 26 January 1791. Photo by author, 2007.

attach a racial label to either Barreau or Cangé. He did not call them *Sieur* either – that title was still reserved for whites. But Cangé was clearly in a different social class on this occasion than he had been signing the marriage contract the previous year.[65] He may not have felt the need to leave an enigmatic sign after his signature (Figure 5).

A second case follows a similar pattern – the free colored signer made the mark when he signed a document involving ex-slaves, but omitted it when signing a contract with social equals or superiors. Pierre Louis Barronnet was a free quadroon who worked and lived on the plantation of a white man at Bainet. In January 1789 he was asked to witness a deed in which a white militia captain and planter freed his five enslaved biracial children, all between the ages of 30 and 40. In that case he made a Masonic mark. But eleven months later, when Barronnet's illegitimate daughter married a white man, Etienne Muelle, who, like Funel, was from Aix-en-Provence, and used a Masonic sign in his own signature, Barronnet did not.[66] Another man of color who made these signs in Funel's register of deeds in the early 1790s was Claude Remougis, *sang mêlé*, who made a Masonic sign when he formed a partnership with a man of color who could barely sign his name to work a 79 acre [25 carreaux] plot of land.

The one signer who broke this pattern was Jacques Runifort, the free biracial man described earlier. At least two whites formally appointed Runifort to look after their plantations and he signed his name confidently. Funel called Runifort *Sieur* in the power of attorney that Bernard DuPeyrat gave the man of color. But Runifort was quite poor, and lived high in the hills of the parish. Unlike other men of color, he made Masonic marks when he signed contracts with the wealthy men who were hiring him. It seems likely that Masonic signs were a way for Runifort to assert a certain social and cultural respectability in a legal document.[67]

Conclusion

The enigma of the so-called Masonic signature lends itself well to the kinds of conspiracy theories that Gustave Bord embraced and which nineteenth- and twenty-first-century historians used to describe Toussaint Louverture's still unexplained role in the outbreak of the

Haitian Revolution. That same enigma also made them attractive in eighteenth-century Saint-Domingue. Signers who left these marks were asserting something about themselves, creating an association that might be interpreted differently by different observers but which was likely to reflect favorably upon them.

This study suggests that marks in signatures cannot be used to show that there a secret network of free men of color involved in Freemasonry in Saint-Domingue. To the extent that Enlightenment concepts influenced such men, transatlantic fraternalism was apparently not involved. Rather, in Bainet and elsewhere in Saint-Domingue, men of color drew enigmatic marks after signing their name to shore up an identity that was perched between respected powerful local property owners, like Julien Raimond, or Pierre Cangé, on the one hand, and free coloreds who were at the edge of slavery, on the other. This strategy was favored by free men whose French cultural skills were strong, but who had little financial resources.

My own conclusions in *Before Haiti* about free colored Masons in Aquin parish, including Depas Medina, illustrated the power of this strategy. I assumed he and other free colored signers were members of an undocumented lodge. Looking more closely at evidence from the neighboring parish of Bainet, I now believe he was merely trying to assert his place as a member of the local elite. Depas Medina was different from other free colored signers in being relatively wealthy. But, like Louverture and Rigaud who also signed in this way, he aspired to civic and political influence and would go on to be one of Saint-Domingue's first free colored notaries. The mysterious sign, with its suggestion of secret knowledge or membership in an influential network, would only strengthen the case that he deserved such a position of respect and trust. Similar motivations, I suggest, inspired Toussaint Louverture to make his mark. If eighteenth-century transatlantic fraternalism did not embrace or include many men like Louverture or Depas Medina, their signatures suggest that these ambitious rising men wanted to claim some of the prestige of that movement.

Notes

1. Bell, *Toussaint Louverture*, 63, 77; Buck-Morss, *Hegel, Haiti, and Universal History*.
2. McClellan, *Colonialism and Science*, 106, says "One out of every twenty-five white males and probably more like one out of every three or four sociologically eligible white men was a mason."
3. Bullock, *Revolutionary Brotherhood*. This is a subject of controversy in Latin America. Simón Bolívar was initiated into a Parisian lodge, but scholars disagree about the masonic credentials of other Latin American independence leaders like Francisco de Miranda or Argentina's José de San Martín because their lodges were not formally connected to pre-existing masonic organizations. Ferrer Benimeli, "Bolívar y la masonería." At least one of Miranda's biographers sees him unequivocally as a Freemason; Racine, *Francisco de Miranda*, 193–195.
4. Le Bihan, "La franc-maçonnerie," identifies de Joly and Lafayette as Freemasons; Saunier, "L'espace caribéen," 49, on the *Amis des Noirs*.
5. The example is from ANOM: SDOM, 0698, and is annexed to a document dated 1 messidor l'an 9.
6. The thesis that Toussaint was involved in a royalist plot has most recently been advanced by Girard, *Toussaint Louverture*, 106–120; Girard describes the evidence that Toussaint was a Freemason in 1791 as "thin." See pages 63, 74, and 281.
7. Geggus, "Toussaint Louverture," 112–132.
8. Bell, *Toussaint Louverture*, 77–78; for other scholarship see Cauna, "Thèse du complot" and Fouchard, "Toussaint Louverture était-il franc-maçon?"

9. Garrigus, *Before Haiti*, 291–306; Buck-Morss, "Hegel and Haiti," 854–856, notes 108, 110, and 111.
10. This is the argument at the core of Dubois, *Avengers of the New World*.
11. Loiselle, "Living the Enlightenment," 5; Bogdan and Snoek, "History of Freemasonry," 20.
12. Le Bihan, "La franc-maçonnerie," 45; Le Bihan, *Loges et chapitres*, 389; Escalle and Guillaume, *Francs-maçons des loges françaises*, 105–106.
13. Le Bihan, "La franc-maçonnerie," 44–45.
14. Ibid., 45–6; Prinsen, *Bonseigneur Rituals*, 8–13.
15. McClellan, *Colonialism and Science*, 91–106, 181–191.
16. Begouën Demeaux, "Aspects de Saint-Domingue," 29.
17. Saintard, *Essai sur les colonies françoises*, 135.
18. Beaurepaire, "Universal Republic."
19. Saunier, "L'espace caribéen," 42–55; Saunier, "Être confrère et franc-maçon."
20. Taillefer, *La franc-maçonnerie toulousaine*, 91–92, provides a brief overview of the scholarly literature on Martinès Pasqually. For a description of his ideology and practices, see Nahon, *Martinès de Pasqually*, 138–139 and 143–144; when Martinism returned to Haiti, it was in the form of it was in the twentieth century. See Saint Victor Hérard, "Gnostic Church of Ambelain Martinism."
21. Le Bihan, "La franc-maçonnerie," 41; Cauna, "Thèse du complot," 301.
22. Maurel, "Une société de pensée à Saint-Domingue," 241; see also Pluchon, "Cercle des Philadelphes," 157–185.
23. Cited in McClellan, "L'historiographie d'une académie coloniale," 83 (translation by the author); for Baudry's lodge membership, Escalle and Guillaume, *Francs-maçons des loges françaises*, 248.
24. Le Bihan, "La franc-maçonnerie," 41, 49.
25. "Nouvelles diverses du Port-au-Prince," *Affiches américaines*, 10 July 1784, 436; [untitled announcement], *Affiches americaines*, 17 July 1788, 354; for a list of public Masonic activities, see Cauna, "Loges, réseaux et personnalités maçonniques," 42–43; for the prominent role Freemasons played in public life in some eighteenth-century British North American colonies, see Harland-Jacobs, *Builders of Empire*, 51–52.
26. Moreau de Saint-Méry, *Loix et constitutions des colonies*, Vol. 6, 497.
27. Le Bihan, "La franc-maçonnerie," 39–62.
28. Combes, "La franc-maçonnerie," 156–157.
29. Escalle and Guillaume, *Francs-maçons des loges françaises*, 3, 167.
30. Beaurepaire, "Fraternité universelle."
31. Garrigus, *Before Haiti*, 141–170.
32. Cited in Beaurepaire, "Fraternité universelle," 211: "que des hommes intacts."
33. Saunier, "L'espace caribéen," 51.
34. Cauna, "Thèse du complot," 306, cites "Lettre à Willermoz du 24 avril 1774," in Le Forestier, *La franc-maçonnerie occultiste*, 502.
35. Debien, *Lettres de colons*, 232. Thanks to Bernard Camier, who alerted me to this quote.
36. Garrigus, *Before Haiti*, 70, 96, describes the history of the Hérard family.
37. Cauna, "Thèse du complot," 312. Bernard Camier was kind enough to give me a photocopy of this document: "Tableau des F.F. composant la R. L. la Réunion Désirée [...] à L'orient du Port-républicain," 1800, from the Bibliothèque nationale de France, Fonds maçonnique 2.
38. Escalle and Guillaume, *Francs-maçons des loges françaises*, 254, 411.
39. Combes, "La franc-maçonnerie," 156, 161, states Bonnet's Freemasonry without proof; Mentor, *Histoire de la franc-maçonnerie*, 168, reproduces this list with the addition of J.C. Imbert and Pierre Noël Léveillé. Mentor's sources are privately held.
40. Ardouin, *Études sur l'histoire d'Haïti*, Vol. 4, 492–493; Bernard Camier reports seeing Laplume's name on the 1801 membership register of the Frères Réunis lodge in Les Cayes, held in the Bibliothèque du Grand Orient in Paris; Camier, "[Newly Available Masonic Archival Documents]," 22 June 2007, personal email.
41. On Boyer's reception in Connecticut, see Hinks, "'Perfectly proper and conciliating'"; also Harvey, *History of Lodge No. 61*; and an untitled article on prisoners from US Warship Trumbull in 1801 in *Bulletin of the Connecticut Historical Society* 26–30 (1961): 58–60.

42. Sheller, "Sword-Bearing Citizens."
43. Cauna, "Quelques aperçus."
44. According to one account, in 1806 Christophe was considering becoming a Freemason, until he became convinced, erroneously, that Haitian Freemasons had helped a handful of French hostages escape from Cap Haïtien, the city he commanded. See Condy Raguet, "Memoires of Hayti, Letter XXI, The Cape, May 1806," *The Port Folio*, January 1811, 52.
45. White, "Prince Saunders"; for an alternative theory of why Christophe named his palace Sans Souci, see Trouillot, *Silencing the Past*, 31–69.
46. Hofman, "Illusion of Opinion."
47. Bord, *La franc-maçonnerie*, 282–288.
48. Agulhon, *Pénitents et francs-maçons*, 207. Thanks to Ken Loiselle for this reference.
49. Guillaume, "Contribution rémoise," 184–186; thanks to Bernard Camier for this reference.
50. Garrigus, *Before Haiti*, 48.
51. Garrigus, "Opportunist or Patriot?"; Combes, "La franc-maçonnerie," 176 on de Joly.
52. Garrigus, *Before Haiti*, 121–122, 182–183, 293–294.
53. Buck-Morss, *Hegel, Haiti, and Universal History*, 856.
54. Taillefer, *La franc-maçonnerie toulousaine*, 77 note 4, provides a reliable summary of the scholarship on Morin who is the subject of very different biographical treatments, especially in Masonic publications.
55. Seal-Coon, *Historical Account*, 23–26 is the basis for much of this paragraph.
56. Prinsen, *Bonseigneur Rituals*, 12.
57. For a full account, see Hinks, "'Perfectly proper and conciliating'"; also Case, *Ancient Accepted Scottish Rite*, 18; Escalle and Guillaume, *Francs-maçons des loges françaises*, 132, show that the Grand Orient de France officially constituted a "Frères Choisis" lodge in Saint-Domingue in 1774, but that lodge was based in the mountain village of Fond des Nègres, not the port city of Jacmel. It is possible that the Connecticut Freemasons confused the two towns, which are about 40 miles apart.
58. Escalle and Guillaume, *Francs-maçons des loges françaises*, 141–146, 411.
59. Ménier, "Comment furent repatriés les griffes de Saint Domingue, 1803–1820."
60. For Rigaud's signature, Archives nationales d'outre-mer, Aix-en-Provence (henceforth ANOM): SDOM, 0687, 13 September 1792, property inventory with attached instructions from Rigaud via a letter written signed Jacmel 12 September 1792; also SDOM, 0688, 9 March 1793, property inventory with attached letter from Rigaud signed 26 February 1793; for Toussaint, see SDOM, 0698, deed dated 1 messidor year 9 with an attached letter from Louverture to Frigouilla, dated 27 prairial year 9.
61. Escalle and Guillaume, *Francs-maçons des loges françaises*, 437.
62. Dessens, *From Saint-Domingue to New Orleans*, 51.
63. Isnard, *Inventaire sommaire*, 40, cites the Registre du greffe de Peyroules, 1739–1778; Agulhon, *Pénitents et francs-maçons*, 203, cites the Archives Départementales Bouches-du-Rhône 24, f. 36, "Necrologie des penitents noirs (1521–1954)" for Funel's death date.
64. ANOM: SDOM, 0684, 25 May 1790.
65. ANOM: SDOM, 0686, 26 January 1791.
66. ANOM: SDOM, 0682, 11 November 1789.
67. Ibid., 25 June 1789; SDOM, 0687, 26 February 1792; SDOM, 0687, 15 October 1792; SDOM, 0688, 31 January 1793.

Acknowledgements

Oscar Alleyne, Bernard Camier, Ken Loiselle, Peter P. Hinks, and Jessica Harland-Jacobs contributed greatly to this paper with comments, documents, and research ideas. All errors are my own. A Research Enhancement grant from the University of Texas at Arlington funded my collection of the archival data analyzed here. Mylynka Cardona coded the notarial contracts I discuss.

Disclosure statement

No potential conflict of interest was reported by the author.

Funding

This work was supported by University of Texas at Arlington: [Grant no. REP].

ORCID

John Garrigus ⓘ http://orcid.org/0000-0002-1091-6122

Bibliography

Agulhon, Maurice. *Pénitents et francs-maçons de l'ancienne Provence : Essai sur la sociabilité méridionale*. New edition. Paris: Fayard, 1984.

Ardouin, Beaubrun. *Études sur l'histoire d'Haïti; suivies de la vie du général J.-M. Borgella*. Vol. 4. Paris: Dézobry et E. Magdeleine, 1853.

Beaurepaire, Pierre-Yves. "Fraternité universelle et pratiques discriminatoires dans la franc-maçonnerie des lumières." *Revue d'histoire moderne et contemporaine* 44, no. 2 (1997): 195–212.

Beaurepaire, Pierre-Yves. "The Universal Republic of the Freemasons and the Culture of Mobility in the Enlightenment." *French Historical Studies* 29, no. 3 (2006): 407–431.

Begouën Demeaux, Maurice. "Aspects de Saint-Domingue pendant la guerre de Sept Ans, d'après les papiers Foäche." In *Mémorial d'une famille du Havre. Vol. 2, Stanislas Foäche, 1737–1806: Négociant de Saint-Domingue*, 1–33. Paris: Société française d'histoire d'outremer, 1982.

Bell, Madison Smartt. *Toussaint Louverture*. New York: Pantheon Books, 2008.

Bogdan, Henrik, and Jan A. M. Snoek. "The History of Freemasonry: An Overview." In *Handbook of Freemasonry*, edited by Henrik Bogdan and Jan A. M. Snoek, 11–32. Leiden: Brill, 2014.

Bord, Gustave. *La franc-maçonnerie en France des origines à 1815*. Paris: Nouvelle Librairie Nationale, 1908.

Buck-Morss, Susan. "Hegel and Haiti." *Critical Inquiry* 26, no. 4 (2000): 854–856.

Buck-Morss, Susan. *Hegel, Haiti, and Universal History*. Pittsburgh, PA: University of Pittsburgh Press, 2009.

Bullock, Steven C. *Revolutionary Brotherhood: Freemasonry and the Transformation of the American Social Order, 1730–1840*. Chapel Hill: University of North Carolina Press, 1998.

Case, James Royal. *A History of the Ancient Accepted Scottish Rite in Connecticut*. Connecticut: Council of Deliberation, 1967.

Cauna, Jacques de. "Quelques aperçus sur l'histoire de la franc-maçonnerie en Haïti." *Revue de la société haïtienne d'histoire et de géographie* 52, no. 189–190 (1996): 20–34.

Cauna, Jacques de. "Loges, réseaux et personnalités maçonniques, de Saint-Domingue à Haïti (XVIIIe–XXe siècles)." In *Villes de la Caraïbe. Réalités sociales et productions culturelles*, edited by Jean-Paul Révauger, 37–54. Bordeaux: Pleine Page, 2005.

Cauna, Jacques de. "Autour de la thèse du complot: Franc-maçonnerie, révolution et contre-révolution à Saint-Domingue, 1789–1791." In *Franc-maçonnerie et politique au siècle des lumières: Europe-Amériques*, edited by Cécile Révauger, 289–310. Pessac: Presses Universitaires de Bordeaux, 2006.

Combes, André. "La franc-maçonnerie aux Antilles et en Guyane française de 1789 à 1848." In *La période révolutionnaire aux Antilles: Images et résonances, littérature, philosophie, histoire sociale, histoire des idées*, edited by Roger Toumson and Charles Porset, 155–180. Schoelcher: Université des Antilles et de la Guyane, 1987.

Debien, Gabriel. *Lettres de colons*. Laval: Madiot, 1965.

Dessens, Nathalie. *From Saint-Domingue to New Orleans: Migration and Influences*. Gainesville: University Press of Florida, 2007.

Dubois, Laurent. *Avengers of the New World: The Story of the Haitian Revolution*. Cambridge, MA: Belknap Press, 2004.

Escalle, Élisabeth, and Mariel Gouyon Guillaume. *Francs-maçons des loges françaises "aux Amériques", 1770–1850: Contribution à l'étude de la société créole*. Paris: Escalle, 1993.

Ferrer Benimeli, José A. "Bolívar y la masonería." *Revista de Indias* 43 (1983): 172–228.

Fouchard, Jean. "Toussaint Louverture était-il franc-maçon?" *Revue de la société haïtienne d'histoire et de géographie* 122 (April 1979): 57–58.

Garrigus, John D. *Before Haiti: Race and Citizenship in French Saint-Domingue*. New York: Palgrave-Macmillan, 2006.

Garrigus, John D. "Opportunist or Patriot? Julien Raimond (1744–1801) and the Haitian Revolution." *Slavery & Abolition* 28, no. 1 (2007): 1–21.

Geggus, David P. "Toussaint Louverture avant et après le soulevement de 1791." In *Mémoire de révolution d'esclaves à Saint-Domingue*, 2nd ed. edited by Franklin Midy, 112–132. Montréal: CIDHICA, 2007.

Girard, Philippe. *Toussaint Louverture: A Revolutionary Life*. New York: Basic Books, 2016.

Guillaume, Pierre. "Contribution rémoise à la question des signatures maçonniques." *Champagne généalogie* 56, no. 3 (1992): 184–186.

Harland-Jacobs, Jessica. *Builders of Empire: Freemasons and British Imperialism, 1717–1927*. Chapel Hill: University of North Carolina Press, 2007.

Harvey, Oscar Jewell. *History of Lodge No. 61, F. and A. M., Wilkesbarré, Pa: Together with a Collection of Masonic Addresses, an Account of the Anti-Masonic Crusade, and Extended Biographical Sketches of Prominent Members of the Lodge, With Portraits*. Wilkes-Barre, PA: E.B. Yordy, 1897.

Hinks, Peter P. "'Perfectly Proper and Conciliating': Jean-Pierre Boyer, Freemasonry, and the Revolutionary Atlantic in Eastern Connecticut, 1800–1801." *Atlantic Studies* 16 (2019).

Hofman, Amos. "Opinion, Illusion, and the Illusion of Opinion: Barruel's Theory of Conspiracy." *Eighteenth-Century Studies* 27, no. 1 (1993): 27–60.

Isnard, Marie Zépherin. *Inventaire sommaire des archives départementales antérieures à 1790: Basses-Alpes*. Vol. 2. Digne: Imprimerie Vial, 1908.

Le Bihan, Alain. "La franc-maçonnerie dans les colonies françaises aux XVIII siècle." *Annales historiques de la Révolution française* 46, no. 1 (1974): 39–62.

Le Bihan, Alain. *Loges et chapitres de la Grande loge et du Grand orient de France (2e moitié du XVIIIe siècle)*. 2nd ed. Paris: Editions du Comité des travaux historiques et scientifiques, 1990.

Le Forestier, René. *La franc-maçonnerie occultiste au XVIII siècle et l'ordre des Elus Coëns*. Paris: La Table d'Emeraude, [1928] 1987.

Loiselle, Kenneth. "Living the Enlightenment in an Age of Revolution: Freemasonry in Bordeaux (1788–1794)." *French History* 24, no. 1 (2010): 60–81.

Maurel, Blanche. "Une société de pensée à Saint-Domingue, le 'Cercle des Philadelphes' au Cap Français." *Revue française d'histoire d'outre-mer* 48, no. 171 (1961): 234–266.

McClellan, James E. *Colonialism and Science: Saint Domingue in the Old Regime*. Baltimore, MD: Johns Hopkins University Press, 1992.

McClellan, James E. "L'historiographie d'une académie coloniale: Le Cercle des Philadelphes (1784–1793)." *Annales historiques de la Révolution française* 320 (2000): 77–88.

Moreau de Saint-Méry, M. L. E. *Loix et constitutions des colonies françoises de l'amérique sous le vent*. Vol. 6. Paris: Chez l'auteur, 1784.

Ménier, Marie Antoinette. "Comment furent rapatriés les greffes de Saint Domingue, 1803–1820." *La Gazette des archives* 100 (1978): 13–29.

Mentor, Gaétan. *Histoire de la franc-maçonnerie en Haïti: Les fils noirs de la veuve*. Port-au-Prince: Imprimerie Le Natal, 2003.

Nahon, Michelle. *Martinès de Pasqually: Un énigmatique franc-maçon théurge du XVIIIe siècle, fondateur de l'ordre des Elus Coëns*. Saint-Malo: P. Galodé, 2011.

Pluchon, Pierre. "Cercle des Philadelphes du Cap-Français à Saint-Domingue: Seule Académie coloniale de l'Ancien Régime." *Mondes et cultures* 45 (1985): 157–185.

Prinsen, Gerry. *Bonseigneur Rituals: A Collection of 18th Century Ecossais Rituals*. Kila, MT: Kessinger, 1998.

Racine, Karen. *Francisco de Miranda: A Transatlantic Life in the Age of Revolution*. Wilmington, DE: S R Books, 2002.

Saintard, Pierre-Louis. *Essai sur les colonies françoises, ou Discours politiques sur la nature du gouvernement, de la population and du commerce de la colonie de S.D.* Paris, 1754.

Saint Victor Hérard, Roger. "The History of How the Gnostic Church of Ambelain Martinism, Etc. Arrived in Haiti, and Its Subsequent Move to the USA," trans. Phillip A. Garver, *The World of the French Gnostic Tradition* (2005). http://www.gnostique.net/documents/haitiens.pdf. Accessed 05 November 2018.

Saunier, Éric. "Être confrère et franc-maçon à la fin du XVIIIe siècle: Les exemples du Havre et de Pont-Audemer." *Annales historiques de la Révolution française* 306 (1996): 617–634.

Saunier, Éric. "L'espace caribéen: Un enjeu de pouvoir pour la franc-maçonnerie française." *Revista de estudios históricos de la masonería* 1, no. 1 (2009): 43–56.

Seal-Coon, Frederick-William. *An Historical Account of Jamaican Freemasonry*. Kingston: Golding Print. Service, 1976.

Sheller, Mimi. "Sword-Bearing Citizens: Militarism and Manhood in Nineteenth-Century Haiti." *Plantation Society in the Americas* 4, no. 2–3 (1997): 233–278.

Taillefer, Michel. *La franc-maçonnerie toulousaine sous l'Ancien Régime et la Révolution, 1741–1799*. Paris: E.N.S.B., 1984.

Trouillot, Michel-Rolph. *Silencing the Past: Power and the Production of History*. Boston, MA: Beacon Press, 1995.

White, Arthur O. "Prince Saunders: An Instance of Social Mobility among Antebellum New England Blacks." *The Journal of Negro History* 60, no. 4 (1975): 526–535.

"Perfectly proper and conciliating": Jean-Pierre Boyer, freemasonry, and the revolutionary Atlantic in eastern Connecticut, 1800–1801

Peter P. Hinks

ABSTRACT

Near the end of the Quasi-War in 1800, Jean-Pierre Boyer, future president of Haiti, was brought to New London, Connecticut with other partisans from the pro-French forces in St. Domingue. Boyer along with others were held in nearby Norwich until April 1801. A Freemason, Boyer was welcomed by Masons in Norwich while plundered by other Masons on the cruiser and in New London. In 1800, internal contention roiling Masonry in New London County readily overlapped with local political partisanry and religious controversy – all of which likewise engaged broader regional and national conflicts. The insertion of a black French partisan initiated into a foreign Masonic order enriched the presence of the Atlantic in all these contests. This essay explores how Boyer and Freemasonry helped to highlight the complex web of local, national, and Atlantic interpenetrating the political and social life of New London County.

In fall 1800, the American Quasi-War with France was winding down. The conflict – rooted in ruptures with France earlier in the 1790s – centered around French and American seizures of each other's vessels on the Atlantic and in the Caribbean where France's prized colony, St. Domingue, was located. The war formally ended with the signing of the Treaty of Morfontaine on 30 September 1800. Yet in early 1799, representatives of President Adams's administration concluded private arrangements with Toussaint Louverture, the island's emerging black leader who aspired to greater independence from France. They agreed to supply him with war materiel and other commodities in his war against the pro-French forces of General Andre Rigaud in the island's south. In return, he guaranteed American merchants access to the island's ports despite a French ban. American naval vessels protected this merchant fleet in St. Domingue's waters as well as supplied armed support to Toussaint.

These events and measures would dramatically deliver this Atlantic to New London County in Connecticut. In late August 1800, the US naval cruiser, *Trumbull*, out of New London and commanded by Capt. David Jewett captured near 150 black pro-Rigaud soldiers, officers, and their family members off the southwestern coast of the island. It was a "most notable exploit" assessed one historian and it reflected the collapse of Rigaud's forces in the south. The prisoners were transported to New London where they debarked in September. Norwich's chronicler, Frances Manwaring Caulkins (born in 1795 in New London), described the prisoners as "natives of St. Domingo, partly of French origin, but with a large admixture of African blood." Soon marched to Hartford and processed before the US District Court, most returned to New London County where some were placed in Norwich and others in New London. There they remained until April 1801 when they were moved to New York City for transport to France.[1]

One of these prisoners was Jean-Pierre Boyer, "Captain and Assistant Adjutant General" to Rigaud, who would become President of a newly united Haiti in 1820.[2] Later described by one Connecticut contemporary as "a young mulatto of manly and dignified deportment," Boyer was born of an enslaved woman from the Congo in 1776 and early sent by his white French father, a shopkeeper in Port-au-Prince, to Paris to be schooled. He returned to St. Domingue in 1793.[3] Boyer was placed in Norwich.

After seizing the vessel, Capt. Jewett realized that Boyer carried various Masonic effects from his lodge of the Grand Orient of France in Jacmel. However, once in New London, Jewett, a Mason from Wooster Lodge in Colchester, Connecticut, allowed his uncle, Eliphalet Bulkeley, Master of Wooster, to seize and retain all of these articles. Neither exhibited any regard for fraternal duties to Boyer. In fact, Jewett and his seamen were accused of pillaging the prisoners. More broadly, they revealed contempt for "a coloured man" and the anarchic republicans of the "piratical" Rigaud, near universally reviled then by American sailors in the Caribbean and by the mainland press as the man responsible for "the depredations, the piracies, plunder and murders" visited upon our "countrymen."[4]

Despite these vivid recriminations, Boyer was embraced in Norwich as a brother by several Masons and domiciled in their houses at the Lodge's expense. The *Norwich Courier* exclaimed "the French prisoners in this city are treated in the most humane and benevolent manner [...] [T]hey are very plentifully provided with both food and raiment." The editor, Thomas Hubbard, noted that "they have the full liberty of the town." He was especially proud for: "Another circumstance reflects great honor on the Masonic Fraternity. – One of the prisoners having been recognized as a brother, was immediately supplied with every convenience, and placed out to board in a private family in this city."[5] In one house, young women taught him English; in another, a local physician healed him of a wasting illness. Boyer's shipboard encounters with Masons differed dramatically from that he received from their landed counterparts in Norwich.

These remarkable and overlooked events provide a singular opportunity to employ the "cis-Atlantic" model proposed by David Armitage for investigating "the interaction between local particularity and a wider web of connections (and comparisons)" on the Atlantic. The web seeks to integrate "seemingly disparate regions within a common Atlantic context" and dissolve such "artificial" boundaries as "internal and external, domestic and foreign, or national and imperial" separating these regions. By concentrating "on smaller units of analysis," "cis-Atlantic history confronts such separations by insisting on commonalities and by studying the local effects of oceanic movements." Norwich and its county were infused with distinctive political partisanship, religious controversy, and Masonic disputes, all overlapping with regional and national conflicts. The insertion of Boyer amplified these controversies in eastern Connecticut as it displayed the locale's close interconnections with the broader seaboard, Caribbean, and Atlantic. Armitage's model asserts the integrality of this "local particularity" to the framing of the Atlantic world, that this local flowed necessarily into the structuring of that bigger world. This cis-Atlantic upends the centering of the Atlantic around its metropolitan nexuses and replaces it with a more complex model where the de-centralized yet interstitched aggregate of the Atlantic's myriad scattered localities and networks actually constituted what that world meant.[6]

Other current historians have argued for a similar model. In his fine work on people of African descent in late eighteenth-century Virginia, James Sidbury asserts that the complex interactions of localities with the broader Atlantic world undercut easy "heuristic distinctions between internal and external influences."[7] Indeed the two cannot be separated from each other, he argues, as they intertwine and forge something different in each local context. Excellent studies by Ashli White and James Alexander Dun have increased our understanding of the experience of St. Domingue and French emigres and transients in Philadelphia in the 1790s and the complex symbiosis they shared with the inhabitants of the national capital.[8] White has observed how the course of these encounters compressed the revolutionary Atlantic of Western Europe, Caribbean, and North America into one specific space where important and diverse representatives and currents from all the realms converged. However, rather than illustrating the conventional model of a hierarchical chain where representatives of imperial and national governments initiated diverse policies and incursions that their telescope of subordinates in such localities implemented, White argues that their criss-crossing interaction in Philadelphia exhibited an intricate stranding of all these realms of the Atlantic into an overarching "web" where their interweaving often revealed local contest and hybridization more than untrammeled centralized command.

Armitage, White, and Sidbury all argue for local particularity as the nexus where the complex interpenetration of local, national, and imperial occurred and most richly revealed the Atlantic at any given time as a diverse and highly contingent tableau of these interconnected sites. The Atlantic, they assert, cannot be understood without these close local studies, which reveal that Atlantic and local were in fact inseparable.

This essay argues that Norwich and New London County in 1800 afforded one of these sites and that investigating the overlooked strands of Freemasonry in their local webbing helps to illustrate how. The multifarious analyses of White and Dun do not include the significant strands of Freemasons from France, St. Domingue, and Philadelphia and other American locales in their webs. The fine work of Jan C. Jansen in this issue on the close interplay of the Masonry of French and St. Domingue emigres with that of others in the Caribbean basin and the American seaboard initiates this greater detailing of, among other sites, the Philadelphia context. The striking example of Boyer in Norwich helps us to understand further how Masonic exchanges in another "local particularity" reveal the rich interaction of this specific strand of the Atlantic web there as well.

American Freemasonry by 1800 remained a fractious body, despite the efforts of Masons nationally after 1783 to establish a federal system of authority in which each state would establish its own grand lodge to charter and regulate all lodges within its territory.[9] While Scottish Rite, the Masonry of the Grand Orient of France, was welcomed in Charleston, South Carolina and elsewhere on the southern seaboard, when Boyer brought it to New London County, it was received with disdain and suspicion by some. New England still remained seized by the Illuminati furor whose leading clerical and Federalist proponents identified his Masonry as the very spearhead in America of Jacobinic revolution and atheism. His experience revealed yet again the varied ways in which localities on the American seaboard mediated the broader conflicts and opportunities traversing the Atlantic. Moreover, along with Scottish Rite, the emergence then of other "higher degree" systems such as Knights Templar and Royal Arch furthered Masonic fractiousness in eastern Connecticut and complicated the consolidating efforts of the grand lodge.

Embracing Boyer represented the persistence among some Masons in Norwich in 1800 of a central characteristic of eighteenth century Atlantic Masonry – cosmopolitanism. This temperament flourished in the Craft in its first century when a diversity of Masonries existed, each claiming the right to charter new lodges. Spread throughout Europe and the Atlantic in the 1700s and often distant from chartering grand lodges, disparate lodges of Masons interacted freely with each other regardless of whether their grand lodges would have considered their interaction "regular" or not. Often profession of ones Masonic *bona fides* and perhaps possession of some credentials and secrets was sufficient to secure one's status as a "brother." As Jessica Harland-Jacobs has observed, "[i]n the British Atlantic world of the eighteenth century, Freemasonry proved to be a highly elastic and adaptable institution."[10] Moreover, embracing a French Mason of African descent from St. Domingue evidently associated their local cosmopolitanism with the Atlantic's revolutionary emancipationism. In Boston and Philadelphia at the same time, black and white Masons actively disputed whether they would share fellowship or not. Masonry in New London County unavoidably engaged this dispute as well.

Obviously not all the county's Masons upheld this cosmopolitanism: Bulkeley, Jewett, and others repudiated Boyer's claims to Masonry and thus comfortably did not accord him a reception due a Masonic "stranger." Some Masons in Connecticut and beyond feared this cosmopolitanism nurtured a laxity that threatened to destroy pure Masonry and its grounding in select membership more than it did any wholesome fellowship. Others feared it allowed subversives to launch or commandeer lodges and use their networks to nurture revolution in an enemy's country. Elsewhere in the Atlantic, the fraternal web strained as well under pressures simultaneously local, national, and oceanic. Bitter conflict with France raged in Great Britain in the 1790s and fears flared that the independence-minded United Irishmen had infiltrated Ireland's lodges. Thus British metropolitan forces worked to join Freemasonry indissolubly with loyalty to state and empire while contracting its distinctive eighteenth century cosmopolitanism.[11] Over the years following 1800, Connecticut's strengthening Grand Lodge came to establish greater "order and uniformity" among its lodges that included checking the cosmopolitanism that enabled Norwich's lodge to open its doors so readily to a foreign Mason of color. Yet in eastern Connecticut in 1800, achieving this level of control for the grand lodge remained in the future. Following very closely the understudied strand of Masonry in New London County in the late 1790s leads us not only into its intricate interweavings within the local web but ineluctably as well down the seaboard, into the Caribbean, and out into the broad Atlantic.[12]

* * *

Freemasonry grew significantly in eastern Connecticut in the 1790s: from a total of twelve lodges in 1789 with only one in eastern Connecticut, the state had forty-four lodges by 1800 with at least eight of them in the eastern counties of New London and

Windham.[13] Some ministers such as Samuel Nott of Franklin, a village of Norwich, opposed "Masonic fever" as a threat to revealed religion and to the clerical authority of mainstream Congregationalism in the state.[14] However, another Masonic drama agitated the state more immediately then. In 1800, Connecticut was still in the throes of the Illuminati controversy, forwarded in the state principally by Yale's President, Reverend Timothy Dwight. The Illuminati referred to a secret society, supposedly organized first in Bavaria, that fomented the French Revolution and the Terror. They channeled their anarchic principles throughout the Continent and beyond principally through Masonic lodges organized under grand lodges in Germany and France. In England in the late 1790s, John Robison and Abbe Barruel published works apparently exposing this conspiracy. By 1798 in the United States, the Boston Congregational minister, the Reverend Jedidiah Morse, had imbibed them and preached a sermon in May echoing the charges of the two while amplifying them by linking the conspiracies to Democratic-Republican agitation in the United States since the arrival of the controversial French ambassador, Edmond-Charles Genet, in 1793.

While Morse struggled to identify a good Masonry that issued from Great Britain, the likely association of some Masons in the US with nefarious sedition remained. Both Morse, born in Connecticut and educated at Yale, and Dwight furthered these charges in the state. Many Masons in Connecticut labored to evince their loyalty, especially at the grand lodge level. The Grand Lodge of Vermont – a state New England Federalists designated a Republican seedbed – scrupulously highlighted its national loyalty in a letter to President Adams in late 1798. In his reply, Adams affirmed that *in general* Freemasonry's secrecy and sense of possessing a special "science of government [...] may be perverted to all the ill purposes which have been suspected." Nevertheless, the Grand Lodge's testament evinced its "characteristics of candor [...] [that] leave no room to doubt [...] that you will risque all in support of your government."[15] Federalists and Congregational ministers in Connecticut and New England had loudly fused the French Revolution with irreligion and democratic excess in the US for the past several years; now Dwight and Morse subordinated all the disorder to the leadership of French and continental Freemasonry. The Vermont Grand Lodge pointed to one remedy to the attacks of the anti-Illuminatists – a bold public statement affirming the devotion of the state's Masons to nation and patriotism.[16]

An anonymous author from Newfield, Connecticut – a small town in eastern Fairfield county – amplified the charges of Morse and Dwight, allaying any suggestion that his fears were an exception. He believed the details and warnings from Barruel and Robison remained perfectly accurate for the current situation in the state; he chided Dwight and Morse for whatever measured retractions they offered of earlier anathemas on alien Freemasonry. Such undermining of their authority was precisely what the agents sought. While uncertain if actual *"Illuminati"* were in the state, he was convinced that "in many of our Lodges," there are those "who act like them." He protested the strength of these "designing men" in many Connecticut lodges and the relative inability of the grand lodge to extirpate them, despite the fact that the recent Illuminati furor had "produced a revolution as to officers in Grand Lodge," a reference to key Federalists elected as top officers in the Grand Lodge by 1798 and an ensuing contraction of lodge creation. Imperiled Masonry in Connecticut for this author was not simply a local or even national problem; it was fundamentally an Atlantic problem, the ultimate source of the state's current infection. And the problem was deep:

> French Philosophers [are] [...] sowing their foul seed in [Connecticut] and the United States, with an expectation of reaping within a few years, a plentiful crop of Democrats, Deists and Atheists [...]. [M]any Masons, are cultivating and tilling the soil.

By no means were these agents in retreat. It is, he continued,

> a fact well ascertained, that the overthrow of all the Republics of Europe, by France, was effected by duplicity, deception, intrigue and stratagem, first practiced in the Society of Masons: There the disbelief of a God, and his religion was promulgated, and those fine and high sounding words, "Liberty and Equality" invented.

He affirmed the Atlantic dimensions of Connecticut's peril: "Their success in Europe, has warranted the attempt in this and the United States." One of the most important tactics of these "designing men" was to use lodge protocol to enable "the vile Infidel and Atheist" along with "Drunkards [...] [and] Whoremasters" to be admitted as members who then sowed confusion and rancor in the lodge as they demoralized true Masons into retreat. "[N]othing, but the united exertions of every well-disposed Mason, will defeat them."[17] John L. Brooke suggests that such fears were not "irrational." Not, however, because of a real presence of Illuminati, but rather because "Freemasonry's open membership" among other factors in the 1790s had allowed for a pronounced influx of oppositional Republicans into the Craft where they challenged earlier Federalist dominance.[18]

For such as the anonymous author, the enormous success of Ancient Freemasonry in America substantiated his fears. The Ancients were first organized in 1751 in London by an Irish journeyman who emphasized the artisanal origins of Freemasonry in the guild of stonemasons who built Solomon's Temple. They proliferated in America and the British Atlantic in the latter decades of the century. By 1800, Freemasonry in America was essentially Ancient Masonry. Despite their name, the Moderns were older and drew heavily from the mercantile and professional elite of the key towns and ports of Great Britain and the colonies. They had dominated late colonial American Masonry. On the other hand, the middling artisan and shopkeeping class of ports and towns flocked to the Ancients. Mobile military lodges chartered among British troops in the late eighteenth century Atlantic helped extend their sway. Chafing under earlier exclusion from Modern lodges, the new men of the Ancient lodges forged a more elastic policy on membership. Yet conflicts between Ancients and the remnant Moderns over the chartering of lodges and practices within them persisted into the 1790s, adding to the jumble of American Freemasonry by 1800. The anonymous author directly assailed the tenets and expanded membership of the Ancients "who know little more of the Society than the name [...] [and] claim it to be of greater antiquity."[19]

He likely imagined that many ill-disposed were already embedded in Norwich and elsewhere in New London County. While Norwich's Somerset Lodge in 1800 included such Federalists as John Trumbull, the vituperative Federalist editor of the Norwich *Packet*, and Ebenezer Huntington, it along with St. James in adjacent Preston also contained Jeffersonian Republicans such as Diah Manning and John and Consider Sterry, all of whom openly embraced Boyer. While not as effusive in their support of Boyer, other local Masons supported the Republicans with the Sterrys and Manning including Asa Spaulding, Samuel Huntington, Christopher Leffingwell, David Nevins, and Samuel Mott. While powerful local leaders held important offices in Somerset, they represented both political orientations while presiding over a lodge of not only merchants, large landholders, and professionals but of teachers, printers, middling farmers, artisans, booksellers, stationers, and paper-makers. As will be discussed further below, Freemasonry proved an important pillar upholding eastern Connecticut's longstanding culture of opposition to Congregational supremacy in the colony and state and to the political dominance of elites in Hartford and New Haven.[20] Such as Morse and the anonym might wonder if these members of Somerset who not only paid for Boyer's lodging but admitted him into their lodge as a valid visitor were complicit with designs he may have had. Morse's model might readily identify Boyer and his cohort with sedition, especially given that he had warned that agents of such would come from St. Domingue as well as France. According to one historian of Freemasonry in Connecticut, Boyer "visited the lodge at least twice."[21] In 1800 Connecticut, Boyer's credentials likely would not have authorized his visit; his admission thus speaks again to the relative autonomy lodges might then still exercise and, in this case, apply to sustaining cosmopolitanism. It is worth recognizing just how frankly seditious was the treatment these Norwich Masons afforded Boyer: New London editor, Charles Holt, convicted under the Sedition Act, had just been released from jail for writing a relatively mild statement while Somerset embraced an officer whose close attachment to Rigaud made him directly complicit in the deaths of Americans and the seizure of local vessels![22]

Yet, despite these possible musings, what made the ominous charges of Dwight and Morse so startling was that a number of French lodges already existed in the US. Several were woven into local grand lodges; some even had a relationship with the Grand Orient of France. For example, the lodge Morse cited as decisive evidence for the conspiracy, *La Sagesse* in Portsmouth, Virginia, was in fact created in 1786 by French emigres when the US was at peace with France. The influx of further emigres in the 90s had reinvigorated it; but they, as Morse's Congressional correspondent had informed him, were "honest and industrious men [...] entirely harmless as far as fomenting hostility to the institutions of the country was concerned." In Philadelphia, *L'Amenite, La Parfaite Union* and others peaceably thrived in the 1790s. In 1800, *L'Amenite* "organized and sponsored a huge memorial service for their deceased 'brother,' George Washington, which earned them praise from [...] President John Adams and Vice-President Thomas Jefferson." Indeed, an organized French "Lodge of Perfection" had been present in Philadelphia as early as 1781 while the Pennsylvania Grand Lodge had chartered several lodges in St. Domingue in the 1780s and 90s. To the south in Charleston in 1796, two emigres from France and St. Domingue, Alexandre Francois Auguste de Grasse and Jean Baptiste Marie Delahogue, organized the *Loge La Candeur*. Moreover, despite the vexing Alien and Sedition Acts, de Grasse became a naturalized citizen in 1799. They both helped to establish Scottish Rite's Southern Jurisdiction there in 1801.[23]

Republicans and their Masonic adherents assailed the increasingly silly charges of Morse and Dwight. In early 1800, Samuel Huntington, a Republican and Secretary of Somerset Lodge, helped launch an expose of the lurid misrepresentations of Robison and Barruel and their New England advocates in the state's press. In Norwich on 4 July 1800, others toasted that "*palsied* be the hand which would attempt to destroy sound and demonstrative reasoning by the foolish hobby of a spurious and frightful *illuminati*." The proponents of the Illuminati conspiracy again grounded it in the Atlantic by fusing it to the rationalism, anti-clericalism, democratic egalitarianism, and amoral trajectory they ascribed to the late Enlightenment of Diderot and Rousseau and the French Revolution.[24]

More locally, Dorothy Ann Lipson too associates the post-revolutionary Masons of eastern Connecticut with Enlightenment ideals, but far more positively. She characterizes them as "latitudinarian," dedicated to universalism, rational inquiry, individual freedom, and happiness which they pursued outside the frame of an established church.[25] Some Somerset Masons exhibited this latitudinarianism. Along with attacking the Illuminati furor, Republicans in Norwich in 1800 also toasted

> True rational Liberty [...]. May thy benign influences extend to the *dark corners of the earth*, and those nations who now sit in darkness *under the curse of tyranny and oppression*; may they shortly enjoy *the just rights of men*.[26]

But their devotion to a rational liberty was not so much about irreligion and anti-clericalism as Lipson suggests, perhaps clustering them with other more notable Connecticut Masons of the 1790s who did display anti-clericalism such as David Daggett and Zephaniah Swift.[27] The Sterrys as well as many other local Republicans and some Masons were deeply devout Baptists and Separate Congregationalists, derided by the state's dominant Federalists and mainstream Congregationalists as unlettered and unruly bumpkins. The ecclesiology of the Baptists and Separate Congregationalists particularly oriented around congregational autonomy: they reviled the longstanding tactics of the state to compel credal and organizational uniformity with mainstream Congregationalism, the established church of the state. It was supported by mandated taxes the "dissenters" loathed. Ever since the 1740s and the Great Awakening, these non-conforming denominations in eastern Connecticut had challenged the authority of the Standing Order to dictate their religious convictions and conscience. More recently, Certificate Laws further infuriated them by requiring they submit to a formal and humiliating registration of their "difference" in order to direct their taxes to their own clergy. For these dissenters this governance in its own way echoed the tyranny of kings, bishops, and popes.[28]

Cosmopolitan freemasonry of the eighteenth century could draw some of these ardent evangelicals because they saw in it the dedication to inquiry, conscience, and liberty undergirding religious freedom. John and Consider Sterry, among Boyer's warmest friends in Norwich, well exemplify them. They were deeply committed both to scientific inquiry and to faith: as they emphasized as early as 1790, "principles of knowledge and virtue [are] engrafted in the soul." Dedicated Republicans and Freemasons, they launched their own newspaper – *The True Republican* – in 1804 at the same time John was becoming established as the beloved minister of Norwich's First Baptist Church. They were also gifted autodidact mathematicians who wrote and published arithmetic textbooks as well as works on astronomy and navigation. By mathematics' "elegant and sublime manner of reasoning, our minds are enlightened and our understanding enlarged, and thereby we acquire a habit of reasoning, an elevation of thought that determines the mind and fixes it for every other pursuit." The Mason's compass and plumb line led one to contemplate the divine mysteries of grace and faith. Those promoting the specter of the Illuminati and their Atlantic span attacked all of this understanding of reason, liberty, equality, and faith.[29]

By embracing Boyer, his Norwich brothers boldly rejected this specter as spurious. For the Sterrys and many others in Norwich and its surrounding towns, French Freemasonry – rather than the seal of atheism and anarchy – was fully legitimate, embodying yet another fine Masonic jewel in the cosmopolitan Craft's quest for rational and divine enlightenment. Boyer's arrival in Norwich created an occasion for them to display with a particular public boldness their positive relationship to that Masonry and other "French" virtues, institutions, and people – of color, no less! They evinced an openness not only to rationalism and inquiry but to a universalism that included the possibility of forging composite lodges and nations from diverse nationalities, races, ideologies, and jurisdictions.

Those Masons in New London County not sharing with the Sterrys and others in this warm embrace of Boyer still did share with them the lodges and fraternity of local Freemasonry. Especially in the Norwich area, they gathered in the same lodges and together promoted fraternal love. When, as we will see, Royal Arch Masonry expanded in the region, many of these diverse men became Companions in the same Chapters. All generally embraced such core Masonic tenets as select fraternity, brotherly love, enlightenment and inquiry, charity and faith. Yet, amid this general consensus, the details and terms of Masonic governance, membership, and rituals remained contested and in flux – certainly in America, but on the broader Atlantic as well. By 1800, wars, insurrections, conspiracies, and electoral suspicions circulating in the nation and Atlantic energized these disputes, infusing them with a partisanship that drew simultaneously on the local, national, and Atlantic. Suspicions in New England in particular about the political and military threat of French Masonry during the Quasi-War were still acute, especially among the Federalist and Congregational elite. And in the very contracted universe of this study in eastern Connecticut, those Masons not sharing those suspicions usually leaned Republican.

These doubts and contests figured significantly into the receptions Boyer received onboard and in New London County. A committee of men representing the Commandery of the Knights Templar – led by its Captain General, Eliphalet Bulkeley – seized, as was remembered bluntly by Bulkeley's son in 1820, all of Boyer's Masonic documents and ceremonial jewels. They were taken not from a Mason but "from a coloured man, (then confined in prison as a prisoner of war.)"[30] Bulkeley retained the effects as mere "curiosities" and never returned them. Amid the jewels and documents were "a catechism of the degrees from Entered Apprentice up to Perfect Master, communications from the Grand Orient at Paris, and a charter for the Loge Freres Choisis at Jacmel (Haiti), issued in 1774, and countersigned by 'S. Morin'". All of these were very valuable and confidential Masonic items. Bulkeley and the others exhibited no fraternal regard to Boyer. Twenty years later, Boyer still sought to regain possession of documents seized from him in 1800![31]

Indeed, Capt. Jewett ravaged all the prisoners. Naval documents from August 1800 and after reveal that the French prisoners passionately protested to Secretary of the Navy Benjamin Stoddert regarding Jewett's harsh treatment of them and his seizure of their money and goods. Captain Alexander Murray, the US Naval Station Master at Cap Francais had requested that Jewett "not plunder the prisoners of their Pocket money." Yet "[h]e I find has taken every penny from them & all their Watches & Swords, & left them to the bounty of the Inhabitants of New London."[32] Indeed, Jewett failed to stop as ordered at Norfolk – where the prisoners were to be placed on Craney Island – and sailed on for twelve days "at the risk of starving his Crew & Prisoners."[33]

Despite the war-time context, Jewett might have recognized Boyer otherwise. Other American Masons in war followed a different protocol. In 1779 in New Jersey, an American General returned Masonic records to a British officer, stating in an enclosed note that although "contending states, call forth their subjects to war, as Masons we are disarmed of that resentment which stimulates to undistinguished desolation [...] [and] ought to promote the happiness and advance the weal of each other." English Masons tolerated and mixed with French Masons organized under "the French system" while they were prisoners of war in England from the 1750s through the 1810s.[34] Particularly infused with an affective gravity binding them all together, Masons were supposed to embrace a sojourning or uprooted Mason, regardless of circumstance, as a brother and offer assistance. As one noted in 1798, none were to know "the name of Stranger."[35]

Yet the anonymous Connecticut Mason of 1799 was certain "the softer accents of *Brotherly Love, Charity, and Universal Benevolence*" uniting all Masons under whatever conditions were only the mellifluous sedition of the *"Democratic School"* and *"French Philosophers"* who "have crept into many Lodges in Connecticut." Their Masonry was in fact not Masonry at all; rather it was perilous partisanry masquerading as *bienfaisance*. His Masonry, on the other hand, was one of "steady observance of Christianity and inviolable attachment to good order and government" – and he had no doubt that that Masonry was then endangered in Connecticut. Core Masonic verities were now suspect as enabling a subversive cosmopolitanism. The proliferating Ancients – wittingly or otherwise – unlocked the lodge door to this peril. France's Atlantic spawn hatched in Connecticut.[36]

Steven Bullock, however, does not identify the celebration of these virtues then with any insidious French influence. Rather the mass of Ancient Masons were more inclined to stress fraternal love and charity than were the Moderns or the more conservative among the Ancients because, he observes, the social roots of the Ancients were in more mobile lodges such as military ones. Likewise, after the Revolution, they were especially concerned to expand their membership and terrain into the interior. The tenet of fraternal love helped bind together the mobile and newly admitted among America's increasingly dispersed Masons. Diasporic people then particularly valued this love. Fledgling and vulnerable African American Masons in Boston – originally Ancients and many of whom itinerated in the maritime world – highlighted these virtues even more so: a black Mason there in 1789 stressed that "christian charity – universal love and friendship – benevolent affections and social feelings [that] unite and knit men together" were the essential attributes of Masonic "brotherly love." Yet, even as ascendant and expanding American Masonry as a whole in 1800 evidently extolled brotherly love, those dishonoring Boyer and his Masonry seemed to share the author's suspicions of its "softer accents."[37]

To be sure, more than adherence to some true Masonry informed Jewett's and others' contemptuous attitude towards these prisoners. In late August 1800, Captain Alexander Murray encountered the *Trumbull* in the harbor at Cap Français as it was about to depart. He was very impressed with the large number of high-ranking officers and notable citizens of color on the captured vessel. Nevertheless he still characterized them in a letter to Benjamin Stoddert as "wretches" for whom he

> saw no alternative but sending them on to America, they are of the Vilest cast a set of Lawless Vagabonds that the Community will be well rid of in this part of the World for had they reached the place of their Destination [i.e., Cuba] there is little doubt but the[y] would again have Soon commenc'd their piracys against our Commerce.

Murray along with all officers and sailors rightly dreaded the armed vessels Rigaud's forces used to attack naval cruisers and American merchant vessels in southern waters. Although likely intended exclusively for escape, the *Vengeance* was armed and these vessels were commonly denominated in the press of Connecticut and beyond as "piratical barges" and "savage." Jewett probably comfortably believed that whatever treatment he doled out to such criminals was appropriate.

While their fears on the one hand were certainly justified, Murray and Jewett also reflected the pronounced tendency then of the Adams administration and of the Connecticut and northern Federalist press to portray Toussaint and his army in benign terms. A remarkable public "domestication" of his forces had occurred by the late 1790s; to use the phrase of a correspondent of Adams's Secretary of State, Timothy Pickering, they now appeared exclusively "humane and mild."[38] Just as readily, they framed Toussaint's opponent, Rigaud, as "capricious and tyrannical." Included among the Trumbull's captives was a supposed commander of some of those barges whom the local *Packet* described as "a vile fellow" in the spirit of Alexander Murray's above descriptions. Apparently they all were complicit with Rigaud's loathsome barges.[39]

Yet over the course of the bitter Haitian Revolution in the 1790s, Toussaint and his officers and allies were as likely to commit horrible atrocities and reprisals as were any other of innumerable participants including Rigaud and his forces. Moreover the specific descriptions above are extreme for nonresisting officers accompanied by children and women. Frances Manwaring Caulkins later scolded that the prisoners' captors might have treated them more "humanely [...] rather than plunder them of their goods and carry them into captivity." These were the same men who some in Norwich would soon characterize as "perfectly proper and conciliating." In fact, a Republican newspaper in nearby Stonington declared that "[t]here is not a captain of a barge [...] among them. They are landmen, belonging to Rigaud's army, and fled with their wives and children."[40] These observations upended the Federalist-sponsored "sanitizing" of Toussaint that scrubbed him of nefarious "frenchness" while retaining it for Rigaud and his partisans.

Eliphalet Bulkeley's confiscation of Boyer's Masonic effects also prompted the first close review of them. It would only deepen his connection to that "frenchness." Boyer had been initiated into the Scottish Rite. This Masonry was actually founded in France in the 1760s as an esoteric higher degree system. It was disseminated from there to the French West Indies later in the decade by the controversial Stephen Morin, especially to the south of St. Domingue where Boyer was later admitted. Scottish Rite arrived in the US principally in Charleston, South Carolina through Christian and Sephardic Masons from America, France, and St. Domingue as early as the 1770s. By 1801 after their numbers had swelled there during the tumultuous 1790s, they would forge the seminal Southern Jurisdiction of the Supreme Council, the first such council in the Atlantic for Scottish Rite. Despite the consolidating enterprise of the grand lodges, the fledgling state of American freemasonry still rendered it porous for such a hybridizing by this "fresh view of Freemasonry."[41] This action began the "domestication" of this Freemasonry in the United States where over the ensuing decades, it would expand, especially in the South. Bulkeley and other Masons in eastern Connecticut likely knew of Scottish Rite both as it pertained to France and the United States for it had had some earlier presence in the Hudson River Valley and possibly even in Norwich.[42]

Boyer contributed to this seaboard engagement with and circulation of Scottish Rite, a Masonry of "French sensibilities [...] [with] its own distinctive mix of the democratic values expressed as liberty, equality, and fraternity." Yet Boyer and this Masonry confronted a very different local context from what that Masonry confronted to the south. A black partisan of Rigaud's regionally loathed forces in southern St. Domingue, Boyer delivered a foreign Masonry to a local context gripped by the Illuminati furor that identified that Masonry as counterfeit, seditious, and irreligious. Despite this hostility, Boyer still likely helped to seed Scottish Rite in the region: an eminent historian of Connecticut freemasonry states that Boyer's knowledge of these higher degrees was so significant that he communicated Scottish Rite's Ineffable Degrees to some unidentified Masons in eastern Connecticut, perhaps his confreres at Somerset. Indeed, he speculated that a Scottish Rite "Lodge of Perfection" may have briefly been present in Norwich as early as 1796![43] The reception of Boyer in New London County points not only to matters of concern to the history of Freemasonry in America by 1800; it reveals more broadly the ways in which a "local particularity" mediated and appropriated the tumult of the late eighteenth-century Atlantic world in terms of the imperatives and context of their own indigenous cultures.

Interest in higher degree Masonry had mounted in New England in the 1790s beside an expanding enthusiasm for the Craft as a whole. The region, however, focused on Royal Arch Masonry and the Knights Templar, both of which had arrived from England. The Knights in particular would prove unreceptive to the arrival of Boyer's higher degree system. While the proliferating lodges under the system of Ancient Freemasonry awarded only three degrees, the Knights Templar and Royal Arch awarded many more degrees signifying supposedly higher levels of Masonic knowledge. Yet many Masons in Ancient lodges rejected the pursuit of these higher degrees as superfluous to Masonic enlightenment and as esoteric and elitist. Moreover the presence of these higher degree orders with their own governing councils posed questions not only about just what relationship they were to have with state grand lodges, but also about just who exactly was a true Mason. They furthered the diversity and contesting of Freemasonry in Connecticut in 1800. The emerging grand lodge system attempted to resolve this conflict: as Modern grand lodges merged with dominant Ancient ones by the late eighteenth century, new charters specified that the three degrees awarded by all local lodges certified any recipient as a fully recognized Mason; he required no further "higher" degrees to be so acknowledged.[44] Yet the Knights Templar in Connecticut then would raise some doubts about this apparent resolution: their founders in the mid-eighteenth century understood the modern Knights as the only true Masons, descended from the Templars of the Crusades among whom, they asserted, Freemasonry originated exclusively.

By 1800, Norwich was the seat for a Royal Arch Chapter and Colchester for a Knights' Commandery. Their fledgling histories further illuminate both the cohering and contesting of Freemasonry in New London County. By 1800, the county had at least thirty-five Companions, or Royal Arch Masons; certainly it had more but that number constitutes relevant men the author has identified. They spanned the regional Masonic and social spectrum: from Consider Sterry, Diah Manning, and Samuel Huntington to Eliphalet Bulkeley, Ebenezer Huntington, and Henry Champion. Companions were centered in Norwich at Franklin Chapter #4 and comprised at least twenty men from that town. Any man initiated as a Master Mason in a state lodge might be admitted into a Chapter. In accord with the system of Ancient Masonry, Royal Arch Masons derived their rituals and iconography from the building of the first and second Jerusalem Temples. Many of them understood their further degrees as complementing the knowledge secured from their first three degrees in their local lodge. The locating of their Chapter in Norwich points to the diversity of Companions there.[45]

The Knights Templar, however, were much more selective and exclusive. Before one could begin the ascent through the chivalric orders culminating in the Knights, one had to be initiated into all Royal Arch degrees. In 1800, no fewer than fourteen Knights existed in New London County; it is not clear how many more existed. They were overwhelmingly concentrated in Colchester: twelve resided there – all from Wooster – with two from Norwich and a few others from New London. The Knights inducted into the Colchester Commandery by 1800 including Eliphalet Bulkeley were all from Colchester's leading families. Many among them were important Templar officers as well as principals in Wooster. The relative social and political diversity among Companions in Norwich was not as evident among the Knights of Colchester.[46]

The Knights in particular initiated more affluent Masons who could pay the additional fees and purchase the uniforms and ritual paraphernalia. Some also sought to distinguish themselves from the more middling people populating Ancient lodges. They addressed themselves as "Sir Knight" and rooted their Masonry not in the building of the two Temples, but in the valiant service their predecessors provided to Christian pilgrims and to the occupation of the Holy Land during the Crusades. The origins of Freemasonry were supposedly in these Knights, not in some stone-builders. They were the most explicitly Christian of all the Masonic orders, requiring a pledge to defend that faith. Alone among Masons, they understood themselves as the *avant garde* of warriors protecting Christendom. The membership of the Knights in their first years in eastern Connecticut strongly points to this search for a greater – and truer – Masonic exclusivity. It was no surprise that their local leadership confiscated Boyer's documents.

They exhibited a turn away from the cosmopolitanism Masons in Somerset modeled. Those dreading the subversive dilution of Masonry in Connecticut urgently beseeched the Knights' service. The anonymous author did not "believe otherwise than that it [i.e., Freemasonry] was instituted by those Christian Princes, who undertook the first Crusade in the year 1096, to drive the Infidels from Jerusalem." He asserted that "[t]hose Princes who instituted this Society [i.e., the Knights Templar] [...] admitted such Characters, and such only, [...] who, by their steady observance of Christianity and inviolable attachment to good order and government, had merited the confidence of all." Only after "seven years close application to Religion, Virtue and Honor were [they] advanced to Masters." Through them alone, "Masonry was spread over Europe." Their exclusive conservative Christian mandate placed them among the vanguard of those combatting the current scourge of Democratic atheism and the "designing men" of the ordinary lodges who enabled their troops of "Drunkards [...] [and] Whoremasters." Supported by a vigilant grand lodge, the Knights would disperse this horde. Fortunately, the author knew a Commandery existed in Colchester.[47]

To this author, the Knights were not only antidote to the evident cosmopolitanism of the Sterrys and Mannings; they scoured the whole of the fraternity of the hucksterism of the Ancients, the dupes of the French. Doubt may certainly be raised that this was the understanding of Bulkeley and his fellow Knights of their mission. After all, they had been raised in Ancient lodges and in Royal Arch. Nevertheless, their treatment of Boyer and dread of the predatory French, their embrace of the Christian chivalric underpinnings of the Knights, and all joined with their overwhelming membership from and quasi-sequestration in conservative Colchester suggests a predisposition to agree with at least some of what the anonymous author asserts about the Masonry and mission of the Knights. In 1800, the Knights had by no means been interwoven into a unified system of American Freemasonry under grand lodge jurisdiction such as would exist more securely by the early 1820s. The Knights did retain in 1800 some authoritative singularity. And it was in this sanative singularity that the anonymous author placed all his hopes.

The microcosm of Norwich, Colchester, and surrounding eastern Connecticut in 1800 focused some of the tensions then existing in an organizationally transitional American Freemasonry. Bitter divisions regionally over politics and religion not only exacerbated the tensions; the very public engagement of this partisanry among Masons themselves illustrated just how they grappled then with who and what was a Mason. Was a Mason, "whether Europe, Asia, or Africa gave him existence," legitimate, one whom a lodge wherever "reflects great honor on the Masonic Fraternity" by embracing?[48] Or, rather, had the Masonic virtues supposedly undergirding that embrace – "the softer accents of *Brotherly Love, Charity, and Universal Benevolence*" – actually obsolesced in an age of fulsome revolution? Had the lax regulation and selectivity they foisted enabled French and democratic agents to subvert the lodge's "steady observance of Christianity and inviolable attachment to good order and government?" While certainly fraternity and benevolence also existed among Masons in eastern Connecticut in 1800, more than enough fraught visions of devious camaraderie and cataclysm circulated as well to make some wonder if the ideals were now only illusions. The arrival of Boyer helped to bring all of this to the fore.

Moreover, this particular contest over Masonic identity in Norwich could not evade the pervasive backdrop of slavery, abolition, and race in New England and the United States. Boyer's Freemasonry was integrally connected with emancipationism, a process the northern United States was then gradually undergoing. Despite the charges of Toussaint and his deputies, Rigaud, his officers, and forces in southern St. Domingue never wavered in their support of emancipation.[49] The universal and benevolent fraternity of humankind regardless of nation, creed, or race was a tenet fundamental to the Craft and would have informed Boyer's embrace of universal freedom. Indeed, Boyer himself was a representative of the very opening of French Freemasonry which did not admit people of color prior to the 1790s.[50] By no means, however, did that tenet predispose all Atlantic Masons to abolition: many Masons were slaveholders and engaged in the Atlantic slave trade; Cécile Révauger argues persuasively that few Masons in the late eighteenth century and early nineteenth century were antislavery, let alone abolitionists. Yet Jacques de Cauna has argued that in fact a white French Mason, Etienne Polverel, launched abolition in the New World. Along with Léger-Félicité Sonthonax, Polverel abolished slavery by military decree in St. Domingue in late August 1793. De Cauna who argues that Polverel, not the usually recognized Sonthonax, engineered this abolition, grounds the policy in his Masonry. An early adjutant of Polverel's in the south was Jean-Pierre Boyer who had even traveled in the same vessel with the civil commissioner across the Atlantic. Several Masons from Norwich, Preston, and New London who had been members of the Connecticut Abolition Society would have shared that sentiment with Boyer including key Republicans Samuel Mott and Christopher Leffingwell as well as Rev. John Tyler. All welcomed him into their lodge.[51] Moreover the emerging Freemasonry of people of color in Boston and elsewhere in the seaboard North was exclusively antislavery: while Prince Hall in his African Lodge in Boston then upheld black freedom in a quieter, nonconfrontational manner, black Masons there by the 1820s under the leadership of John Telemachus Hilton publicly excoriated slavery, demanded black freedom and equality, and praised the example of revolutionary Haiti. Throughout the nineteenth century, African American Masons stood as the most dramatic example of enduring cosmopolitanism in the American fraternity. The arrival of Boyer explicitly drew Norwich and New London County into this vast web of Atlantic emancipationism.[52]

The embrace of black Boyer also occurred within the context of ongoing disputes within American Freemasonry over to what degree, if at all, white and black Masons would share fellowship. While it cannot be explored in detail here, this issue was very much in play in the 1790s throughout the northeastern seaboard; after 1800, the infrastructure of exclusion would become more ossified. What happened in Norwich in 1800–1801 affords one vivid example of white Masons in particular positively exploring the boundaries of this fellowship.[53]

Perhaps we might distinguish Republican Masons from Federalist ones in New London County as follows: one cluster welcomed a fraternal and benevolent embrace with a man of color and his racial colleagues in their town, homes, and lodge while the other recognized an important but far less personally and domestically transformative strategic engagement with Toussaint. Local Federalists commonly supported an end to slavery, yet they overwhelmingly favored a cautious gradualism that was informed by their dread of swelling the numbers of common working people – white and black – they identified as inherently tumultuous. Certainly, some Republicans there may have leaned towards this position. Yet some did not including Charles Holt, ally of Norwich Republicans and stalwart editor of the Republican New London *Bee*. He along with others in nearby towns published in late 1798 the seminal *Narrative* of Venture Smith, a local man formerly enslaved, in whose virtue and industry they envisioned "a Franklin and Washington." Key to this position of the opposition was its relative openness to including African Americans in its broad-based drive to expand democracy for the adult male citizenry. Positive positions on black freedom and inclusion were integral to that culture, especially in the 1790s, and created the dynamics for overlooked regions like eastern Connecticut to transform racial sensibilities and practices during this "First Emancipation" in the North more than contemporary historians have recognized.[54] Embracing Boyer extended that inclusion.

Local Freemasonry and its indigenous controversies proved crucial to making possible this engagement with revolutionary emancipationism on the Atlantic. While this Republican opposition in New London County was certainly premised on much more than Freemasonry, its Masonry provided it a particularly supple vehicle for engaging some of the more important dimensions of its contest with Federalist dominance locally, nationally, and on the Atlantic: religion, freedom of conscience and inquiry, and the assessing of France, its revolution, and its partisans in St. Domingue. The greater opportunity for lodge autonomy in 1800 allowed a mixed lodge like Somerset to evince more partisanship, despite Masonic ordinances against such expression within the lodge's walls. The simultaneous interpenetration of the myriad networks of Atlantic Freemasonry with the local, national, imperial, and trans-national necessarily bound it up with all the both parochial and broader common conflicts – Masonic and otherwise – of the Atlantic.[55] When the arrival of a representative of one of the more important of those Masonrys explicitly renewed many of these levels of network and association in Norwich and New London County, their complex intertwining with the world of a small New England port created a remarkable occasion for summarizing how "local particularity" helped to structure and define the Atlantic.

After 1800, expanding grand lodge control in Connecticut would contract opportunities for its lodges to engage with such turbulence from the Atlantic. Federalists in Connecticut barely reconciled themselves to Jeffersonian rule; in part, they responded by reinforcing their state dominion. Masons in Connecticut and New England witnessed their own turning inward as well. The grand lodges oversaw an evolving fraternal insularity that – fueled by the rising popularity of higher degrees – focused the brothers on reinforcing their Masonic identity and exclusivity through attention to the rituals and lore of freemasonry. The lodge existed as exclusive refuge for this work. Whatever political partisanry or worldly preoccupation compromised that work was to be muted and banished. Over the ensuing years, the Masonic devotion and organizational brilliance of men such as Thomas Smith Webb and Jeremy Cross would prove essential in New England and the North to resolving competing claims among the higher degree orders and the grand lodges and to uniting them all by 1820 under an Americanized York Rite that acknowledged grand lodge state supremacy. That supremacy included its power to determine what Masonic credentials any prospective visitor to a lodge must possess. The cohesion of this supremacy would contribute to constricting the channels of cosmopolitanism in Masonic Connecticut that made the ready confluence of one of its lodges with a black partisan of France so possible in 1800.[56]

Notes

1. For all records obtained and generated by the District Court in Hartford and its officials in New London, see the records for "U.S. v. Schooner Vengeance, 1800 Oct, Admiralty." National Archives at Boston, Waltham, MA, Records of the District Courts of the United States (Record Group 21), U.S. District Court for the District of Connecticut, Case Files, 1790–1915 (Identifier 2240989). Save for a few other newspaper references, the contemporary sources in footnotes 1–5 are all the sources the author identified after an extensive search for sources regarding the presence of Boyer and the other prisoners in New London County.
2. See designation of his office in note by the physician who treated his "Infirmities" in Tracy, P [hilemon], Physn, 26 February 1801. Connecticut Historical Society (hereafter CHS), Documents related to prisoners from Haiti, 1800–1801; see also Caulkins, *History of Norwich*, 428, 515, 526.
3. Caulkins, *History of Norwich*, 526; Baur, "Mulatto Machiavelli," 307–309; Kihn, "French San Domingo Prisoners," 47–63.
4. Perkins, *Old Houses of Norwich*, 94; Caulkins, *History of Norwich*, 519–520; New York *Commercial Advertiser*, 4 November 1800, as cited in *Naval Documents*, Vol. 6, 423.
5. *Norwich Courier*, 3 December 1800.
6. Armitage, "Three Concepts of Atlantic History," 23–28.
7. Sidbury, "Saint Domingue in Virginia," 535.
8. White, *Encountering Revolution*, 6–9, quote on 7. See also Dun, *Dangerous Neighbors*; Rugemer, *The Problem of Emancipation*, 42–44; Scott, "The Common Wind"; Jansen, "Brothers in Exile," esp. 10–16, 21, 23–25.
9. For the early history of Connecticut's Grand Lodge, see Storer, *Records of Freemasonry*, 95–141; Lipson, *Freemasonry*, 62–72.
10. Harland-Jacobs, *Builders of Empire*, 127.
11. Ibid., 99–129.
12. Lipson, *Freemasonry*, 79.
13. Wheeler, *The Centennial*, 89; Lipson, *Freemasonry*, 80–81; Storer, *Records of Freemasonry*, 127–129.

THE FRATERNAL ATLANTIC, 1770–1930   103

14. Lipson, *Freemasonry,* 104–109.
15. *Impartial Herald* (Suffield, CT), 1 January 1799.
16. Stauffer, *Bavarian Illuminati*, esp. chapter 4; Lipson, *Freemasonry*, 97–104; Bullock, *Revolutionary Brotherhood*, 172–175; Brooke, "Ancient Lodges," 319–322, 325–326.
17. *A Hint to Freemasons*, 3, 8–9, 12; Lipson, *Freemasonry*, 90–97, 104, 342.
18. Brooke, "Ancient Lodges," 325–326, 354, 358.
19. See esp. Bullock, *Revolutionary Brotherhood*, and Tabbert, *American Freemasons; A Hint to Freemasons*, 4.
20. See Carter, *Centennial History of Somerset Lodge.*; Di Bonaventura, *For Adam's Sake*, admirably reveals the vigor of religious opposition in New London since the late seventeenth century and the earliest days of the Rogerenes. Loucks, "Let the Oppressed Go Free" explores religious and political opposition in Norwich and eastern Connecticut for the revolutionary era; see also Caulkins, *History of Norwich,* 365–426; Grossbart, "The Revolutionary Transition," explores the post-1783 context. See also generally Purcell, *Connecticut in Transition*. For specific information on the affiliations and degrees of the Connecticut Masons mentioned in this paragraph see "Historical Biographical Master Card Files of All Connecticut Masons." Connecticut Grand Lodge, Wallingford, CT.
21. Case, *Ancient Accepted Scottish Rite*, 18 (Through the generosity of Brothers Richard Allen and Leslie King of Somerset-St. James Lodge no. 34 in Preston, I was privileged on 2 September 2016 to examine the minute books of Somerset for the late 1790s. Unfortunately, minutes for the relevant time period appear to no longer exist.) Stauffer, *Bavarian Illuminati, 292–293.*
22. Pasley, *"The Tyranny of Printers,"* 132–147.
23. Jansen, "Brothers in Exile," 14–19, 21; Childs, *French Refugee Life*, 105–108; McClellan, *Colonialism and Science*, 184–8; Stauffer, *Bavarian Illuminati*, 291–321, esp. 319–321; Upton, *Negro Masonry*, 74–75; Fox, *Lodge of the Double-Headed Eagle*, 3–29, esp. 27–28; Baynard, *Scottish Rite Freemasonry*, Vol. 1, 80–83.
24. Regarding the role of Huntington, see Stauffer, *Bavarian Illuminati*, 319, note 1; Lipson, *Freemasonry,* 102; Grossbart, "Revolutionary Transition," 264; *Norwich Courier,* 16 July 1800. See *Bee,* 24 September 1800, for Dwight et al. as "our modern Illuminati." See also *Bee,* 17 September 1800, for "the pretended friends […] to order and good government […] retailing stories of Illuminati […] [in order to alarm] the public with horrible ideas of the principles and designs of their opponents, the republican citizens." John L. Brooke notes these assertions elsewhere in the US: "Ancient Lodges," 358. See the thorough review of Republicans' counter-charges against Morse, Federalists, and the Congregational elite as the true Illuminati in Stauffer, *Bavarian Illuminati*, 345–360. On the very relevant controversy of the Illuminati in England at the same time, see Harland-Jacobs, *Builders of Empire*, 137–143.
25. Lipson, *Freemasonry,* 63.
26. *Norwich Courier*, 16 July 1800.
27. A more precise term to use for their orientation might be "anti-episcopacy". Lipson also overstates the degree to which Connecticut Freemasonry "was inherently antithetical to Connecticut Congregationalism" and "an expression of dissent from Connecticut's cultural traditions." Lipson, *Freemasonry,* 63–64, 78–79. Connecticut Freemasonry in the late eighteenth century included numerous elite Congregationalists and Federalists. Bullock finds Freemasonry in late eighteenth-century America as much more compatible with Christianity, especially Protestantism: Bullock, *Revolutionary Brotherhood*, 163–183.
28. Goen, *Revivalism and Separatism*, 68–93, 258–275, 288–295. See also McLoughlin, *New England Dissent*, and Bushman, *From Puritan to Yankee*.
29. Sterry and Sterry, *The American Youth*, iv–vii. In the same work, the Sterrys identified Newton's development of "Fluxions," or the calculus as "his almost divine invention": Ibid., vi. See also Sterry and Sterry, *Complete Exercise Book in Arithmetic.* For Consider Sterry and navigational schools, see *Norwich Packet*, 31 July 1798, and *Norwich Courier*, 1 May 1799; Perkins, *Old Houses of Norwich*, 120–121.
30. *The Times*, 10 January 1821.

31. Harvey, *History of Lodge no. 61*, 189; Case, *History of the Ancient Rite*, 18; Garrigus, "Secret Brotherhood"; *The Times*, 28 November 1820; 10 January 1821. See also *Poulson's American Daily Advertiser* (Philadelphia), 1 December 1820, and *Weekly Aurora*, 4 December 1820.

32. *Naval Documents*, Vol. 7, 72. On 7 February 1801, Murray wrote to Joshua Huntington, Justice of the Peace of Norwich, that "[i]t is not in my power to return the Commissions or private papers belonging to the officers, as they have never been in my possession." CHS, Documents related to prisoners from Haiti, 1800–1801.

33. *Naval Documents*, Vol. 7, 72. See Stoddert's concern regarding Jewett's depositing of them in New London "contrary to my instructions": *Naval Documents*, Vol. 7, 76. Phyllis Kihn incorrectly assumes that Jewett stopped as ordered at Norfolk and Washington, DC: Kihn, "French San Domingo Prisoners," 55. Jewett may have failed to leave them in the Chesapeake and report to Stoddert because he sought a better prize determination in Connecticut. Stoddert even suspected Jewett of embezzlement: *Naval Documents*, Vol. 7, 72.

34. Bullock, *Revolutionary Brotherhood,* 128–129. For further examples of such returns to combatants during the American Revolution and for fraternity shared between French and English Masons, see Harland-Jacobs, *Builders of Empire,* 84–88; Upton, *Negro Masonry*, 128–130, 218.

35. Bullock, *Revolutionary Brotherhood*, 191–198.

36. *A Hint to Freemasons*, 3, 4, 7.

37. Bullock, *Revolutionary Brotherhood*, 104–106; Hinks, "John Marrant," 111–112. See also Wood, *Radicalism of the American Revolution*, 213–225, esp. 222–225.

38. Johnson, *Diplomacy in Black and White*, 117.

39. *Norwich Packet*, 23 September 1800.

40. *Naval Documents*, vol. 6, 273–274; Caulkins, *History of Norwich*, 526. See CHS list for complete accounting of occupants of *Vengeance*. See also *Naval Documents*, Vol. 6, 300–1. *Impartial Journal* (Stonington), 30 September 1800.

41. Fox, *Lodge of the Double-Headed Eagle*, 23.

42. Case, *History of the Ancient Rite*, 17–21. See also Tabbert, *American Freemasons*, 28–32, 51–54, 193–197; Baynard, *Scottish Rite Freemasonry*, Vol. 1, 25–153; Burgess et al., *A Sublime Brotherhood*, 1–3, 75–84; Fox, *Lodge of the Double-Headed Eagle*; Newbury and Williams, *A History of the Supreme Council*, 35–73; Perkins, *Old Houses of Norwich*, 94; Caulkins, *History of Norwich*, 519–520.

43. Case, *Ancient Accepted Scottish Rite*, 17–19.

44. Tabbert, *American Freemasons*, 54.

45. See "Historical Biographical Master Card Files of All Connecticut Masons." Connecticut Grand Lodge; *Proceedings of the General Grand Chapter of Royal Arch Masons*, 5–28; see also McNulty, *Freemasonry*, 179–199; Tabbert, *American Freemasons*, 93–97.

46. See "Historical Biographical Master Card Files of All Connecticut Masons." Connecticut Grand Lodge; Sturdy, *History of the Grand Commandery of Knights Templar*, 107–113; *Proceedings of the Grand Commandery of Knights Templars*, v–viii, 4–9.

47. Bullock, *Revolutionary Brotherhood*, 239–273, esp. 253–263; Tabbert, *American Freemasons*, 29–32, 93–97; Ridley, *The Freemasons*, 23–28; *A Hint to Freemasons*, 4. John L. Brooke also asserts, but without any further substantiation, that Royal Arch Masonry was spreading on the seaboard in the 1790s in part "through the French lodges established by Haitian exiles." Brooke, "Ancient Lodges," 326, note 93, 350–351.

48. Bell, *An Oration Delivered at Amherst*, 8.

49. Fick, *The Making of Haiti*, 161, 185, and Dubois, *Avengers of the New World*, 173–176, 231–236.

50. Garrigus, *Before Haiti,* 267, 291–296, and Garrigus, "Secret Brotherhood." Also Jansen, "Brothers in Exile," 22–23.

51. Révauger, *Black Freemasonry*; de Cauna, "Autour de la Thèse du Complot," 310–314; de Cauna, "Étienne de Polverel," 170; Stein, *Léger-Félicité Sonthonax*.

52. Hinks, "To Commence a New Era."

53. For example, see Hinks, ibid., 42–44, and Winch, "A Late Thing," 81–83.

54. See for example Melish, *Disowning Slavery*; Sweet, *Bodies Politic*; and, more generally, Takaki, *Iron Cages*.

55. See Jansen's excellent summary of this key characteristic, "Brothers in Exile," 11–13.
56. See especially Bullock, *Revolutionary Brotherhood*, 239–273.

Acknowledgements

The author acknowledges the invaluable comments and critiques of Jessica Harland-Jacobs, Jan C. Jansen, and Elizabeth Mancke. Jessica commented trenchantly on a much lengthier and very different version of this essay, which led to me writing the current essay. Both Elizabeth and Jessica pointed me to models to help situate the locality of New London County more decisively in the Atlantic while Jan helped me to contextualize the interpenetrations of St. Domingue and French Masonry with that of the United States. I am the beneficiary of extraordinary critiques from the two anonymous readers of my essay and cannot thank them enough for their time and insight. Mark Tabbert afforded yet again sage observations on the remarkable complexities of American Freemasonry after the Revolution.

Disclosure statement

No potential conflict of interest was reported by the author.

Bibliography

A Hint to Freemasons. Newfield, CT: Lazarus Beach, 1799.
Anderson, James. *Anderson's Constitutions of 1723*. Washington, DC: The Masonic Service Association of the United States, 1924.
Armitage, David. "Three Concepts of Atlantic History." In *The British Atlantic World, 1500–1800*, edited by David Armitage, and Michael Jonathan Braddick, 11–29. Basingstoke: Palgrave Macmillan, 2002.
Baur, John E. "Mulatto Machiavelli, Jean Pierre Boyer, and the Haiti of His Day." *The Journal of Negro History* 32, no. 3 (1947): 307–353.
Baynard, Samuel Harrison. *History of the Supreme Council, 33° Ancient Accepted Scottish Rite of Freemasonry, Northern Masonic Jurisdiction of the United States of America and its Antecedents*. 2 vols. Boston: Supreme Council Ancient Accepted Scottish Rite, 1938.
Bell, Samuel. *An Oration Delivered at Amherst, June 25, A.L. 5798 Before the Benevolent Lodge of Free and Accepted Masons, at the Celebration of the Festival of St. John the Baptist*. Amherst, NH: Samuel Preston, 1798.
Brooke, John L. "Ancient Lodges and Self-created Societies: Voluntary Association and the Public Sphere in the Early Republic." In *Launching the Extended Republic: The Federalist Era*, edited by Ronald Hoffman, and Peter J. Albert, 273–377. Charlottesville: University Press of Virginia, 1996.
Bullock, Steven C. *Revolutionary Brotherhood: Freemasonry and the Transformation of the American Social Order, 1730–1840*. Chapel Hill: University of North Carolina Press, 1998.
Burgess, Richard B., Jeffrey Croteau, Alan E. Foulds, Aimee E. Newell, Jerry A. Roach, and Catherine C. Swanson. *A Sublime Brotherhood: Two Hundred Years of Scottish Rite Freemasonry in the Northern Masonic Jurisdiction*. Lexington, MA: Supreme Council 33°, Ancient Accepted Scottish Rite, Northern Masonic Jurisdiction, 2013.

Bushman, Richard L. *From Puritan to Yankee: Character and the Social Order in Connecticut, 1690–1765*. Cambridge, MA: Harvard University Press, 1967.

Carter, Charles William. *Centennial History of Somerset Lodge, No. 34, F. and A.M., of Norwich, Conn., 5795–5895*. Norwich, CT: Record Job Print, 1896.

Case, James R. *A History of the Ancient Accepted Scottish Rite in Connecticut*. Hartford: Connecticut Council for Deliberation, 1967.

Caulkins, Frances M. *History of Norwich, Connecticut: From its Possession by the Indians to the Year 1866*. Hartford, CT: Case, Lockwood, and Brainard, 1873.

de Cauna, Jacques. "Autour de la thèse du complot: Franc-maçonnerie, révolution et contre-révolution à Saint-Domingue (1789–1791)." In *Franc-maçonnerie et politique au siècle des lumières: Europe-Amériques*, edited by Cécile Révauger, 289–310. Pessac: Presses Univ. de Bordeaux, 2006.

de Cauna, Jacques. "Etienne de Polverel, un projet abolitionniste d'inspiration maçonnique (Saint-Domingue, 1793)." In *La Société des plantations esclavagistes: Caraïbes francophone, anglophone, hispanophone*, edited by Jacques de Cauna, and Cécile Révauger, 159–175. Paris: Les Indes savantes, 2013.

Childs, Frances S. *French Refugee Life in the United States, 1790–1800*. Baltimore: The Johns Hopkins University Press, 1940.

Di Bonaventura, Allegra. *For Adam's Sake: A Family Saga in Colonial New England*. New York: Liveright Publishing Corporation, 2014.

Dubois, Laurent. *Avengers of the New World: The Story of the Haitian Revolution*. Cambridge, MA: Harvard University Press, 2004.

Dun, James Alexander. *Dangerous Neighbors: Making the Haitian Revolution in Early America*. Philadelphia: University of Pennsylvania Press, 2016.

Fick, Carolyn E. *The Making of Haiti: The Saint Domingue Revolution from Below*. Knoxville: The University of Tennessee Press, 1990.

Fox, William L. *Lodge of the Double Headed Eagle, Two Centuries of Scottish Rite Freemasonry in America's Southern Jurisdiction*. Fayetteville: University of Arkansas Press, 1997.

Garrigus, John D. *Before Haiti: Race and Citizenship in French Saint-Domingue*. New York: Palgrave Macmillan, 2006.

Garrigus, John D. "A Secret Brotherhood? The Question of Black Freemasonry before and after the Haitian Revolution." *Atlantic Studies: Global Currents*.

Goen, C. C. *Revivalism and Separatism in New England, 1740–1800: Strict Congregationalists and Separate Baptists in the Great Awakening*. Waco, TX: Baylor University Press, 2012.

Grossbart, Stephen R. "The Revolutionary Transition: Politics, Religion, and Economy in Eastern Connecticut, 1765–1800." PhD diss., University of Michigan, 1989.

Harland-Jacobs, Jessica L. *Builders of Empire. Freemasons and British Imperialism, 1717–1927*. Chapel Hill: University of North Carolina Press, 2007.

Harvey, Oscar J. *History of Lodge no. 61, F. and A. M., Wilkesbarre, Pa*. Wilkesbarre, PA: E.B. Yordy, 1897.

Hinks, Peter P. "John Marrant and the Meaning of Early Black Freemasonry." *William and Mary Quarterly* 3rd Series 64, no. 1 (2007): 105–116.

Hinks, Peter P. "'To Commence a New Era in the Moral World': John Telemachus Hilton, Abolitionism, and the Expansion of Black Freemasonry." In *All Men Free and Brethren: Essays on the History of African American Freemasonry*, edited by Peter P. Hinks, and Stephen David Kantrowitz, 40–62. Ithaca, NY: Cornell University Press, 2013.

Jansen, Jan C. "Brothers in Exile: Masonic Lodges and the Refugees of the Haitian Revolution, 1790s–1820." *Atlantic Studies: Global Currents*.

Johnson, Ronald A. *Diplomacy in Black and White: John Adams, Toussaint Louverture, and their Atlantic World Alliance*. Athens: The University of Georgia Press, 2014.

Kihn, Phyllis. "The French San Domingo Prisoners in Connecticut." *Bulletin of the Connecticut Historical Society* 28, no. 2 (1963): 47–63.

Lipson, Dorothy A. *Freemasonry in Federalist Connecticut, 1789–1835*. Princeton, NJ: Princeton University Press, 1977.

Logan, Rayford W. *The Diplomatic Relations of the United States with Haiti, 1778–1841*. Chapel Hill: The University of North Carolina Press, 1941.

Loucks, Rupert C. "Let the Oppressed go Free: Reformation and Revolution in English Connecticut 1764–1775." *PhD diss.*, University of Wisconsin, 1995.

MacNulty, Kirk W. *Freemasonry: Symbols, Secrets, Significance*. London: Thames & Hudson, 2006.

McClellan, James E. *Colonialism and Science: Saint Domingue and the Old Regime*. Chicago: The University of Chicago Press, 2010.

McLoughlin, William G. *New England Dissent, 1630–1833: The Baptists and the Separation of Church and State*. 2 vols. Cambridge, MA: Harvard University Press, 1971.

Melish, Joanne Pope. *Disowning Slavery: Gradual Emancipation and "Race" in New England, 1780–1860*. Ithaca, NY: Cornell University Press, 2000.

Naval Documents Related to the Quasi-War between the United States and France. 7 vols. Washington, DC: U.S. Government Printing Office, 1934–1937.

Newbury, George Adelbert, and Louis Lenway Williams. *A History of the Supreme Council, 33° of the Ancient Accepted Scottish Rite of Freemasonry for the Northern Masonic Jurisdiction of the United States of America*. Lexington, MA: Supreme Council, A.A.S.R., N.M.J., 1987.

Pasley, Jeffrey L. *"The Tyranny of Printers": Newspaper Politics in the Early American Republic*. Charlottesville: University of Virginia Press, 2001.

Perkins, Mary E. *Old Houses of the Antient Town of Norwich, 1660–1800*. Norwich, CT: The Bulletin, 1895.

Proceedings of the General Grand Chapter of Royal Arch Masons of the United States, from its Organization, in 1797, up to and Including The Triennial Convocation of 1856. Buffalo, NY: The General Grand Chapter, 1877.

Proceedings of the Grand Commandery of Knights Templars for the State of Connecticut. Norwich, CT: The Grand Commandery, 1873.

Purcell, Richard J. *Connecticut in Transition: 1775–1818*. New ed. Middletown, CT: Wesleyan University Press, 1963.

Révauger, Cécile. *Black Freemasonry: From Prince Hall to the Giants of Jazz*. Rochester, VT: Inner Traditions, 2016.

Ridley, Jasper. *The Freemasons: A History of the World's Most Powerful Secret Society*. New York: Arcade, 2011.

Rugemer, Edward. *The Problem of Emancipation: The Caribbean Roots of the American Civil War*. Baton Rouge: Louisiana State University Press, 2008.

Scott, Julius S. "The Common Wind: Currents of Afro-American Communication in the Era of the Haitian Revolution." *PhD diss.*, Duke University, 1986.

Sidbury, James. "Saint Domingue in Virginia: Ideology, Local Meanings, and Resistance to Slavery, 1790–1800." *The Journal of Southern History* 63, no. 3 (1997): 531–552.

Stauffer, Vernon. *New England and the Bavarian Illuminati*. New York: Columbia University Press, 1918.

Stein, Robert L. *Léger Félicité Sonthonax: The Lost Sentinel of the Republic*. Cranbury, NJ: Associated University Presses, 1985.

Sterry, Consider, and John Sterry. *A Complete Exercise Book in Arithmetic: Designed for the Use of Schools in the United States*. Norwich, CT: J. Sterry, 1795.

Sterry, Consider, and John Sterry. *The American Youth: Being a New and Complete Course of Introductory Mathematics: Designed for the Use of Private Students*. Providence, RI: Bennett Wheeler, 1790.

Storer, E. G. *The Records of Freemasonry in the State of Connecticut*. New Haven, CT: Henry S. Storer, 1859.

Sturdy, George A. *History of the Grand Commandery of Knights Templar of Connecticut*. Norwich, CT, 1923.

Sweet, John Wood. *Bodies Politic: Negotiating Race in the American North, 1730–1830*. Philadelphia: University of Pennsylvania Press, 2006.

Tabbert, Mark A. *American Freemasons: Three Centuries of Building Communities*. Lexington, MA: National Heritage Museum, 2005.

Takaki, Ronald T. *Iron Cages: Race and Culture in 19th-Century America*. New York: Oxford University Press, 1990.

Upton, William H. *Negro Masonry: Being a Critical Examination of Objections to the Legitimacy of the Masonry Existing Among the Negroes of America*. Cambridge: The M.W. Prince Hall Grand Lodge of Massachusetts, 1902.

Wheeler, Joseph K., ed. *The Centennial: One Hundredth Anniversary of the Most Worshipful Grand Lodge of Connecticut, New Haven, July 10th. A.L. 5889*. Hartford, CT: Peck & Prouty, Printers, 1889.

White, Ashli. *Encountering Revolution: Haiti and the Making of the Early Republic*. Baltimore: The Johns Hopkins University Press, 2010.

Winch, Julie. "'A Late Thing I Guess': The Early Years of Philadelphia's African Masonic Lodge." In *All Men Free and Brethren: Essays on the History of African American Freemasonry*, edited by Peter P. Hinks, and Stephen David Kantrowitz, 63–83. Ithaca, NY: Cornell University Press, 2013.

Wood, Gordon S. *The Radicalism of the American Revolution*. New York: Vintage Books, 1993.

Part III
Tensions

& OPEN ACCESS

Atlantic antagonism: Revolution and race in German-American Masonic relations, 1848–1861

Andreas Önnerfors

ABSTRACT
After the 1848 revolutions in Europe, waves of European émigrés, many of them Germans, settled in the United States. These Forty-Eighters faced challenging choices in their relationship to American society, oscillating around assimilation, adaptation, alienation and open antagonism. The arrival of thousands of refugees from revolutions repositioned US politics within a transatlantic world, one increasingly shaped by multiple intersections and exchanges. Through the activities of German-speaking lodges in New York, this article analyses ideological tensions between Masonic universalism as espoused by émigrés and US Masonic practices, particularly with regard to racial biases. Persistent prejudices and significant differences in organizational culture led to escalating transatlantic Masonic tensions, pointing to deeper divergences in worldviews and self-perceptions. These tensions exposed the limits of the cosmopolitan ethos of Freemasonry when faced with the realities of cross-cultural negotiations between immigrant and US-born Freemasons.

Immigration and identity: The complex case of the German Forty-Eighters

The Napoleonic Wars (1803–1815) severely disrupted the political state of Germany. Without the legal and dynastic framework of the Old German Empire (disbanded in 1806), Germans questioned whether Germany represented a unified political space or even culture at all, and how political order should be organized in the future. Germans considered a number of alternatives, ranging from revolutionary republicanism in the Rhineland to conservative restoration in Prussia. During the period called "Vormärz" – stretching from 1815 to the revolution of 1848 – the liberal and social legacy of the French revolution and the reactionary authoritarian and absolutist legacy of the old empire characterized the poles of the political struggles. These antagonisms finally erupted in the failed revolution of 1848–1849, known as the "March revolution." In its aftermath, radical liberals went into exile, some by choice, others by necessity, and many of them emigrated to the United States.

This is an Open Access article distributed under the terms of the Creative Commons Attribution-NonCommercial-NoDerivatives License (http://creativecommons.org/licenses/by-nc-nd/4.0/), which permits non-commercial re-use, distribution, and reproduction in any medium, provided the original work is properly cited, and is not altered, transformed, or built upon in any way.

The German émigré Forty-Eighters – an estimated 4,000 to 10,000 individuals – faced multiple tensions in refashioning a durable political identity in exile.[1] They began these processes of resettlement and refashioning with a transnational perspective on American politics. To conceptualize and negotiate their particular position, they drew on the revolutionary legacy of 1848, asserting "the value of German culture in their adopted home," while at the same time trying to articulate a "German language of American citizenship."[2] Events in Europe had inspired some Americans, particularly abolitionists, to stand in transatlantic solidarity with revolutionaries in Europe. The European struggle for liberty was thus profoundly transformed by the emigration of many of its champions to the United States.[3]

These tensions manifested themselves in the world of Freemasonry. Shortly after emigrating to the United States, German émigrés began to join, run, and then reorganize Masonic lodges in their new homeland. Masonic lodges were one of many forms of association and sociability in German immigrant communities. As Bruce Levine has pointed out, these associations "offered spiritual refuge, camaraderie [and] material assistance" and strengthened "community cohesion and ethnic identity" within the émigré community.[4] This examination of émigré Freemasonry in New York contributes to scholarship on German American associational life, as well as analyses how émigrés, through the universal fraternal network of Freemasons, became embroiled in transatlantic disputes over Freemasonry, and American political culture more generally.

Recently, scholars such as Alison Clark Efford, Mischa Honeck and Daniel Nagel have made important contributions towards a more sophisticated understanding of the political identity formation among German immigrants in the decades following 1848. They highlight the first generation of Forty-Eighters as particularly articulate and politically engaged, promoting the image of "'the freedom-loving German' who abhorred slavery as much as he prized immigrant rights."[5] These Forty-Eighters experienced serious tensions between their utopian expectations of American society and political and social realities they experienced upon arrival in the United States. Many émigrés turned into sharp critics of US politics and society and published their positions in a number of German American press outlets.[6]

This essay contributes to that body of scholarship by showing how German émigré Freemasons did not retreat or separate themselves from larger midcentury US political controversies, but rather reflected the increasingly polarized ethnic and racial sensibilities on both sides of the Atlantic. They forcefully engaged with explosive issues such as slavery, abolitionism, ethnicity, race, and nationalism. German émigré Freemasons responded to these political issues, struggling to reconcile both universalist ideals and particularist interests. They often found themselves at odds with their American counterparts in areas such as Masonic organizational culture, the interpretation of the limits of Masonic universalism, and the acceptance of heterogeneous ideological positions in Freemasonry. Through these ideological debates, German American Freemasons in New York thus made original and radical contributions to the political thinking of the time.[7] If the antebellum period saw a "transatlantic dialogue about human equality" and a "transnational web of reform," as Honeck has argued, it is worth investigating the lodges of German American Freemasonry as hubs and nodes "embedded in concurrent democratic endeavors on both sides of the Atlantic."[8] It is no accident that the German émigré press of the period published a Masonic journal – *Der Triangel: Oder Akazienzweig am Lebensbaum*

THE FRATERNAL ATLANTIC, 1770–1930   113

ächten Maurerthums (1855–1879) – with close links to the lodges examined in this article. It positioned itself against the rapidly growing nativist movement in the antebellum era that led to the establishment of the xenophobic and anti-immigrant Know-Nothing party.[9]

A "life-giving spark" across the Atlantic? German-speaking lodges in New York

On 2 May 1851, Pythagoras Lodge No. 86, organized in 1841 by German Americans under the Grand Lodge of New York (GLNY), separated from the GLNY and was consecrated as Pythagoras No. 1 in Brooklyn under the Grand Lodge of Hamburg (GLH).[10] In its first printed circular letter, Pythagoras No. 1 declared that this step aimed

> not only to bring about a more intimate union of our German brothers *here* with those across *there* in the old fatherland, but particularly to facilitate this more intimate union between our German and American brothers, in order to further the best of Freemasonry in general.

By placing themselves under the GLH, lodge members ostensibly believed that they "may become the binding force of the Arch uniting the basic pillars, the grand lodges on this and that side of the Atlantic, or the chain of union, through which the life-giving spark flows from the one to the other."[11] Lodges in the newly adopted American fatherland of German émigrés, the letter highlighted, could help immigrant Germans respect and love their new home country.

At first sight, this new relationship between the Pythagoras lodge in New York and the Grand Lodge of Hamburg appears to be merely a positive step in the establishment of organized sociability in the age of great transatlantic migration. A closer look, however, reveals deeper dimensions. The members of Pythagoras Lodge No. 1, by forming this formal relationship between their Brooklyn lodge and the Grand Lodge of Hamburg, brought into view and transatlantic debate the distinctly American form of Masonic self-jurisdiction, the complex dynamics of transnational affiliations with non-American Masonic lodges, and the realities of a racially segregated society.[12] When these German Americans affiliated with the GLH, they almost certainly did not realize the controversies their decision would engender. From an historian's vantage point, the history of Pythagoras Lodge No. 1 offers a lens through which to study more general phenomena, especially relating to the adjustments of immigrants to the United States and American Freemasonry. The intriguing tension between moral universalism as propagated in Freemasonry and the particularism of societal realities on both sides of the Atlantic reflected broader sociopolitical forces of the mid nineteenth-century Atlantic world.[13]

The German Freemasons who separated from the GLNY and affiliated with the GLH had found themselves perplexed by persistent prejudices and significant differences in Masonic organizational culture in the US. Re-establishing transatlantic ties made sense within their understanding of Freemasonry. Yet from an American perspective, they had violated the jurisdiction of the Grand Lodge of New York, and by extension the jurisdictional structure of American Freemasonry more generally. Immigrants were not to challenge the state of affairs through affiliation with European grand lodges. Contrary to the early vision of Pythagoras No. 1, bridging the Atlantic though Masonic affiliation proved tendentious rather than harmonizing. When faced with particular socio-political realities, the cosmopolitan ethos of Freemasonry arrived at serious and contradictory limitations. On both sides of the Atlantic, arguments were brought forward pointing at deeper divergences in worldviews and self-perceptions, essentially a recourse to the polarizing comfort zones of cultural exclusivity and entrenchment. Far from representing an ideal of homogenization, the North Atlantic, in the case examined here, emerges as a heterogeneous zone of contrast and antagonism where the streams of the Old and New World collided. The decade explored here, during which representatives of European Freemasonry styled themselves as progressive and attacked their counterparts in the New World for their backwardness, provides an important piece of the puzzle of German American political identity formation in the period 1840–1860. It shows that many Forty-Eighters did not see the US as more politically progressive, but rather positioned themselves as émigré reformers, a stance which provoked a backlash from US-born Freemasons, as well as earlier German American Freemasons.

The organizational history of Freemasonry in New York is complex. After American independence, Freemasons sometimes attempted to organize a union-wide Masonic umbrella, but ultimately failed. Rather in each state, Freemasons founded a grand lodge, and American Freemasons enforced a principle of "exclusive territorial jurisdiction", meaning that only one grand lodge would be allowed to operate in each state, effectively preventing various kinds of territorial trespassing.[14] Despite a fierce anti-Masonic movement during the 1820s and 1830s, Freemasonry in the United States continue to grow, thanks to a growing influx of European immigrants. By 1860, 13.5 percent of the population in New York was of German-born origin, and German American Freemasonry occupied a relatively significant position in New York.[15]

Tensions within Freemasonry in New York manifested themselves in conflicts relating to voting rights in the general assembly of the Grand Lodge of New York. Past masters of lodges were allowed to vote in the general assembly of the GLNY. Those residing in the New York City area could more easily attend quarterly assemblies and vote, while past masters from upstate lodges could not, thus creating a marked imbalance in favor of lodges in NYC and Brooklyn, which also were numerically in a majority. Upstate lodges complained that these voting practices disadvantaged them, and a number of metropolitan lodges (including Pythagoras No. 86) supported them. During the 1830s and 1840s, these conflicts resulted in the GLNY splitting into four competing organizations: St. John's Grand Lodge (1837–1850), Phillips Grand Lodge (1849–1858), and St. John's Grand Lodge (revived, 1853–1859). The GLNY was officially represented by a fourth body, Willard's Grand Lodge. In 1841, in the midst of this organizational upheaval German Americans founded Pythagoras Lodge No. 86.

Within German American Freemasonry, there was a parallel narrative of tension. During its first phase from 1819 to 1851, lodges emerged out of existing immigrant associations, such as lodge Trinity No. 13 or L'Union Française No. 17. Then in 1851 a second phase began when Pythagoras No. 86 transferred its affiliation to the Grand Lodge of Hamburg, thus forging transatlantic Masonic ties. This second phase (1851–1854) is characterized by fierce battles over organizational and ideological matters. The third phase (1854–1861) begins when some members of Pythagoras No. 1 withdrew and re-affiliated with the GLNY as Pythagoras No. 86, a split that reflected fierce debates among German Americans over whether to engage in appeasement, assimilation and adaptation relative to American society, or continue a sense of alienation, conflict and controversy. While German-affiliated lodges in New York, and the United States more generally, continued during and after the Civil War and well into the twentieth century, the antebellum period offers the most intriguing insights into different transatlantic lines of development.

When Pythagoras No. 86 shifted affiliation from the GLNY to the GLH in 1851, a transatlantic Masonic relationship began that lasted half a century. While some lodge members broke away from No. 1 in 1854 and revived the original patent from the GLNY – which had never withdrawn the charter – their actions did not check subsequent affiliations of German American Freemasons with the GLH. The position of GLH Freemasonry in New York was strengthened by the constitution of a daughter lodge (i.e. by the initiative) of Pythagoras No. 1, called Franklin No. 2 in the Tremont neighborhood of New York City in 1853. In 1871, German Americans founded a third GLH lodge, Zeton zum Licht No. 3, located in Hoboken, in the Masonic jurisdiction of the Grand Lodge of New Jersey. Historians of Freemasonry have not established when these three lodges ceased to work, but in 1884 only Pythagoras No.1 was operating; by the early 1900s, the three GLH lodges had vanished completely. Extensive and untapped archival sources allow us to reconstruct the course of events in the tumultuous years from 1851 to 1860.

Secession from the GLNY and affiliation with the GLH

In the late 1840s, Pythagoras No. 86 commented upon the contemporary political situation in Europe:

> Under the impression of the events unfolding in Europe in our time [we can see how] in the old fatherland, new life aims to create itself. – Society aims to become reborn and painful are the works, rocking her! – These shockwaves are of significance to world history and they force some of our brothers out from peaceful coastal sea-travel to the oceans of the world![16]

Although the lodge acknowledged that Freemasonry embraced a principle of political neutrality, it found it necessary to "further a new creation, as it belongs to sage men, as our immemorial, great Brethren in America did at the end of the last century."[17] Thus, Pythagoras No. 86 interpreted the revolutions of 1848 as a European analogy to the American Revolution.

German Freemasons arriving in New York during the 1840s belonged to a "politically hyper-conscious" faction, in many cases leaving Germany with deep frustrations concerning the slow pace of societal and democratic development.[18] When these men became involved in the decision-making process of the GLNY, they perceived the voting practices of the general assemblies as disturbingly undemocratic. An intensification of the controversies over voting, among other issues, led members of Pythagoras No. 86 to withdraw from the GLNY and apply for a patent from the GLH, at the time arguably one of the most progressive grand lodges in the world.[19] In the correspondence applying for affiliation with the GLH, Pythagoras stressed its aim to "liberate itself completely from the machinations of the American lodges, which it could not subscribe to, and as German lodge [aimed] to work for the strengthening of German-ness [Deutschtum] and relations to the old fatherland."[20] Behind such patriotic language the larger frustrations caused by exile are discernable, particularly unfulfilled socio-political expectations and the complexities of German American political identity formation. In the request to affiliate with the GLH was an intimation of qualms about US Masonic governing practices that went beyond the voting issues of the GLNY.

Simultaneously, Grand Master Willard of the GLNY tried to calm emotions by welcoming one returning German insurgent who had decided to side with the (seceding) Phillips Grand Lodge. Willard declared that he regarded "Pythagoras Lodge No. 86 and Trinity Lodge No. 12, which are composed chiefly of our intelligent and respected German fellow-citizens" as integral parts of the GLNY.[21] But most members of Pythagoras disregarded this olive branch and in December 1850 the lodge declared itself independent. Somewhat paradoxically, the lodge also adopted a motion to appoint the Grand Master of the GLNY as an honorary member of the lodge, "to prove to our American Brothers that Pythagoras Lodge has the sincere desire under all conditions to remain in friendly and fraternal agreement in the future with the sister lodges as well as with the [GLNY]."[22] Even more inclusive were the words spoken at a cornerstone ceremony for their new building, one of the most prestigious lodge buildings in New York City located on Walker Street (now located in Chinatown). The building would eventually host a number of ambitious projects and initiatives, such as a library and a social-philanthropic club. One member of Pythagoras lodge made a festive speech highlighting that "a brother remains a brother in all parts of the world, that no external situation, no position in society, no differences in opinions, no differences of religion do or are able to separate us."[23] The sentiment suggested that affiliation with the GLH reflected not distancing from the GLNY, but an expansion of the connections of New York area Freemasons, a sentiment not shared much beyond the membership of Pythagoras No. 1.

"Open the door to misrule and anarchy": The conflict over territorial jurisdiction

On the ground, the German émigré ideal of a borderless Masonic brotherhood collided with an established bureaucratic Masonic practice in the United States – the principle of exclusive territorial jurisdiction. That practice allowed only one grand lodge to exist in any single state or federal territory. Only the grand lodge recognized by grand lodges in other states could charter lodges within its jurisdiction. Such a rigid interpretation of Masonic jurisdiction was unknown in Germany, which only became a unified national state in 1871. From the perspective of the GLH, its affiliation with Pythagoras No. 1 posed no problem. Across the Atlantic in the US, however, the official position of the GLNY was unapologetically opposed to it. According to GLNY Grand Master Milnor, the GLH erroneously thought that "the law, as they understood it, simply prohibited the existence of two [US] Grand Lodges within the boundaries of the State, but did not forbid the exercise of foreign jurisdiction."[24] Although Pythagoras was "a Lodge composed of German Brethren, who hitherto occupied a high place in our estimation, and who were considered second to none in this community for intelligence and moral worth," the separation could not be tolerated and could only end in discord. Contrary to Hamburg's intentions, its affiliation with Pythagoras No. 1 had the effect of provoking the GLNY to defend vigorously its jurisdictional authority, thereby strengthening the principle of territorial jurisdiction in American Freemasonry.[25] The issue sparked a fierce debate on the general principle of exclusive territorial jurisdiction and whether it had any foundation in the historical principles of Freemasonry. By September 1851, the GLNY had sought and received support from other American grand lodges for resisting "this invasion of her rights and prerogatives by a foreign power" and decided to suspend its relations with the GLH until it revoked the charter for Pythagoras No. 1.[26]

The controversies caused by the measures taken by Pythagoras No. 1 did not, however, preclude other Freemasons in New York from applying for a charter from the GLH.[27] In May 1853, the GLH unanimously voted to accept an application to establish Franklin No. 2, and in June, the lodge was consecrated. Before making its decision, the GLH carefully deliberated, fully aware of the transatlantic irritation it might likely cause. It was convinced, however, on the merits of its decision given "the unbearable condition of Masonic affairs in America, the struggles and splits among the Grand lodges."[28] The GLH opined that the right of exclusive territorial jurisdiction was nothing more than a mutual agreement among American grand lodges, not a general principle of Freemasonry, while the GLH position was derived from older European practices.

The positions forwarded on both sides of the Atlantic were contradictory. German Freemasons in America claimed a right to interpret the true nature of universal Freemasonry. When they found American practices flawed or failed, they resorted to their German origins and even "German-ness" to shield themselves from what they perceived as degraded Masonic practices in the US. American Freemasons, on their part, defended themselves against foreign intrusion and condemned the organization of Masonic lodges based upon nationality as a violation of Masonic universalism. As historian Carl Wittke explains, American German Freemasons might have been "split over the meaning of German ethnicity but united in constituting themselves as a specific ethnic group, a cultural minority within a plural nation," and a minority which sometimes perceived itself as politically superior to others in their new homeland.[29] Wittke goes further and claims that an element of the German Forty-Eighters even saw themselves as part of a "cultural mission" to Germanize America and "to resist assimilation to an inferior culture."[30] His assessment helps to explain how the brothers of Pythagoras No. 1 reconciled themselves to their isolated position; for most, it was a moral high ground. Among that group of German émigrés, however, were a few who found the organizational isolation problematic and decided to adopt a strategy of appeasement, assimilation and adaptation.

The split between Pythagoras No. 1 and No. 86

In 1854, three years after the chartering of Pythagoras No. 1, about twenty members took the initiative to break away from the Grand Lodge of Hamburg, and reactivate their affiliation with the Grand Lodge of New York (Willard) on the basis of the old warrant for Pythagoras No. 86, which the GLNY had not formally withdrawn. At a meeting of the Pythagoras Lodge, this faction stated its opinion that the GLH affiliation had driven Pythagoras Lodge into a social isolation, a state contrary to their understanding of Freemasonry.[31] In adopting the USA as a "new fatherland," these German Americans also believed it implied following its laws, including Masonic laws – in order to live in peace with American brothers. These members split away and in 1854, the GLNY returned the original charter to Pythagoras No. 86.

The re-established Pythagoras No. 86 frequently restated its contention that isolation runs contrary to the aim of Freemasonry. In adapting to the US, they forcefully stated that

118   THE FRATERNAL ATLANTIC, 1770–1930

> We, together with our children, don't ever want to be estranged from this country or from its institutions, because it is – in spite of all its deficiencies – the country of our free choice, the country which gives protection to the persecuted and liberty to the dissenter.[32]

Within a year, Pythagoras No. 86 had more than 50 members and started to raise its profile within the GLNY, for instance in organizing charitable work. Starting in 1856, they helped facilitate the re-uniting of Willard GLNY with the competing Phillips Grand Lodge, culminating in 1858, with articles of union closely resembling the ones proposed by the old Pythagoras No. 86 seven years earlier, when the dispute over voting caused the split. German Freemasons established an educational and social club, "Masonia" (paradoxically administered together with Pythagoras No. 1), and even developed an employment bureau for German brothers in need.[33] The lodge continued to sponsor significant activities in New York Freemasonry and existed until 1993.

Pythagoras No. 86 also made substantial demands on No. 1, including return of property and giving up its name. These claims prompted No. 1 to publish documentation on the split entitled *Papers relating to the late occurrences in Pythagoras lodge No. 1* (1855). That tract exposed larger issues behind the split. "The said division of our Lodge into two unequal parts, in connection with certain incidents of political and social life in the United States seems after all to be by no means destitute of a deeper significance". For some members, the arrival of the Forty-Eighters had pulled Pythagoras Lodge too far away from American society. The reconstituted Pythagoras No. 86 had reputedly stated "that the novel notions imported [by] brethren arrived here since the year 1848 are in opposition to the spirit of Freemasonry here." For the remaining members of No. 1, however, the Forty-Eighters' emigration was understood as a "new migration of the nations from the East to the West." These émigrés made it possible for "the nations from themselves [to] join hands across the oceans," and

> to amalgamate in time into one grand union, the union of mankind, of peace and of enlightenment, in spite of the political barriers, in spite of the posts and toll-gates, in spite of the diplomatic embroilments of the courts, and of the various constitutions of the states.

The "intrinsic intellectual power" of the immigrating Germans merited appreciation: "It is a union of the best qualities and peculiarities of the American and German people which promises a remunerative and fruitful future."[34]

The tract included documentation from the proceedings of the GLH pointing out that one of the defectors had "meddled in a suspicious manner with the higher degrees of French Masonry," also called "the 'Jesuit intrigues' of the French high degrees." Pythagoras No. 1's criticism of former members engaging in higher degree Freemasonry referred to the so-called Ancient and Accepted Scottish Rite (AASR, a 33-degree system of French-Caribbean origins, established in Charleston, SC in 1801), rituals that they thought created invidious social distinctions. Another defector had double standards; at the time of the secession from the GLNY, he had wildly criticized American Freemasonry, referring to "the chaos of the Masonic discrepancies of this place," "particular prejudices," and "the oppressive fetters" of the GLNY. The new GLH affiliation, he believed, demonstrated "humanitarian masonry against those antiquated forms which have already outlived themselves."[35] Three years later he again embraced the GLNY.

This evidence indicates that the split within Pythagoras was engendered by the arrival of a more radical and revolutionary generation of émigrés who not only brought new concepts of Freemasonry with them, but also a political consciousness that could not be reconciled with American realities. The Forty-Eighters blended this spirit of critique and opposition with cosmopolitan visions of a "German" mission in America. Infused in it was a far more contentious issue – racial segregation, both within American Freemasonry and in American society more broadly, an area of profound disagreement in the decade leading up to the Civil War.

Racial segregation as an issue in transatlantic conflicts

Until the 1855 publication of *Papers relating to the late occurrences in Pythagoras lodge No. 1*, the divisions between Freemasonry as practiced in the German-speaking lodges and their American counterparts manifested largely as organizational. But underlying organizational disputes were differences in political culture between democratically-sensitized German émigrés, who were concerned with participation in decision making and the "heart" of Freemasonry, and more legalistically inclined American Freemasons for whom the major issue was to obey rules, and who were accused by some Germans of formalism. The defensiveness of American grand lodges also triggered a justified fear of opening the door to trespassing from European Masonic bodies, and thereby adding to already existing organizational confusion such as that occurring in New York. Beyond these areas of controversy, it is possible to discern subtle, and occasionally open, comments relating to cultural adaptation and isolationism, two dominant coping strategies of European immigrants to the US.

During the late 1850s, another contentious issue of the smoldering transatlantic tensions flared into open conflict, namely a profound disagreement between the GLH and the GLNY concerning racial segregation in US Freemasonry. The controversy unfolded in an intricate interplay among lodges in Monrovia (Liberia), Hamburg and New York. During the quarterly communications of the GLH in February 1858, a letter was read from a German Freemason who had visited a lodge, Oriental No. 1 in Monrovia, Liberia, consisting almost entirely of Black members. On behalf of this lodge and the Grand Lodge of Liberia (GLLi), the correspondent asked about initiating communications with German lodges. The GLH resolved that "however willing [they] would be to respond to this proposal, as it would be desirable for German brethren visiting Liberia to find a friendly lodge there, still he had hesitated to meet this wish without preliminary inquiry." The GLH investigating the matter through its representative at the United Grand Lodge of England (UGLE), and learned that the GLLi was not a recognized Masonic body. Moreover, it was "highly improbable" that a US grand lodge had constituted the GLLi because "a majority of its members were colored persons." The GLH responded to the GLLi through its correspondent that it had to rectify organizational shortcomings and then its request would be reconsidered.[36]

Three months later a German member of Orient No. 1 in Monrovia reported to the GLH that he believed the GLLi was constituted by the Grand Lodge of Massachusetts, "but probably the Negro Grand Lodge of that state," referring to the so-called Prince Hall Grand Lodge, named after its founder and established in various phases (1791/1808/ 1827). This information put the issue in a new light because the question now revolved around whether African American grand lodges in the USA were considered lawful or not. To gain knowledge about their status, in May 1858 the GLH disseminated a lengthy circular to other grand lodges in Europe asking what they knew about these lodges and grand lodges of people of African descent. The circular included a statement concerning racial segregation and prejudice in US Freemasonry, which was strong even in the non-slaveholding states, noting that "it is sad but true that our American brethren have not emancipated themselves from this prejudice." The GLH referenced a passage in GLNY transactions of 1855 calling the admission of African American persons "a monstrosity to be excluded from discussion." American grand lodge representatives in Europe had advised European grand lodges that they should abstain from admitting African American members.[37]

Clearly, Europeans should not expect American grand lodges to recognize lodges and foreign grand lodges with members of African descent. But did this exclusion also apply to European lodges? Were they bound, the GLH queried, "also to refuse to recognize a great number of lodges [...] and to refuse admissions of members of the same, merely because their complexion is somewhat darker"? The Prussian grand lodges, for instance, had recognized the Grand Lodge of Haiti, and the same might be the case with the Grand Lodge of Liberia. Now the dispute turned on the principle of exclusive territorial jurisdiction among US grand lodges. The non-recognition of African American lodges was possibly the outcome of the "*monopoly* claimed by them, according to which there can be but one Gr. Lodge in every state," and Massachusetts, for example, could not have the Massachusetts Grand Lodge and the Prince Hall Grand Lodge at the same time. The GLH acknowledged that "on account of disregarding this monopoly as regards German lodges in North America, [it] has come into collision with the North American Gr. Lodges" on a more general level. But more appalling, in its estimation, was the fact that individual lodges composed of African Americans wishing to join a regular state grand lodge not would be admitted "from a prejudice which cannot be approved of from a *masonic* point of view." The American lodges may be "politically, if not masonically right. But they cannot demand that European lodges should adopt their views or practice concerning colored persons." This matter was of growing concern, because "the intercourse of Europe with other parts of the globe is annually increasing."[38]

We do not know if the GLH realized its circular would elicit vehement reactions from its American counterparts, but the ensuing voluminous transatlantic exchange of letters and statements, as well as articles and opinion pieces in the American and German Masonic press prove how contentious the issue of racial exclusion was. Moreover, this dispute reflects profound national differences concerning Freemasonry, tolerance, and political culture, in general. At its annual meeting in June 1859, the GLNY lamented that the "puny offsprings of Hamburg" were endangering Masonic harmony, maintaining, as they were, a "sullen existence, and a dogged defiance to the solemn edits and resolutions" of the GLNY and almost all other grand lodges in the USA. But worse, the

> parent body of these offsprings, across the Atlantic, is seeking to wreak vengeance upon the fraternity of the U.S., for the reprobation with which it acts and its illegitimate subordinances have been visited, by arousing the prejudices of the Grand lodges of Europe against us.[39]

The GLNY had most likely received the GLH circular through Friedrich August von Mensch, its official representative to the Grand Lodge of Saxony (GLS), one of the many German grand lodges at the time. In his civilian career, he worked for the diplomatic service of his native country.[40] In four reports to the GLS from October 1858 to April 1859, von

Mensch outlined the position of the GLNY.[41] Masonic grand lodges operated in a system of a loosely self-organized international diplomacy, appointing mutual representatives along lines of allegiance and sometimes of pure coincidence. Most grand lodges also had a Committee of Foreign Correspondence (CFC) with the task of coordinating all contacts with other grand lodges.[42] In June 1859, the CFC of the GLNY issued a lengthy 13-page, sharply-worded reply to the GLH circular (based upon von Mensch's letters to the GLS) that it attached to the grand lodge minutes. The GLNY endorsed the report, the primary aim of which was to convince the GLS not to support the GLH circular.

The report's statements reflected how entrenched the racial bias in American Freemasonry had become. It opened by charging that the GLH had made "an unwarranted invasion of our jurisdictional rights" and claimed that the GLH in "retaliation of her supposed grievances" had "adopted a system of reprisals."[43] The GLH circular from May was summarized followed by extensive commentary on it, written in a style to convey a sense of scandal. In his first report to GLS, von Mensch argued against recognition of African American lodges in the USA and against the right of African American Freemasons to visit the GLS. First, he compared the different situations of Freemasonry in German states and the USA to justify the principle of exclusive territorial jurisdiction. It was "not only the question here of the existence of colored, near the present legitimate, Grand Lodges, but also of the constitutionally declared incapacity of the reception in the Masonic order of colored men in the United States." Von Mensch explained to his brethren in Saxony that while Americans commonly believed that African Americans stood on the "lower rounds of the social ladder, and generally speaking of mental development." Their acceptance into Freemasonry was therefore impossible. Moreover, "the initiation of colored men [...] would not fail to produce between the brethren of the Northern and Southern States of the Union dissentions and discord," compromising the interests of the entire country. Since "masonic interests always and everywhere" were "subordinate to the welfare of the state," it would "disturb the order and peace of the country" to act against the foundations of political order. Von Mensch ridiculed the prospect of any African American men visiting the GLS as an absurdity, and denied the legality of the Prince Hall Grand Lodge. The exclusion of black men from Freemasonry, he argued further, was based upon "national customs, historical influences, the power of tradition, social and political relations, and even for physical particularities of the negroes." To make his case, von Mensch quoted outright racist judgements from a German ethnographer concerning the state of civilization in Haiti.[44]

The GLNY interpreted the GLH's critique of exclusionary practices among American lodges not to accept black lodges under the Prince Hall Grand Lodge as reverse "vengeance," because of its criticism of the German grand lodges for not accepting Jewish members.[45] Furthermore, the GLNY attacked the GLH for its "illiberal and unmasonic policy" and "for seeking to create dissentions between the Grand Lodges of Europe and America." Last, but not least, von Mensch's report noted that the GLH attempted

> to recognize and to induce the other Grand Lodges of Europe to recognize bodies of colored men in the United States as Masonic Lodges and Grand Lodges, when it is a notorious fact that no legal organization of the kind exists in the American Union.[46]

Thus, the CFC made clear that it did not recognize Prince Hall Grand Lodge, any lodge with African American members, or their admission in other lodges. The GLNY, however, was apparently unaware of that the GLH definitely belonged to the vanguard of the liberal and reform-oriented wing of German Freemasonry advocating Jewish membership in Masonic lodges and the discontinuation of exclusionary practices based on any factors of religion or race.

Johann Barthelmess, Master of Pythagoras No. 1, penned a lengthy and ardent rebuke to the GLNY's CFC report in August 1859. His letter, preserved in GLH archives, counts no fewer than 40 handwritten pages, in which English quotes and German replies are mixed.[47] In it, Barthelmess systematically refuted arguments against Pythagoras No. 1 and the GLH going back a decade. He began by refuting the claim of exclusive territorial jurisdiction with reference to historical precedents and contemporary practices on both sides of the Atlantic. In Barthelmess's view, the GLNY could not force members of Pythagoras "who [...] in part are not, as you suppose, American citizens, into conditions abhorrent and perhaps repulsive to their own feelings?" He argued that to "compel uniformity of conflicting opinions" leads Freemasons into the "allurements of the systems of higher degrees" or simply leaves them homeless when trying to escape the grand lodge "straight jacket." In response to allegations of the GLH making reprisals against the GLNY, he reiterated the background of the GLH circular on African American lodges and their status. Indeed, in Barthelmess's eyes, the CFC's attempt "to stigmatize its circular as *reprisal*" was made even more disturbing when one knew that the GLNY had repeatedly discussed the issue of African American members since 1812. Only more recently had it turned against African American members and lodges. Barthelemess thus fervently attacked the CFC's position that the GLH had no business "to be meddling with this matter [recognition of 'negro lodges'] more than 3000 miles away" He listed many instances of racial biases in American Freemasonry and concluded forcefully that the northern lodges had subordinated themselves to the interest of southern slaveholders placing profit over human rights.[48]

Barthelmess argued that the GLH, "which has ever energetically defended the universality and the humane substructure of the masonic fraternity" had a moral duty to take notice of African American Freemasons which they "frequently meet in public," although "they live at a distance of 3000 miles." For the GLNY to prohibit intercourse with African American lodges "whose members the extensive commerce of the Hanse Town [Hamburg] leads to that city and to the very door of its lodges" was immoral and absurd. The GLNY's CFC boldly stated that "no German brother has ever visited these negro lodges in New York!," an assertion Barthelmess discredited with evidence to the contrary.[49] He outlined his views on racial segregation in the USA, especially the lack of educational access and structural discrimination, as reasons for the inferior status of African Americans. He pointed out that the ancient charges of Freemasonry included no suggestion that membership could be based on "a difference of colour." Barthelmess accused the CFC of defending "southern interests," and reminded readers of when American grand lodges had displayed positive attitudes with regards to the acceptance of African American Freemasons, but increasingly lodges in the northern states were "afraid to provoke the ill-will of the slave states by even the semblance of favour towards colored persons." The GLNY, having emphatically accused the Prussian grand lodges of excluding Jewish members, now "degrade[d] the masonic fraternity into an instrument of the southern slaveholders. Even at the risk of a split between the Southern and Northern Grand lodges" the "equal rights of all men as regards initiation to masonry" had to be advocated, even if it entailed a "political separation." In hindsight, Barthelmess's words were chillingly prophetic, and point to the profound tensions within the USA at the time.[50]

Barthelmess defended the legality of the Prince Hall Grand Lodge with a historical analysis of the maze of Masonic self-jurisdiction, especially the issue of the formation and recognition of grand lodges without formal permission of the United Grand Lodge of England. He emphasized the superiority of German Freemasonry as compared with American Freemasonry, particularly apparent in ritual differences, a primary reason for Pythagoras No. 1 to remain affiliated with the GLH and a reason for not rejoining the GLNY. For want of uniformity, the soul of Freemasonry was destroyed, Barthelemess claimed.[51]

Von Mensch replied politely in October, pleading ignorance of the issues at hand, and claiming the CFC misquoted him. But he held on to his contention that the troublemaker and instigator of the transatlantic antagonism was Barthelmess himself, in his aversion to American Freemasonry.[52] Finally, in February 1860, the GLH responded directly to the CFC report capturing the transatlantic rifts in question. The GLH wholeheartedly supported Barthelmess and likened the accusation that the GLH had invaded GLNY territory to the Oregon boundary dispute. (Between 1818 and 1846 the British and Americans jointly occupied the Oregon Country, and only in 1846 agreed to extend the international boundary along the 49th parallel to the Pacific, because Americans threatened war). The GLH noted that German Freemasons had separated from the GLNY because of "hollow ceremonials," excessive additional degrees, and an emphasis on social distinctions that made Germans uneasy. Therefore, to create German lodges in the US based on "descent, language, education and that national contemplation of the world" reflected the "beautiful and sublime art of Freemasonry," not a violation of it. The GLH felt bound to support lodges for German émigrés that espoused a "*Weltanschauung*" estranged by the shallowness of their American counterparts.[53]

In addressing racial segregation in American Freemasonry, an even more vitriolic topic, the GLH accused the GLNY of double standards. A German lodge would not bar recognition of "a lodge of red-skins," nor one with members of "the black colour, for the American lodges would consider it a crime to refuse admission to a Hindostane or Malay, were he even blacker than the blackest Abyssinian, nay even to an African Jew." The entire issue might appear trivial, the GLH noted, were it not connected to "baneful negro slavery." European Freemasonry, it averred, would never make difference of color "a bar against [...] initiation or admission." Concerning the regularity of the Prince Hall Grand Lodge, the GLH avoided any final conclusion and deferred to the UGLE. It noted, however, that "as the English nation has made immense sacrifices of money and men for the emancipation of negro slaves in her own colonies, and for the prevention of the slave trade on the coast of Africa," the UGLE certainly would not refuse any future petition for recognition. The GLH's closed with an appeal "to the colored brethren in the United States" to show patience and cultivate "masonic self command, from regard for the weakness of your brethren."[54]

Hot-wiring trans-Atlantic Masonic communications

In his analysis of conflicting concepts of universalism in European Freemasonry, Stefan-Ludwig Hoffmann notes how the "traditional metaphors of light and darkness mingled with the new language of scientific and technological progress."[55] In the case analyzed here, the transatlantic cable occupies an important role as metaphor both of hope for better communications and disappointment at the slow improvement. In 1851 Pythagoras No. 1 imagined itself sending "a life-giving spark across the Atlantic." In 1858, one of its members, Rudolph Garrigue, presented a talk to lodge members on the topic of "The completion of the transatlantic telegraph, the giant progress of our century."[56] At the GLNY, however, "disturbances [...] had defiled the solemnities [...] upon the occasion of the transatlantic cable celebration (scenes which even American papers mention with the utmost indignation)."[57] Although the GLNY hailed the telegraph "a triumph of science," and in August 1858 indicated an interest in participating in municipal celebrations of this "new proof of the triumph of mind over matter," in the end, it withdrew from the September 1 festivities. Instead Grand Master Macoy offered a number of programmatic resolutions, hailing the telegraph as a "material chain of concord [...] encouraging the inhabitants of the earth to dwell together in peace and unity," leading to a "fraternization and union of the families of man," and "uniting the nations of the earth."[58]

According to the GLH, the technological progress accelerating global communications would be of little value without simultaneously promoting universal morality. Metaphorically speaking, the transatlantic cable between the GLH and the GLNY went hot in the 1850s over conflicting notions of progress. At the time, many continental European grand lodges were battling "conceptual enem[ies]," first and foremost the Roman Catholic Church.[59] This battle intensified in Germany during 1870s, the so-called "Kulturkampf" or "culture war" between secular progressives and religious conservatives. Without a clear institutional enemy like the Catholic Church, progressive Freemasons in the US (backed in some instances by foreign lodges like the GLH) directed their agitation against nativism, racial segregation, and formalism in American grand lodges.

The German-US antagonism of the 1850s foreshadowed other fault lines in international Masonic relations, such as the rupture between German and French Freemasons during the war of 1870–1871, and the 1877 split between the United Grand Lodge of England and continental European Freemasonry over freedom of conscience. These conflicts demonstrate that Freemasonry's ambition to operate above national differences as a "moral international" imploded when faced with the realism of international politics. As Hoffman notes, the "internationalization of European societies exposed the particular character of the universalist pretensions of individual lodge systems."[60]

Scholars frequently stress the advantage of the less rigid German model of Freemasonry, in which several grand lodges could operate within the borders of one political territory, as showing greater acceptance of ideological heterodoxy. Georg Simmel, in his influential *Untersuchungen über die Formen der Vergesellschaftung* (1908), argues that this heterodoxy is a response to more authoritarian models of government in society. Paradoxically, greater uniformity or orthodoxy in ritual forms and organization is a feature of Freemasonry in more liberal societies, such as in the US.[61] Pythagoras No. 86 and No.1 argued against formalism in American lodges, against "association articles least adapted to the free soil of America."[62] The lodge imagined itself as a bulwark of "the true and pure principle of humanitarian Freemasonry against the obsolete rule of formalism."[63] The lodge subscribed to an agenda of reform and in 1860 adopted the motto: "No standstill, but advance!"[64] In 1866, rejoicing at the end of the Civil War and the coming of peace,

Pythagoras No. 1 exclaimed: "'Reform!' – this is the cry that now moves thousands of spirits on this side and beyond the Ocean." It appended to its annual communication a long list of areas in need of reform.[65] German Freemasons transported their political awareness and acceptance of heterodoxy, nurtured in an authoritarian context, to the new more politically liberal context of America, without truly engaging with the constitutional culture that had emerged in the US that strove for egalitarianism through law and union-wide compromise.[66] The uniformity and orthodoxy of American lodges, in an ostensibly more liberal political context, was hard for Forty-Eighters to accept. In the US, a relatively young federal union of independently governed states, major internal political conflicts related to spatial organization and power relations were not settled yet, and eventually contributed to the outbreak of the Civil War. The issue of exclusive territorial jurisdiction was therefore far more sensitive to American Freemasons and is representative for tensions in the large US society. German émigrés arriving in the US in the late 1840s could clearly see the problems within American Freemasonry, of territorial exclusivity, problems that American-born Freemasons and some German immigrants who had been in the US longer could tolerate.[67]

Since the American Revolution (1775–1783), American society was based on a constitutional model of rights, on the idea of a rule of law as the basis of political order. For such a political community, the essence of the law and its interpretation had primacy in political deliberation. Without pushing the argument too far, it would be possible to make the claim that German émigré Freemasons were not familiar or not accustomed enough to truly grasp the implications of this way of organizing political communities, which they regarded as based on external form rather than on imminent spirit or soul (or even a particular German "*Weltanschauung*").

On the other hand, German humanitarian passion or pathos painfully touched upon one of the most enduringly sensitive issues of American society: racial segregation. American Masonic universalism ideally, even rationally, meant an embrace of a self-confident society ruled by law, as opposed "misrule and anarchy" or by an absolute monarch. At the same time, that society excluded huge parts of its population, due to skin color alone, from enjoying equal rights. Not even African American Freemasons and their organizations were accepted into this community, despite dogged interference from the GLH and other European grand lodges. German Freemasonry also preserved ideas of cultural particularity, despite the cosmopolitan pathos of Freemasonry in general and of liberal German Freemasonry in particular.[68] The German émigré community confidently stressed its German-ness, or "*Deutschtum*," as a common inclusionary denominator, notwithstanding it being simultaneously exclusionary vis-à-vis the surrounding US society. The split between old members of Pythagoras No. 86 and No. 1 in 1854 and the plans to form an entirely German grand lodge in the US reflect the different stances on cultural assimilation that could be taken. American Freemasonry intentionally omitted a national principle in Freemasonry, which potentially could lead to chaos in the society of immigrants. Yet, paradoxically, American Freemasonry embraced exclusion based on race.

All these issues – territorial hegemony, a national principle in Freemasonry, and race – demonstrate the boundaries of "egalitarian morality" and conflicting models of civilization and society in transatlantic Freemasonry in the nineteenth century.[69]

Notes

1. Nagel, *Von republikanischen Deutschen*, 33–37. For a general introduction to the emigration of Forty-Eighters see also Levine, *The Spirit of 1848*, 15–19. See also Wittke, "The German Forty-Eighters," 713. Although Wittke published his article seven decades ago, current research does not contradict his principal findings.
2. Efford, *German Immigrants*, 17–52, quotes on 18; and a closely related argument in Nagel, *Von republikanischen Deutschen*, 26–27.
3. Honeck, *We are the Revolutionists*, 13–15.
4. Levine, *The Spirit of 1848*, 83–88. It would be valuable to see the patterns of German American civil society formations compared to other immigrant communities arriving at the same time. Was Freemasonry representative of the Forty-Eighter's sociability? Did they also engage in other fraternal orders emerging at the time such as the "International Order of Good Templars" (1851) or did they rather form other ethnically based organizations (for mutual aid) such as the "Hermannssöhne" (1840)?
5. Efford argues that the political attitudes expressed by German immigrants also always were shaped by an awareness of European development and thus were trans-Atlantic in their character. Up to German unification in 1871, German immigrants rather embraced ideas of liberal and inclusive patriotism and individual rights, including Black suffrage, but later shifted towards American nationalism and white reconciliation. Efford, *German Immigrants*, 2–10, 53–85, quotes on 13–14.
6. For their function in shaping a (German) language of American citizenship in the public space, see Efford, *German Immigrants*, 12. In his extensive analysis of the German American press Nagel, *Von republikanischen Deutschen*, 27–29, speaks about an emerging German "ethnic semi-public space."
7. Levine, *The Spirit of 1848*, 160, contends that "[i]n New York City, German America had by far its biggest and most economically and politically heterogeneous center. The various political currents in German America tended to find their clearest and most forceful expressions here." Levine's statement lends a study of NY German American Freemasonry some representative gravity.
8. Honeck, *We are the Revolutionists*, 1–3.
9. Ibid., 16–23; and Nagel, *Von republikanischen Deutschen*, 33 and 325–402, who speaks of the "nativist challenge."
10. The most comprehensive "positive" historical account of the lodge's history is Hoffmann, "The First Twenty Years," 33–54; and "Pythagoras Lodge No. 1," 320–342. The latter has a printed membership list.
11. The Freemason Teubner printed this first annual return at his publishing house.
12. Leroy T. Hopkins, "The Craft vs. Color': German Freemasonry and Race Relations in the Nineteenth Century," Typed manuscript ca. 1995. Livingston Library and Museum, Grand Lodge of New York, Series 2, Individual Lodge Papers, Pythagoras No. 86 (No. 1), first observed these tensions in detail.
13. Hoffmann, "Nationalism," 263. For a general introduction, see Önnerfors, *Freemasonry*.
14. On "territorial sovereignty," see Önnerfors, *Freemasonry*, 86–87.
15. Levine, *The Spirit of 1848*, 59.
16. "Jahresbericht 1868." Staatsarchiv Hamburg (hereafter StH), 614-1/72_5.1.10 777, Mitgliederverzeichnisse der Loge Pythagoras Nr. 1 in New York, 1852–1872 (hereafter Mitgliederverzeichnisse), quoting a circular from 1849.
17. Ibid.
18. Wittke, "The German Forty-Eighters," 715.
19. Hoffmann, "Pythagoras Lodge No. 1," 320–321.
20. Wiebe, *Die grosse Loge*, 263–265.
21. Hoffmann, "The First Twenty Years," 38.
22. Ibid., 40.
23. *Die Ger. und vollk.*, 14.

24. Hoffmann, "The First Twenty Years," 44.
25. Ibid., 45.
26. Ibid., 46; and *Proceedings 1852*, 52.
27. Wiebe, *Die grosse Loge*, 269.
28. Hoffmann, "The First Twenty Years," 48.
29. Efford, *German Immigrants*, 13.
30. Wittke, "The German Forty-Eighters," 714–715; and Honeck, *We are the Revolutionists*, 22.
31. Hoffmann, "The First Twenty Years," 49.
32. Hoffmann, "The First Twenty Years," 50. Nagel, *Von republikanischen Deutschen*, 73–129 develops how the newly arrived Germans or "greens" were confronted with an earlier generation of "grays". Whereas the "greens" wrongly assumed cultural homogeneity among the German immigrant community in their political struggle, the "grays" referred to their American citizenship and loyalty to their new homeland and its constitutional order.
33. Here we again can observe the function of Freemasonry outside its narrower orbit, as a friendly society and part of German American community organizations with charitable goals.
34. *Papers*, 9.
35. *Papers*, quotes on 13, 18, 19, and 20.
36. *Documents*, quotes on 1 and 2.
37. *Documents*, quotes on 2 and 4.
38. *Documents*, quotes on 4 and 5.
39. *Transactions 1859*, 81; Hoffmann, "The first twenty years," 52; and *Documents*, 34.
40. In 1846, von Mensch published a *Manuel pratique du consulat*. He worked as counsel for several German states.
41. These letters are printed in English translation in *Transactions 1859*, 199–214.
42. In 1840 the GLNY installed the first foreign representative, ironically from the GLH. At the occasion the Grand Master claimed that the "duties of Masonic governments correspond with those of the civil governments of the State." *Transactions 1840–1841*, 8.
43. *Transactions 1859*, 199. Subsequent references cited parenthetically in text.
44. *Transactions 1859*, quotes on 203, 204, 210, and 211.
45. Hoffmann, "Nationalism," 272.
46. *Documents*, 35.
47. "Repräsentanten der Gr L des Staates N Y bei der Gr Landesloge von Sachsen (5/1 1859. Report of the Committee of foreign Correspondence 123–136) über die Stellung der farbigen Logen und Brüder in den Verein: Staaten." StH, 614-1/72_5.1.10 1547, Angelegenheiten der Freimaurerlogen in New York, XVIII A24. Barthelmess was born in 1820 in Bavaria, joined Freemasonry in the lodge Zu den drei Pfeilen in Nuremberg, and was affiliated to Pythagoras No. 1 in 1852. The membership records listed him as a medical doctor. He defended a dissertation on ovarian infections at Würzburg University in 1844. He was very active as a printer and publisher for the lodge. Eventually, he moved back to Germany.
48. *Documents*, quotes on 11, 13, 14, and 15.
49. *Documents*, quotes on 15–16.
50. *Documents*, 17–20. Barthelemess's rhetoric is concordant with the more radical factions of German American resistance to slavery, and with abolitionists and the Republican Party. See Honeck, *We are the Revolutionists*, 23–32; and Nagel, *Von republikanischen Deutschen*, 523–524 and 552.
51. *Documents*, 22.
52. Honeck, *We are the Revolutionists*, 10, notes that 1848 refugees were frequently perceived as troublemakers by previous generations of immigrants.
53. *Documents*, quote on 40. Nagel, *Von republikanischen Deutschen*, 49–50 and 530, highlights this recurring theme in German American discourse.
54. *Documents*, quotes on 46, 47, and 48.
55. Hoffmann, "Nationalism," 271.
56. "Jahresbericht 1859." StH, Mitgliederverzeichnisse.

57. *Documents*, 36. Unfortunately no further information about this thrilling incident could be found.
58. *Transactions 1859*, quotes on 4 and 5.
59. Hoffmann, "Nationalism," 273.
60. Ibid.
61. Simmel, *Untersuchungen*, 293, translated to English in "The sociology of secrecy and secret societies" in *The American Journal of Sociology*, 11 (1906): 441–498.
62. "Jahresbericht 1859." StH, Mitgliederverzeichnisse.
63. "Jahresbericht 1867." StH, Mitgliederverzeichnisse.
64. "Jahresbericht 1860." StH, Mitgliederverzeichnisse.
65. "Jahresbericht 1866." StH, Mitgliederverzeichnisse. See also Hoffmann, "Nationalism," 266 and 271, on the concept of progress in German Freemasonry.
66. Nagel, *Von republikanischen Deutschen*, 50–57 develops the German émigré frustration with understanding how their ideal of a democratic republic corresponded to the political realities of the dynamic and racially diverse US society. They did not fully grasp the praxis of self-governance in US-politics.
67. Hoffmann, "The First Twenty Years," 46.
68. Hoffmann, "Nationalism," 261.
69. Ibid., 260.

Acknowledgments

I would like to express my thanks to Distriktsloge Hamburg e.V., who granted me permission to use their private archive at Staatsarchiv Hamburg. I also would like to thank Catherine Walter, Tom Savini, and Bruce Renner from the Livingstone Library of the Grand Lodge of New York for their kind assistance in my research. Thanks also to Thad Peterson at Deutsches Freimaurermuseum in Bayreuth for providing me with additional information as well as especially to Dr. Leroy T. Hopkins who kindly shared his research into German American Freemasonry with me. I would also like to thank the two anonymous reviewers of this paper who contributed with valuable input.

Disclosure statement

No potential conflict of interest was reported by the author.

Bibliography

Die Ger.: und vollk.: St. Johannis Loge Pythagoras No. 1. im Aufgang von New-York an die geliebten Schwester Logen und Brüder unseres Bundes. New-York: Teubner, 1852.
Documents Respecting the Controversy between the Grand Lodges of Hamburg and New York: On the Exclusive Territorial Jurisdiction of Grand Lodges: On the Inquiry Concerning the Regularity of Colored Lodges. Brooklyn: Masonic Historical Society, 1860.
Efford, Alison Clark. *German Immigrants, Race and Citizenship in the Civil War Era*. Cambridge: Cambridge University Press, 2013.
Harland-Jacobs, Jessica. *Builders of Empire: Freemasons and British Imperialism, 1717–1927*. Chapel Hill: The University of North Carolina Press, 2007.

Hoffmann, Karl F. "The First Twenty Years of Pythagoras Lodge No. 86, F. & A.M., – 1841– 1861." *Transactions of the American Lodge of Research* 7 (1957): 33–54.

Hoffmann, Stefan-Ludwig. "Nationalism and the Quest for Moral Universalism: German Freemasonry, 1860–1914." In *The Mechanics of Internationalism: Culture, Society and Politics from the 1840s to the First World War*, edited by Martin H. Geyer, and Johannes Paulmann, 259–284. Oxford: Oxford University Press, 2001.

Hoffmann, Karl F. "Pythagoras Lodge No. 1 (Hamburg) in Brooklyn, N.Y." *Transactions of the American Lodge of Research* 7 (1957): 320–342.

Honeck, Mischa. *We are the Revolutionists: German-Speaking Immigrants & American Abolitionists After 1848*. Athens: The University of Georgia Press, 2011.

Levine, Bruce. *The Spirit of 1848. German Immigrants, Labor Conflict and the Coming of the Civil War*. Urbana: The University of Illinois Press, 1992.

Nagel, Daniel. *Von republikanischen Deutschen zu deutsch-amerikanischen Republikanern: Ein Beitrag zum Identitätswandel der deutschen Achtundvierziger in den Vereinigten Staaten 1850–1861*. St. Ingbert: Röhrig Universitätsverlag, 2012.

Önnerfors, Andreas. *Freemasonry: A Very Short Introduction*. Oxford: Oxford University Press, 2017.

Papers Relating to the Late Occurrences in Pythagoras Lodge No. 1. New York: Teubner, 1855.

Proceedings of the Most Worshipful Grand Lodge of Free and Accepted Masons of the State of Louisiana (1852). New Orleans: Crescent Office, 1852.

Simmel, Georg. *Untersuchungen über die Formen der Vergesellschaftung*. Berlin: Duncker & Humblodt, 1908.

Transactions of the Grand Lodge of the Most Ancient and Honorable Fraternity of Free and Accepted Masons of the State of New York (1859). New York: Robt. Macoy, 1859.

Transactions of the Right Worshipful Grand Lodge of the Ancient and Honorable Fraternity of Free and Accepted Masons of the State of New-York (1840–1841). New York: Marsh, 1841.

Wiebe, Carl. *Die grosse Loge von Hamburg und ihre Vorläufer*. Rademacher: Hamburg, 1905.

Wittke, Carl. "The German Forty-Eighters in America: A Centennial Appraisal." *The American Historical Review* 53, no. 4 (1948): 711–725.

The great divide: Transatlantic brothering and masonic internationalism, c. 1870–c. 1930

Joachim Berger ⓘ

ABSTRACT
This article demonstrates the interplay between national, international and transatlantic dimensions within fraternalism. From the late nineteenth century, masonic lodges took part in the broader push towards the formation of transnational organisations and institutions. They were mainly based in western and southwestern Europe. However, transatlantic channels were established that went beyond the individual and local level. The article analyses these waves of transatlantic brothering and relates them to the tides of confrontation and rapprochement between the United States and Europe. It argues that the First World War marked a moment of intensified interactions when English and French masonries rivalled over the Americans' favour, followed by a period in which transatlantic internationalist initiatives were shaped by masons based in New York. These inner-masonic alliances embraced the rationale of international relations in the realm of state policy and promised to overcome the divides between the various camps in European and World freemasonry.

In the mid-nineteenth century, European masonic umbrella associations maintained diverse relations with the grand lodges in the USA, which became of practical significance due to the mass migration of Europeans across the Atlantic.[1] The Grand Lodge of the State of New York was in a key position, as it was considered the "door" to America. The Swiss Grand Lodge "Alpina" established relations via the exchange of representatives with the Grand Lodge of New York in 1866, as it was

> in the interests of brethren and their relatives who had emigrated [...] to connect with a Grand Orient [sic] that could provide them with advice and practical assistance, and, where they experienced difficulties, could contact the authorities there directly or indirectly through influential brethren.[2]

At that time, bilateral relations between the umbrella associations were primarily understood as brotherly networks of individual members. Lodges consisting of emigrants served as institutional connectors, as they "worked" in the native languages of the members under the authority of American umbrella associations – it is estimated that in 1875 there were 25 German-speaking lodges with around 3,000 members in the city of New York alone.[3]

These connections between European and American freemasonries[4] only existed between certain umbrella associations, and they fluctuated over time.[5] These fluctuations were reflected particularly conspicuously in the phenomenon of masonic internationalism that emerged from the 1870s onward. "Internationalism" denotes both a normative goal and a process of ever closer communicative ties (as well as intensifying conflicts) between national bodies and individuals.[6] I conceive of masonic internationalism as an interplay of three levels of actions: It covers, first, transnational movements[7] at the level of masonic bodies and their consolidation in transnational structures and organisations. They manifested themselves in international conferences and congresses, in transnational organisations such as the International Confederation of the Supreme Councils of the Scottish Rite (founded in 1875), the International Bureau of Masonic Relations (established 1903) and the International Masonic Association (founded in 1921). These transnational movements and organisations correspond to a narrow understanding of "internationalism" prompted by their contemporary activists and opponents.[8] Second, these organized transnational movements were embedded in a network of bilateral relationships between masonic bodies, some of which – like the English and the Prussians – tried to actively counteract the transnational movements.[9] And third, the latter were augmented – and sometimes rivalled by – international grassroots movements arising from the initiatives and associations of individual freemasons such as the masonic peace demonstrations and the "Universal Freemasons' League". This three-dimensional approach allows an integration of the masonic proponents as well as the opponents of transnational co-operation into the picture without reproducing or refuting the "narratives of failure" or the conspiracy theories of the time.[10] By studying the interplay of national actors, bi- and multilateral relations and transnational movements, this study opts for an approach to fraternal history that "adopt[s] multiple and intersecting units and scales of analysis."[11] Freemasonry thus can serve as an example of the "the inherent malleability" of internationalism: Whereas "their ideology and operations were global in scope," masonic actors in international forums had to juggle overlapping allegiances and multiple belongings.[12] They tried to balance diverging understandings of religious commitment alongside the postulate of freedom of conscience, and had to relate their national loyalties and their colonial respectively imperial ambitions to an ideal of "humanity" that hoped to bridge all these differences.[13] It is through the study of its international relations and transnational movements that Freemasonry most clearly appears as "a kind of ideological palimpsest where different identity projects have written one over the other, one through the other, with older scriptures eventually shimmering through, cosmopolitanism being one amongst them."[14] Geographically, masonic internationalism was very much driven by European movements – like other kinds of internationalism.[15] In the last third of the nineteenth century, European-transatlantic channels between freemasons were expanded – mirroring the intensification of worldwide travel and communication. In European freemasonries, as in their societies generally, interest in the USA increased from the 1890s onward – due to the growing economic power of the latter and as a reaction to the general "sense of crisis in Europe." However, prior to the First World War the USA remained one nation among others from a masonic perspective; America was not (yet) a model.[16]

This article investigates the transatlantic dynamics in masonic internationalism, which evolved in the context of internal masonic differences (particularly on religious and territorial issues) as well as societal and state-political developments. The First World War served as a catalyst in this process and represented a (temporary) turning point. Historian Mary Nolan's observation also applies to international masonic relations: "war and its aftermath [made] Europe and America both more entangled and more distant."[17] The article analyses this development between c. 1870 and c. 1930 from the perspective of a number of European masonic bodies[18] on North American freemasonries, primarily in the USA.[19] In these transatlantic relations, it will be argued, religious differences and territorial conflicts could be bridged for a time, with European freemasons promoting the formation of global concepts of space. I thus treat transatlantic masonic relations in the framework of transnational history, dealing with interconnections, transfers and conflicts between (primarily nationally bound) actors and organisations, rather than focussing on comparisons.[20]

Transatlantic forums and fault lines, 1855–1889

In the formative phase of internationalism, the universal exhibitions played a decisive role in facilitating transatlantic masonic encounters. At the "Congrès universel," which the Grand Orient of France convened during the Paris Exposition of 1855, both the Grand Lodge of Virginia and the Grand Lodge of the District of Columbia were represented.[21] Official delegations of the Grand Lodges of Indiana, Louisiana and Ohio participated in the celebration organised by the Grand Orient during the next Paris world exhibition (1867), and five other grand lodges were represented by individual members.[22] The Americans also utilised the forum of the universal exhibitions. In 1893, during the World's Columbian Exhibition, the Supreme Council of the USA (Northern Jurisdiction) convened an international meeting of the Supreme Councils of the Ancient and Accepted (Scottish) Rite in Chicago. Delegates of the Supreme Council of France were among those who attended from Europe.[23]

The Ancient and Accepted Scottish Rite (A.A.S.R.) was a ritual system of 33 degrees that had emerged in France in the eighteenth century and was reimported from the USA to Europe after 1801, spreading over the entire continent and Great Britain (with the exception of, for example, Scandinavia and Germany). In most countries, the Supreme Councils as leading authorities confined their rule to the higher degrees (4–33) and their organisational units, whereas the first three or basic degrees or "Craft Masonry" were administered by the so-called "obediences" (Grand Lodges and Grand Orients).[24] Through their delegations and meetings, the Supreme Councils served as pacesetters for masonic internationalism generally and for transatlantic relations specifically. This manifested itself most clearly in 1912 during the International Conference of the Supreme Councils in Washington, DC, with individual delegations being sent from Europe by the Councils of France, Greece, Italy, Switzerland and Serbia.[25] This partial shift of congress tourism from Europe to America occurred in other internationalisms as well.[26] Nonetheless, transatlantic differences of opinion emerged between the Supreme Councils at an early stage. For example, in 1875 the Supreme Councils of the USA argued with the Supreme Council of France about the administration of the higher degrees in Honolulu. As a result, the Americans did not attend the international conference of the Supreme Councils in Lausanne in that year (initially, this conference had been scheduled for Washington, DC).[27]

This and other disagreements, which in the Scottish Rite primarily involved religious as well as organisational and territorial issues, also manifested themselves in the grand orients and the grand lodges for the first three or basic degrees in the form of conflicts over admission conditions – regarding religion and skin colour or race. At the "Universal Congress" in Paris in 1855, the representative of the Grand Lodge of the District of Columbia defended slave ownership. Anyone who argued for an end to the practice, he asserted, was threatening the social and economic position of the slave owners – including the masons among them. To bolster his argument, he cited the geographical and cultural differences between the North and the South and the masonic principle of non-intervention. The delegate also warned that a large fault line would open up if the Europeans continued to found lodges in America and to award degrees to people who were not suitable because they were citizens of a different country. He thus voted against both the foundation of European lodges in the USA and – with no great attempt hide it – against the admittance of African Americans. By contrast, the representative of the Grand Lodge of Virginia declared that he bowed to the majority vote of the congress, thereby distancing himself from his counterpart from Washington, DC. Regarding the admittance of "coloured men," the congress ultimately decided that prior to the initiation of a candidate from another country, the consent of the masonic body of that country must be sought, the majority yielding to the American objections from the District of Columbia.[28] This dissent continued in the Grand Orient of France in particular and was a source of strain in its relations with the North American grand lodges for some time.[29]

Schisms and rapprochements

Relations between the continental European masonic bodies and the "white" grand lodges in the USA, which by the 1880s had spread to all of the American states,[30] varied considerably. For example, the Grand Orient of Italy exchanged representatives with the Grand Lodges of Ohio (1877), Indiana (1881), Georgia (1896), Montana (1897), West Virginia (1901) and the District of Columbia (1906). In 1897, it also sought the recognition of the Grand Lodge of New York – the "gateway" to the USA.[31] Relations between the latter and the eight established grand lodges in Germany were also varied. It maintained permanent relations with the "Eklektische Bund" in Frankfurt am Main from the 1840s, while relations with the Grand Lodge of Hamburg were suspended in the 1850s and did not resume until 1906–1907.[32] Below the official level of mutual representatives, the access of German freemasons to the lodges in the USA as "visiting brethren" remained a constant topic of discussion in the German Federation of Grand Lodges.[33]

The United Grand Lodge of England also tried to establish close relations with the Americans. When dealing with the "brethren" in the former "colonies," its leadership even dispensed with the usual English understanding of itself as the "mother lodge of global freemasonry," in order to stress the Anglo-American commonalities. The English Grand Master (George Frederick Samuel Robinson, Earl de Grey and Earl of Ripon) described the overwhelming reception that he received from thousands of American freemasons during his stay in the USA in 1871. Ripon's official mission was to lead the British delegation in the Joint Anglo-American High Commission, which was to reconcile the tensions between the UK and the USA. He transferred the political goal of his trip to masonic relations – it was, he said, "a mission the great object of which was to cement the friendship between the two great branches of the Anglo-Saxon race."[34] As a representative of the British government Ripon put his political mission in almost identical terms – it was "animated by a sincere desire to promote the friendship and the alliance of the two great portions of the Anglo-Saxon race."[35] In the context of Anglo-American relations, the category of "race" did not relate exclusively to the distinguishing feature of skin colour, and Ripon did not link "race" to "slavery." His organisation had opened its lodges to emancipated slaves only in 1847, and the English were at pains not to exasperate US-Americans. "Race"[36] in the Anglo-American context, it seems, emerged as a general differentiating term with regard to all "different-minded" freemasonries, referring primarily to the French.

The British-French schism after 1878 alienated the grand lodges in the USA from the Grand Orient of France. In 1877, the French body had removed the passage that Freemasonry was founded on a belief in God and the immortality of the soul from its constitution. As a reaction, the United Grand Lodge of England instructed all private lodges only to accept as "true and genuine Brethren" those freemasons who had been initiated in lodges requiring a belief in (the existence) of the "Great Architect of the Universe."[37] What started as a partial interruption of masonic intercourse gradually evolved into a European (and global) schism in Freemasonry with the formation of an "Anglo-Saxon" and a "Latin" camp. While the rift occurred on grounds of diverging opinions on the transcendental basis of Freemasonry, it was underpinned by opposing positions on the involvement of Freemasonry in societal and political discussions and actions. In Belgium, France, Italy, Portugal, and Spain, masonic lodges were frequented by freethinkers, anticlericals, and peace activists. To them, the mission of Freemasonry was to repel the dominant position of the Catholic Church in society, especially in the field of education. This activist stance found little support among freemasons in predominantly Protestant (respectively Anglican) countries like Scandinavia, Prussia, Britain – and the USA.[38] In 1879, the Grand Master of the Grand Lodge of Arkansas, referring to the change in the French constitution, noted "that we have few common interests with freemasonry as it is organized on the European continent."[39] Recurring conflicts regarding the American doctrine of unrestricted territorial jurisdiction also played a role in alienating the Americans from the French.[40] The schism hardened in the decades before 1900 and affected the emerging transnational movement of the national umbrella organisations. Americans and Canadians kept their distance from the international congresses of the grand lodges and grand orients, which began with the congress in Paris in 1889. The North American grand lodges wanted to have nothing to do with the Grand Orient as they viewed it as an "irregular and spurious body." The anti-clerical attitude of the French also contributed to this.[41] In 1900, the Grand Lodges of Vermont and Idaho even threatened to suspend their relations with the Belgian Grand Orient if it did not separate itself from the Grand Orient of France.[42]

The international conference in Antwerp (1894) was attended by but one representative from America – from Florida.[43] Representatives were sent to the Geneva congress in 1902, at which the International Bureau of Masonic Relations was founded by three masonic bodies that were not recognised by the established grand lodges or the two Supreme Councils of the USA: the "Grande Loge de Couleur" of the District of Columbia, the Supreme Council of Ohio and a connected grand lodge of the same state. The participation of these bodies prompted the "regular" Grand Lodges of the District of Columbia and of the State of Ohio to boycott the subsequent international congress in Brussels (1904) – the latter also explained its decision to boycott by stating that the agenda contradicted the fundamental principles and statutes of Freemasonry. This criticism was directed towards the question of international arbitration and towards the discussion of the position paper of the Belgian Pierre Tempels, who criticised "dogmatic" prescriptions in Freemasonry.[44]

Edouard Quartier-la-Tente, the director of the International Bureau of Masonic Relations, bemoaned the distance, which the North Americans maintained from the transnational movement. He suspected that it was the membership of the Grand Orient of France that was keeping them away from the International Bureau, thereby thwarting its global and transatlantic pretensions.[45] The role of mediator, which Quartier-la-Tente and his Grand Lodge Suisse "Alpina" sought to play in international relations, was contradicted by the fact that "Alpina" was not recognised by about 20 North American grand lodges because of its connections with the Grand Orient of France. Quartier-la-Tente asserted at the Brussels conference in 1910 that the fault line primarily resulted from disagreements regarding the minimum religious requirements for lodge membership. By contrast, on the issue of how to deal with African American freemasons, he perceived a possibility that the principles of both sides would converge over time.[46] The French themselves suspected that they had been cut off by the Americans because they had recognised African American lodges and had demanded that the categories of race and skin colour should – like the issue of religious beliefs – be no impediment to admittance. Quartier-la-Tente pointed out that the European masonic bodies were infringing on the territorial sovereignty of the American grand lodges by founding their own lodges and by accepting existing lodges there under their umbrella.[47]

Thus, it appears that transatlantic masonic relations had come to a standstill prior to the First World War. However, the gulf between the Americans and the continental European transnational movement was not an absolute. At the conference of Supreme Councils in Brussels (1907), the Canadian and the two North American Councils were present; the follow-up conference in Washington has been referred to earlier.[48] While none of the American bodies officially joined the International Bureau, seven grand lodges and the Supreme Council of the Northern Jurisdiction nonetheless supported it financially on a temporary or continuing basis.[49] Like the Prussian National Mother Lodge, they wanted to avoid meeting at congresses of bodies that they had not recognised. However, they were by no means entirely averse to the idea of a transnational point of contact and information.

The Great War: political alliances versus religious-secular differences

The First World War, or more precisely the year 1917, was a turning point for transatlantic relations. The shared "brotherhood in arms" of the French, the British and ultimately also the American freemasons seemed a good way of bridging the gulf between the "Latin" and the "Anglo-Saxon" freemasonries.

Initially, the French approached the North Americans, and the latter responded positively. Freemasons in the US armed forces were permitted to visit French lodges from 1917 onward.[50] The French obediences also attempted to bring the American grand lodges into the international forums, which had been dominated by Europeans up to that point. The two events that the Grand Orient and the Grand Lodge of France organised in 1917 in Paris established the future direction. At the conference of the freemasonries of the allied states held in January of that year, the delegates sent brotherly salutations to freemasons in the USA. These signals were received positively – initially by individual American masons and later more generally. While no American grand lodge participated in the second Paris congress in June of the same year, which was for the freemasonries of the allied and neutral states, the Grand Lodge of Arkansas, which excused itself due to the large distance involved, expressed its support for the aim of the conference. The Grand Lodge of Ohio retrospectively declared its adhesion. The congress supported the political agenda of US President Woodrow Wilson by supporting the right of nations to self-determination and the foundation of a League of Nations.[51]

By this time, the USA had entered the war on the side of the Allies. This prompted various American grand lodges to overcome their previous reservations regarding the Grand Orient of France and they offered to establish masonic connections with the latter on various levels.[52] In 1918, the Grand Lodge of Alabama first permitted the exchange of visitors between itself and the Grand Orient and subsequently moved to full recognition. The Grand Lodge of Iowa, which established official relations with the Grand Orient, Louisiana and New Jersey, even offered to exchange representatives, the highest level of "diplomatic" relations. New Jersey explained its decision to take this step in political terms. It stated that, since the military forces of both countries were united in the struggle for the principles of democracy and the freedom of the world, the freemasons of both countries would have to follow suit.[53] The Grand Lodges of California and Nevada permitted the exchange of visitors with the lodges or individual members from France, Belgium and Italy. Thus, the gulf between the American and the "Latin" camps was bridged. In communication with the United Grand Lodge of England, the Californian Grand Lodge stressed the criteria that prevented it from recognising the Grand Orient of France (in particular, it objected to the fact that the Grand Orient did not insist that its members profess a belief in the existence of God). However, as the Californians pointed out, there was a strong current in favour of "fraternal intercourse," due to the political alliance between the USA and the United Kingdom, which had brought thousands of American freemasons to France. Differences concerning the transcendental basis of Freemasonry were thus effectively ignored for pragmatic reasons.[54]

For its part, the leadership of the Grand Orient viewed the Americans as a means of bringing an end to its ostracism by the English Grand Lodge. Shortly before the end of the war, Council member Andrey Lebey expressed the view that the Americans could come to an acceptance of the anti-clerical stance of the French, as they were able to appreciate the differences between the two countries in terms of the relationship between the church(es), the state and society, and they could thus defend the French against English criticism. Attempting to build on the two Paris congresses in 1917, Lebey argued that the freemasonries of the allied countries should form "a kind of permanent committee," and the French should work with the Americans on this.[55]

The English did not engage in this fraternisation across the boundaries between the masonic camps, which was driven by national and political aims. Instead, the idea emerged in the English Grand Lodge of an "English-speaking freemasonry," which would unite all the lodges in the British Empire and the rest of the English-speaking world – particularly the USA. This Anglo-American brotherhood was staged in the celebrations of the English Grand Lodge to mark its bicentenary in 1917 and the end of the war in 1919. Thousands of freemasons including visitors from both sides of the Atlantic participated in both events.[56] A veritable competition emerged between the English and the

THE FRATERNAL ATLANTIC, 1770–1930   137

French for the goodwill of the Americans. These internal masonic developments came in the aftermath of strong intervention by the USA in the political affairs of Europe.

Avant-garde or gravedigger of the transnational movement?

After the war, the Grand Lodge of New York took on a leading role in transatlantic fraternisation. Lead by its past Grand Master Townsend Scudder, it founded so-called "Sea and Field Lodges" in four French towns. These lodges facilitated mutual visits of American and French masons, including members of the Grand Orient of France. Under Scudder's influence the Grand Lodge of New York itself at times acted as the avant-garde by claiming responsibility for the Geneva Congress in 1921 and the foundation of the International Masonic Association (Association Maçonnique Internationale, A.M.I.) the same year; this also coincided with US President Wilson's claim to responsibility for founding the League of Nations.[57] This act of bridge building succeeded due to a distinct pragmatism. The leading freemasons in New York at the time attempted to use the political and national links with the French, which the war had brought about, to paper over the gulf between them in terms of religion and worldview. In Geneva, the committed internationalist Townsend Scudder promised the delegates of the Grand Orient of France that he would intercede on behalf of the Grand Orient with the American grand lodges and even with the United Grand Lodge of England.[58] The leadership of the New York Grand Lodge did indeed encourage the English to show some "charity" to the French for the sake of the greater goal of "world reconstruction."[59] In doing this, the New Yorkers went considerably further than other US-Americans grand lodges were prepared to go. Other American grand lodges, such as that of the State of Georgia, revoked permission for its members to visit French lodges in 1919, claiming that from the onset it was intended as a temporary measure in the context of the war.[60]

While not even the political circumstances were able to improve bilateral relations between the United Grand Lodge and the Grand Orient, nonetheless, in 1921/1922 it appeared that masonic internationalism might become a joint venture of continental Europeans and US-Americans. Communication between the New Yorkers and the "Latin" bloc around the French and Belgian obediences strengthened. For example, in order to appeal to its 280,000 members, the Grand Lodge of New York wanted to have the suggestion of the Grand Orient of France – to encourage all freemasons to study the maintenance of peace – published in the bulletin of the A.M.I. Grand Orient's president Gérard praised the American "brothers" for this – in spite of their "confessional intransigence!"[61]

The New Yorkers sought to establish good relations with all the masonic camps, even the German-speaking freemasons, whom they could count on to respond positively. Shortly after the armistice had been signed, the German federation of Grand Lodges had called upon the English and American grand lodges in the name of "humanity" to come to the aid of the suffering German population.[62] The appeal was based on the idea of a "brotherly" connection with the "Anglo-Saxon" freemasonries that (so they claimed) continued to exist in spite of the temporary break in relations caused by the war – in contrast with relations with the umbrella associations of the Allied states of the "Latin" camp (France, Belgium and Italy). Thus, in December of 1921, the Frankfurt "Eklektischer Bund" responded positively to the offer of the New Yorkers to re-establish relations that had been dormant since the war, now that "peace has been concluded between

Germany and America."[63] New York wanted to raise this bilateral normalisation to the international level and encouraged the German grand lodges to join the A.M.I. To this end, a three-person delegation travelled around Germany in August of 1923. However, the Grand Lodge of Saxony and the "Eklektische Bund" could not consider joining the A.M.I. while the occupation of the Rhineland continued. At the quarterly meeting of the "Eklektische Bund" on 1 August 1923, Grand Master Heinrich Becker depicted the German people as victims of the war, the treaty conditions and the occupation, and he called on the American guests present to propagate this view internationally.[64]

However, disagreements recurred also in relations with the "Latin" freemasonries and with the transnational movement. One bone of contention led back to the Supreme Councils of the Ancient and Accepted (Scottish) Rite. Through the international networks of the Rite, the Americans had exerted pressure on the international relations networks of the grand orients and the grand lodges. They advocated for the permanent exclusion of the Supreme Councils of the Grand Orients of France and Italy from the international conferences of the Rite, as they had a fundamentally critical attitude towards the "grand orient" model (exerting authority both on the first three and the higher degrees of the Rite). Consequently, the Grand Lodge of New York demanded that the highest authorities for the lodges of the first three or basic degrees should be clearly separated from the Supreme Councils, which were – in accordance with the division of labour between the Supreme Council and the Grand Lodge of France – to administer only the higher degrees of the Rite. The Italians understood this separation as a prerequisite for the American grand lodges' establishing official relations with the continental European grand orients. The Grand Orient of Italy thus excluded the two Italian rites (the Symbolic Rite and the Ancient and Accepted Scottish Rite) from the administration of the Italian lodges, and was then able to exchange representatives with the New York Grand Lodge in April 1923. This step was preceded by mutual visits by leadership figures.[65]

In the same meeting, the New York lodge decided to join the A.M.I. as a full member. According to one attendee, the Italian Grand Master Domizio Torrigiani, the discussion revealed two main trends within American freemasonry. One preference was to keep "American action" independent of worldwide movements – particularly the European ones; others argued in favour of cooperation "with the other families of the world."[66] The accession of the New Yorkers, which they had left suspended for a year and a half, was thus highly controversial. At the end of the year, a decisive turn in transatlantic relations finally occurred. Both sides began to distance themselves from each other. In December 1923, the Grand Orient of France discussed relations with the USA. The religious tendency of the York Rite was viewed with general scepticism. It was described as running contrary to the demand of the Grand Orient for absolute freedom of conscience and as hindering the strengthening of connections. However, these connections had already deteriorated, as pointed out in the meeting. At the time, the Grand Orient only maintained official relations with five grand lodges in the USA (Alabama, Iowa, Minnesota, New Jersey and Rhode Island), but not with the Grand Lodge of New York. The latter was refusing to accept members of the Grand Orient as guests in its New York City lodges, as it claimed that the French lodge was infringing on its territorial sovereignty. The Grand Lodge of Louisiana had suspended relations in March 1921 for the same reason. And now a new territorial conflict was igniting with the Grand Lodge of New Jersey, which subsequently also broke off relations with the Grand Orient in 1925.[67]

Territorial disputes again became entangled with differences of opinion regarding religion and worldview. Prior to the Brussels Convention of the A.M.I. (25–27 September 1924), the Grand Lodge of New York announced that it was leaving the association because some of its members did not recognise the "ancient landmarks" of Freemasonry. This was primarily directed at the German "Masonic Federation The Rising Sun" (*Freimaurerbund zur aufgehenden Sonne*), which was branded as "irregular," but was also directed at the Grand Orient of France, which had supported the German group.[68] To underpin their rejection, the New Yorkers asked all member obediences of the A.M.I. whether their new members had to swear the reception oath before God, and whether the Bible was placed in front of the chairman.[69] Townsend Scudder, who as an internationalist by now was isolated in his grand lodge, stated in the A.M.I. that in the USA a mood had developed that was against the Association. According to Townsend, this sense of hostility was primarily fed by ignorance of conditions in France, but also by annoyance at the fact that the bulletin of the A.M.I. was no longer published in English (for financial reasons).[70]

The decision of the Grand Lodge of New York to leave was a heavy blow for international masonic cooperation.[71] From the German perspective, the fact that the Americans had separated "from international freemasonry" meant that they had split with the French and the Belgians (in 1925 Italian freemasonry was almost at an end anyway). However, the New Yorkers did not retreat into isolationism, but made "efforts to found an Anglo-German bloc of freemasonry" and had "severed its ties to international freemasonry."[72] They were not successful in this. The English Grand Lodge did not establish relations with German grand lodges until 1932 (and then only three of them). The hopes of the French to re-establish connections with the Americans failed as well.[73]

Conclusion: transatlantic relations and masonic internationalism

From the last third of the nineteenth century, bilateral relations between the masonic umbrella associations on both sides of the Atlantic received considerable impetus, particularly from international cooperation between the Supreme Councils. After the First World War, the re-emerging transnational movement benefited from encounters between French and American freemasons "in the trenches." The Grand Lodge of New York sought to utilise these convergences in its bilateral and multilateral relations with all of the camps within Freemasonry.

This re-orientation of the New York freemasons coincided with an increased focus on Europe in American politics; the "order rhetoric of Woodrow Wilson"[74] was echoed by the masonic rhetoric of a "world reconstruction." In the political controversy about the accession of the USA to the League of Nations, which never happened[75], one can hear echoes of the vacillating attitude of the Grand Lodge of New York towards the International Masonic Association. The ambivalence of the Americans regarding how much of a leading role they should adopt in Europe is visible in both spheres. However, the similarities between political relations between states and international masonic relations should not be overstated. Ultimately, they were governed by different rationales. Even before the First World War, transatlantic (US-American–European) masonic relations were already influenced by a combination of religious and ethical disagreements (for example, regarding the universality of human rights) and questions of territorial authority. The various actors emphasised one of these main differences or retracted it depending on the situation. From the First World War onward, the Americans and the Germans, just like the French and the Italians, engaged in the politicisation of masonic relations. The partial alliances between the American and the "Latin" European freemasonries – alliances that were primarily political in nature – were able to temporarily obscure the divides regarding religion. For the New York Grand Lodge, being a member of an international association that included bodies who did not respect the so-called "landmarks" of Freemasonry remained very problematic; in retrospect, its decision to leave the association is not surprising. Thus, over the longer term, it proved impossible to ignore the fundamental difference of views regarding the minimum religious requirements, especially as it became connected with the problem of territoriality again in the 1920s. In contrast, the question whether or not initiating "coloured" men to Freemasonry ceased to be a matter in dispute after the Great War.

Due to these ambivalences, the intensifying transatlantic relations between 1917 and 1923 were both an indicator and a pacesetter of globalisation within Freemasonry. Parallel to the European-North American encounters, Central and South American obediences entered into the A.M.I.[76] As a result of this – and particularly as a result of the (temporary) membership of the Grand Lodge of New York – the transnational movement of the obediences lost its exclusively "European" orientation. Of course, "America" did not become a "model" for the continental European freemasons;[77] the latter were too sure of their independence for this. Neither was the presence of American freemasons in Europe and in the international arenas so dominant that the diverging bodies of the old continent drew on "Europe" as a common reference point.[78] Rather, the ephemeral transatlantic fraternisations promoted among the leaderships of the European freemasonries a "[t]hinking in global terms,"[79] which sat well with their universalist utopia.

Notes

1. See generally Nolan, *Transatlantic Century*, here 23–25.
2. Es sei "im Interesse der auswandernden Brüder und ihrer Angehörigen," "mit einem Großoriente [sic] in Verbindung zu treten, der ihnen mit Rath und That beistehen und sich für sie im Nothfalle bei den dortigen Behörden unmittelbar und mittelbar durch einflußreiche Brüder verwenden kann." Printed report on the assembly of the Grande Loge Suisse "Alpina," Berne, 27–28 August 1864. Geheimes Staatsarchiv Preußischer Kulturbesitz, Berlin-Dahlem, Germany (hereafter GStAPK), Freimaurer, Bestand Großlogen und Protektor, 5.1.4., Große National-Mutterloge der Preußischen Staaten genannt "Zu den Drei Weltkugeln," No. 7652, fs. 87–97, quote on f. 88 of the report.
3. Große Mutterloge des eklektischen Freimaurerbundes (hereafter GMLEklBd), extraordinary meeting (Außerordentliche Versammlung), 5 February 1875. *Mittheilungen aus den Protokollen der Großen Mutterloge des eklektischen Freimaurerbundes zu Frankfurt am Main (1872–1878)*. Archives of the Lodge "Zur Einigkeit," Frankfurt/Main, Germany, Collection Große Mutterloge des eklektischen Freimaurerbunds zu Frankfurt/Main (hereafter LzE, GMLEklBd 5.1.9.), no. 385.
4. Note on capitalisation and the use of the singular or plural: I speak of "Freemasonry" when referring to the institution, its general organisational features and ideology, whereas the terms "freemasonry" resp. "freemasonries" denote specific branches with their peculiar shapes and characteristics (French, German, Latin, Christian etc. freemasonries).
5. On the "Atlantic masonic system" ("système maçonnique atlantique") see Beaurepaire, *Europe*, 90–99; Mollès, "Triangle atlantique."
6. See Paulmann, "Internationalismus," 182; following Friedemann and Hölscher, "Internationalismus," 392–397.

THE FRATERNAL ATLANTIC, 1770–1930   141

7. See, for example, Clavin, "Time, Manner, Place"; Pernau, *Transnationale Geschichte*; Rosenberg, "Transnationale Strömungen," 825–850.

8. Scholarship on Freemasonry, "largely encased in national (or subnational) frameworks" (Jansen, "Atlantic Sociability," 84), has for a long time neglected these movements. If at all, historians have treated these masonic movements by highlighting its "perceived failures" rather than its "actual activities" (Orzoff, "Interwar Democracy," 272). See Lubelski-Bernard, "Peace"; Combes, "Relations maçonniques I"; Combes, "Relations maçonniques II"; Combes, "Relations maçonniques III"; Martin, "Internacionalismo"; Martin, "Asociación Masónica Internacional"; Beaurepaire, *Europe*; Berger, "European Freemasonries." Like the contemporary masons they study, these scholars assess the attraction and impact of the movements by the masonic utopia of a universal brotherhood, the implementation of which was bound to fail (e.g. Conti, "Masonic International," 25: "the idea of gathering all the Masonic families from around the world into a single coordinating body in the name of universalism and a supposed commonality of values and ideal references was nothing but a vain chimera."). Furthermore, these studies contrast the national(ist) framing of the masonic actors with their universalist and cosmopolitan aspirations. However, research on non-masonic movements has shown that in actual fact nationalism was an ideological and organisational building block of internationalism. See Geyer and Paulmann, "Mechanics. Introduction," 7; Rosenberg, "Transnationale Strömungen," 826; Kott, "Organisations internationales," 14.

9. There is no comprehensive study of this multilateral network in the nineteenth and twentieth centuries from a pan-European or global perspective. For a systematic perspective see Snoek, "Relationships." Studies from national (English, French, and Belgian) perspectives are, among others, Daniel, *Networks*; Bauer and Rochigneux, *Relations internationales*; Maes, *Belges et Francs-Maçons*, 260–271.

10. On the League of Nations, see Herren, "Völkerbund," 273 ("Narrative des Scheiterns").

11. Harland-Jacobs, "World of Brothers," 13.

12. Laqua, "Transnational intellectual cooperation," 236; Harland-Jacobs, "World of Brothers," 23.

13. On the hiatus between cosmopolitan or universalist ideals and exclusive practices see Harland-Jacobs, *Empire,* 64–98; Berger, "Rituelle Grenzziehungen," 186–188.

14. Tyssens, "Nationalism," 463.

15. See Herren, *Internationale Organisationen*; Laqua, *Age of Internationalism*; Sluga, *Internationalism*.

16. See Gräser, "Model America," cit. section 23; Nolan, *Transatlantic Century*, 10.

17. Nolan, *Transatlantic Century*, 52.

18. These are the United Grand Lodge of England, the Grand Orient of France, the Grand Orient of Italy and the German Confederation of Grand Lodges with two of its member bodies – the "Grand Mother Lodge of the Eclectic Masonic Federation" (Große Mutterloge des Eklektischen Freimaurerbundes) based in Frankfurt on the Main and the large "Grand National Mother Lodge of the Prussian States, called 'The Three Globes'" (Große National-Mutterloge der Preußischen Staaten, genannt "Zu den drei Weltkugeln") with headquarters in Berlin.

19. The freemasonries of Central and South America with their characteristics (anticlericalism, free-thinking, political engagement) cannot be dealt with here. See Mollès, "Libre-pensée."

20. Although David Armitage labels his concept of "Trans-Atlantic history" an "international history of the Atlantic world," he confines it to a "history of the Atlantic world told through comparisons" (Armitage, "Atlantic History," 15, 18). On his "Trans-Atlantic" approach see Jansen, "Atlantic Sociability," 89; Games, "Atlantic History," 746.

21. *Compte-rendu congrès Paris 1855*, 11–12.

22. Grand Orient de France (hereafter GODF), "Fête de l'Ordre," 15 June 1867. *Bulletin du Grand Orient de France* (hereafter *BullGODF*) 23 nos. 4–6 (1867): 275–279. The Grand Lodges of California, North Carolina, Kentucky, Massachusetts and New York had themselves represented by individual members.

23. See Centre de Documentation Maçonnique du Grand Orient de Belgique, Brussels, Belgium, "Archives de Moscou" belges (hereafter CEDOM, AdM), 114–1–0079: fs. 84–85.

24. See Naudon, *Hauts grades*, 180–193; Viton, *R.E.A.A.*, 39–45.

25. *Transactions Conference Washington 1912*, 5–6. In the case of Italy and France, it was the two independent Supreme Councils – competing with those under the roof of the resp. Grand Orients – that were present in Washington. The Italian Supremo Consiglio under Saverio Fera had separated from the Grand Orient of Italy in 1908. See Cordova, *1892–1908*, 241–242, 286–293, and Conti, *Massoneria italiana*, 178–194.

26. Herren, *Internationale Organisationen*, 39.

27. See Viton, *R.E.A.A.*, 46; Mandleberg, *Ancient and accepted*, 261.

28. *Compte-rendu congrès Paris 1855*, 43–47, 67, quote from page 44.

29. See, for example, the discussion in the Council of the Order (Conseil de l'Ordre): *BullGODF* 25, no. 5 (1869): 267–269.

30. See Mollès, "Triangle atlantique."

31. Grande Oriente d'Italia (hereafter GOI), Seduta, 19 May 1877. *Processi Verbali delle sedute del Grande Oriente d'Italia* 2, no. 1 (1865–1879). GOI, Archivio Storico, Rome, Italy (hereafter GOI, *Processi Verbali*); GOI, Seduta, 6 April 1881. GOI, *Processi Verbali* 2, no. 2 (1879–1887); GOI, Consiglio, 17 October 1897. GOI, *Processi Verbali* 1, no. 3 (1887–1904): f. C 110–110'; GOI, Consiglio, 20 April 1901. *Processi Verbali* 1, no. 3 (1887–1904): f. C 200'.

32. Circular letter of the German Confederation of Grand Lodges (with extracts from annual report of the Grand Lodge of Hamburg 1907–1907), 22 January 1908. *Mitteilungen des Deutschen Grosslogenbundes* No. 4 (1907–1908). 2

33. See, for example, the minutes of the diet of the German Confederation of Grand Lodges in Bayreuth, 6 July 1908. *Mitteilungen des Deutschen Grosslogenbundes* No. 1 (1908–1909); circular letter of the German Confederation of Grand Lodges (with extracts from annual report of the Grand Lodge of Hamburg 1911–1912), 24 December 1912. *Mitteilungen des Deutschen Grosslogenbundes* No. 2 (1912–1913).

34. United Grand Lodge of England (hereafter UGLE), Quarterly Communications, 7 June 1871. *Proceedings of the United Grand Lodge of Ancient Free and Accepted Masons of England* (1869–1876): 2 (hereafter UGLE, *Proceedings*). UGLE, The Library and Museum of Freemasonry, Freemasons' Hall, London, UK (hereafter UGLE, FHL), BE.140.Uni.

35. Quoted in Daniel, *Networks*, 115. On Ripon's mission see ibid., 106–17, 153.

36. See Harland-Jacobs, *Empire*, 80–81, 219–220, 232–239.

37. See Ligou, *Desmons*, 95–112; Daniel, *Networks*, 274–275.

38. See Conti, "Masonic International," 17; Hivert-Messeca, *Europe*.

39. "[…] dass wir wenig gemeinsame Interessen haben mit der Maurerei, wie sie auf dem europäischen Continent organisiert ist." Circular letter of the German Confederation of Grand Lodges (with extract from minutes of US-American grand lodges, here Grand Lodge of Arkansas, 14 January 1879), 25 March 1880. LzE, GMLEklBd, 5.1.9., no. 585.

40. See Berger, "Territoriality," 102–103.

41. GODF, Conseil, 20 January 1890. *BullGODF* 45, no. 11 (1889–1890): 547.

42. GODF, Conseil, 3 December 1900. *BullGODF* 56, no. 5 (1900–1901): 41.

43. *Conférence Anvers 1894*, 7–8; Grand Lodge of Florida, certificate of authority for James Veit, Jacksonville, 21 April 1894. CEDOM, AdM, 114-1-0213: f. 33.

44. *Compte-rendu congrès Genève 1902*; *Compte-rendu congrès Bruxelles 1904*.

45. Quartier-la-Tente, Edouard to GODF (Conseil). Neuchâtel, 25 March 1905 and 2 December 1907. Bibliothèque nationale de France, Paris, France (hereafter BnF), Manuscrits Occidentaux, Fonds maçonnique, Rés. FM2 154 (BIRM/2). On the transatlantic objectives of the International Bureau see Mollès, "Le système-monde maçonnique," 18.

46. *Compte-rendu conférence Bruxelles 1910*, 50–51, 76.

47. Ibid., 130, 179–181.

48. *Transactions Conference Brussels 1907*; *Transactions Conference Washington 1912*.

49. See the survey of donations to the International Bureau of Masonic Relations, 1906–1919 (n.d., unpag.). BnF, Manuscrits Occidentaux, Rés. FM2 154 (BIRM/2).

50. This reports the semi-offical *Rivista Massonica* (Pegasus, "America ed Europa"); it is confirmed for the Grand Lodge of New York by its Grand Master (Robert H. Robinson), quoted in: Scudder,

THE FRATERNAL ATLANTIC, 1770–1930   143

Townsend to Alfred Robbins. New York, 16 February 1922. UGLE, FHL, In Archives Store, AS BY 362/5, Bundle "International Relations."

51. *Conférence Paris 1917*, 71–72; *Congrès Paris 1917*, 6, 46. See Beaurepaire, *Europe*, 250.

52. See the discussion in the General Assembly of the GODF, 20 September 1918. *BullGODF* 74 (1918): 140–141.

53. Alabama: GODF, Conseil, 8 March 1918. *BullGODF* 74 (1918): 24; GODF, Conseil, 28 January 1919. *BullGODF* 75 (1919): 38. Louisiana: GODF, Conseil, 30 March 1918. *BullGODF* 74 (1918), 28. Iowa, California, New Jersey and Nevada: GODF, Conseil, 21 August 1918. Ibid., 23; GODF, Conseil, 16 October 1918. Ibid., 36,

54. Hervey, Rhodes (Grand Master of the Grand Lodge of California) to UGLE (Grand Secretary). Los Angeles, 22 July 1918. UGLE, FHL, Historical Correspondence in Biog Room (Grand Orient de France), Box 5.

55. GODF, Assemblée générale, 20 September 1918. *BullGODF* 74 (1918): 140–141. "une sorte de Comité permanent": GODF, Conseil, 20 September 1918. Ibid., 34.

56. UGLE, Especial Grand Lodge, 23 June 1917, Royal Albert Hall, London. *UGLE Proceedings* 16 (1916–1918): 179–209; UGLE, Especial Grand Lodge, 27 June 1919, Royal Albert Hall, London. *UGLE Proceedings* 17 (1919–1921): 45–71.

57. See, for instance, Nolan, *Transatlantic Century*, 74; Ellwood, "'America' and Europe," 426–427. For the "sea and field lodges" see Hivert-Messeca, *Grande Guerre*, 188–191.

58. GODF, Conseil, 7 November 1921. *BullGODF* 77 (1921): 31–32.

59. Robinson, quoted in Scudder to Robbins, 16 February 1922 (see above note 50).

60. Daniel, *Peace celebrations*, 8–13.

61. "intransigeance confessionnelle!" GODF, Assemblée générale, 22 September 1922. *BullGODF* 78 (1922): 53.

62. See the "Funkspruch" (radio transmission) of the Deutsche Großlogenbund to UGLE and the grand lodges of the USA, printed in: Süß, "An die deutschen Freimaurer!"

63. "[…] nachdem nun 'Friede zwischen Deutschland und Amerika geschlossen' worden sei." GMLEklBd, Vierteljahresversammlung, 28 November 1921. LzE, GMLEklBd, 5.1.9. with No. 64–75 (special file, Heinrich Becker papers).

64. LzE, GMLEklBd, 5.1.9., no. 593: fs. 7–13; GMLEklBd, Vierteljahresversammlung, 21 November 1923. LzE, GMLEklBd, 5.1.9. with no. 64–75 (special file, Heinrich Becker papers). Relations had only been suspended during the war (rather than broken off). See the membership roles of the GMLEklBd (varying titles) in: LzE, Collection Loge "Zur Einigkeit," Frankfurt/M., 5.2.

65. GOI, Governo dell'ordine, 2 July 1922. GOI, *Processi Verbali* 2, no. 14 (1921–1923); GOI, Giunta esecutiva, 16 November 1922. Ibid.; GOI, Giunta esecutiva, 21 June 1923. Ibid.; GOI, Governo dell'ordine, 7 October 1923. GOI, *Processi Verbali* 2, no. 15 (1923–1925).

66. "azione americana," "con le altre Famiglie del mondo." GOI, Giunta esecutiva, 21 June 1923. GOI, *Processi Verbali* 2, no. 14 (1921–1923).

67. GODF, Conseil, 16 December 1923. *BullGODF* 80 (1923/24): 53–56; GODF, Conseil, 26 May. *BullGODF* 82 (1925): 36.

68. GODF, Conseil, 14 December 1924. *BullGODF* 81 (1924/25): 45; GOI, Conseil, 22 September 1922. *BullGODF* 80 (1923/24): 10.

69. GODF, Conseil, 18 February 1925 (minutes of the "Comité consultatif" of the A.M.I., Lyon, 7 December 1925). *BullGODF* 82 (1925): 27.

70. Minutes of the financial commission of the A.M.I., 24 September 1924. GODF, Archives, Paris, France, Fonds russes, 92–1–13658: fs. 1–3.

71. See Beaurepaire, *Europe*, 257.

72. The Grand Lodge of New York was "bestrebt, einen anglo-germanischen Block der Freimaurerei zu gründen" (GMLEklBd, Vierteljahresversammlung, 31 August 1925. LzE, GMLEklBd, 5.1.9. with no. 64–75, special file, Heinrich Becker papers) and "hat sich von der internationalen Freimaurerei getrennt." (GMLEklBd, Vierteljahresversammlung, 25 November 1925. Ibid.).

73. GODF, Conseil, 3 February 1926. *BullGODF* 83 (1926): 2.

74. Osterhammel, "Weltordnungskonzepte," 426 ("Ordnungsrhetorik Woodrow Wilsons").

75. See. Nolan, *Transatlantic Century*, 74–75.

76. From 1922 to 1932, 20 obediences from Central and South America became members of the A.M.I.; three of them resigned from it or were excluded during that period. See Beaurepaire, *Europe*, 255.
77. Gräser, "Model America," section 2.
78. Nolan, *Transatlantic Century*, 103, states that after 1918 "Europe" became a "frame of reference" for political, economic and social challenges of the day.
79. Harland-Jacobs, "Global Brotherhood," 81.

Acknowledgements

Archival research for this article was facilitated by a Gerald D. Feldman Travel Grant of the Max Weber Foundation, Bonn, Germany. The author wishes to thank Jessica Harland-Jacobs (University of Florida) and Jan C. Jansen (GHI Washington) as well as the anonymous reviewers for *Atlantic Studies* for their stimulating suggestions and constructive criticism.

Disclosure statement

No potential conflict of interest was reported by the author.

ORCID

Joachim Berger ⓘD http://orcid.org/0000-0002-4809-9033

Bibliography

Antic, Ana, Johanna Conterio, and Dora Vargha. "Conclusion: Beyond Liberal Internationalism." *Contemporary European History* 25, no. 2 (2016): 359–371.
Armitage, David. "Three Concepts of Atlantic History." In *The British Atlantic World, 1500–1800*, edited by David Armitage, and Michael J. Braddick, 11–27. New York: Palgrave Macmillan, 2002.
Bauer, Alain, and Jean-Claude Rochigneux. *Les relations internationales de la franc-maçonnerie française*. Paris: Colin, 2010.
Beaurepaire, Pierre-Yves. *L'Europe des francs-maçons. XVIIIᵉ–XXIᵉ siècles*. Paris: Belin, 2002.
Berger, Joachim. "European Freemasonries, 1850–1935: Networks and Transnational Movements." In *EGO Europäische Geschichte Online= European History Online*, edited by the Institute of European History (IEG). Mainz: Inst. f. Europ. Geschichte, 2010-12-03. Accessed 10 January 2019. http://www. ieg-ego.eu/bergerj-2010-en, urn:nbn:de:0159–20100921522.
Berger, Joachim. "Regimes of Territoriality: Overseas Conflicts and Inner-European Relations, c. 1870–1930." *Journal for Research Into Freemasonry and Fraternalism* 5, no. 1 (2014): 101–115.
Berger, Joachim. "'une institution cosmopolite'? Rituelle Grenzziehungen im freimaurerischen Internationalismus um 1900." In *Bessere Welten. Kosmopolitismus in den Geschichtswissenschaften*, edited by Bernhard Gißibl, and Isabella Löhr, 167–192. Frankfurt/Main: Campus, 2017.
Bulletin de l'Association maçonnique internationale. Genève: Ed. Quartier-la-Tente / J. Mossaz 1922–1939.

THE FRATERNAL ATLANTIC, 1770–1930   145

Bulletin du Bureau international de relations maçonniques. Neuchâtel, 1903–1905.

Bulletin. Organe officiel du Bureau international de relations maçonnique dévoué à la franc-maçonnerie universelle. Neuchâtel, 1906–1921.

Bulletin [trimestriel] du Grand Orient de France. Paris, 1846–1932.

Clavin, Patricia. "Time, Manner, Place: Writing Modern European History in Global, Transnational and International Contexts." *European History Quarterly* 40, no. 4 (2010): 624–640.

Coclanis, Peter A. "Atlantic World or Atlantic/World?" *William and Mary Quarterly* 63, no. 4 (2006): 725–742.

Combes, André. "Les relations maçonniques (1877–1940)." *Humanisme* 214–215 (1994): 85–96.

Combes, André. "Les relations maçonniques internationales (2) (1877–1940)." *Humanisme* 216 (1994): 95–101.

Combes, André. "Les relations maçonniques internationales 1877–1940. 3e partie: les années 1925–1935." *Humanisme* 217/218 (1994): 75–89.

Compte-rendu du congrès maçonnique universel, réuni à l'Orient de Paris en Juin 1855, par décret de Son Altesse Royale le Prince Lucien Murat, Grand-Maître de l'Ordre Maçonnique en France. Paris: Lebon, 1856.

Conférence des Maçonneries des Nations Alliées. 14–15 janvier 1917. Paris: Ch. Renaudie, 1917.

Conférence maçonnique internationale de 1910 à Bruxelles. Compte rendu des séances les 9, 10 et 11 septembre. Brussels: Guyot, 1912.

Conférence maçonnique universelle d'Anvers du 21e au 24e jour du 5e mois 5894 (21 au 24 juillet 1894). Brussels: Weissenbruch, 1894.

Congrès des Maçonneries des Nations alliées et neutres les 28, 29 et 30 juin 1917. Paris: Impr. de A. Mangeot, 1917.

Congrès maç. international 1904 à Bruxelles: Compte rendu des séances du congrès du samedi 27 au mardi 30 Aout 1904. Berne: Büchler, 1905.

Congrès maç. international de 1902 à Genève: Compte rendu des séances du congrès. Les 5, 6 et 7 septembre 1902. Berne: Büchler, 1902.

Conti, Fulvio. "The Masonic International and the Peace Movement in the Nineteenth and Twentieth Centuries." In *Reconsidering Peace and Patriotism during the First World War*, edited by Justin Quinn Olmstead, 15–30. Cham: Springer International Publishing, 2017.

Conti, Fulvio. *Storia della massoneria italiana: Dal Risorgimento al fascismo.* Bologna: Soc. Ed. il Mulino, 2003.

Cordova, Ferdinando. *Massoneria e politica in Italia 1892–1908.* Rome: Laterza, 1985.

Daniel, James W. *Masonic Networks & Connections.* London: Library and Museum of Freemasonry, 2007.

Daniel, Raymond. *The Peace Celebrations of the Grand Lodge of England: With Reports on Masonic Conditions in France.* Macon, GA, 1919.

Ellwood, David W. "'America' and Europe, 1914–1945." In *The Oxford Handbook of European History, 1914–1945*, edited by Nicholas Doumanis, 423–439. Oxford: Oxford University Press, 2016.

Friedemann, Peter, and Lucian Hölscher. "International, Internationale, Internationalimus." In *Geschichtliche Grundbegriffe: Historisches Lexikon zur politisch-sozialen Sprache in Deutschland*, edited by Otto Brunner, Werner Conze, and Reinhart Koselleck, Vol. 3, 367–397. Stuttgart: Klett-Cotta, 1982.

Games, Alison. "Atlantic History: Definitions, Challenges, and Opportunities." *American Historical Review* 111, no. 3 (2006): 741–757.

Geyer, Martin H., and Johannes Paulmann. "Introduction: The Mechanics of Internationalism." In *The Mechanics of Internationalism: Culture, Society, and Politics from the 1840s to the First World War*, edited by Martin H. Geyer, and Johannes Paulmann, 1–25. Oxford: Oxford University Press, 2001.

Gräser, Marcus. "Model America." In *EGO Europäische Geschichte Online = European History Online*, edited by the Institute of European History (IEG). Mainz: Inst. f. Europ. Geschichte, 2011-02-08. Accessed 10 January 2019. http://www.ieg-ego.eu/graeserm-2010-en, urn:nbn:de:0159-20101025397.

Harland-Jacobs, Jessica. *Builders of Empire: Freemasons and British Imperialism, 1717–1927.* Chapel Hill: University of North Carolina Press, 2007.

Harland-Jacobs, Jessica. "Global Brotherhood: Freemasonry, Empires, and Globalization." *Revista de Estudios Históricos de la Masonería Latinoamericana y Caribeña* Special Issue (October 2013): 73–88. http://revistas.ucr.ac.cr/index.php/rehmlac/article/view/22543/22685. Accessed 10 January 2019.

Harland-Jacobs, Jessica. "Worlds of Brothers." *Journal for Research into Freemasonry and Fraternalism* 2, no. 1 (2011): 10–37.

Herren, Madeleine. *Internationale Organisationen seit 1865: Eine Globalgeschichte der internationalen Ordnung*. Darmstadt: Wissenschaftliche Buchgesellschaft, 2009.

Herren, Madeleine. "Der Völkerbund – Erinnerung an ein globales Europa." In *Europäische Erinnerungsorte*, edited by Pim den Boer, Heinz Duchhardt, Georg Kreis, and Wolfgang Schmale, Vol. 3, 271–280. Munich: Oldenbourg, 2012.

Hivert-Messeca, Yves. *L'Europe sous l'Acacia: Histoire des franc-maçonneries européennes du XVIIIe siècle à nos jours, Vol. 2: Le XIXe siècle. Le temps des nationalités et de la liberté*. Paris: Dervy, 2014.

Hivert-Messeca, Yves. *Hiram et Bellone: Les francs-maçons dans la Grande Guerre (1914–1918)*. Paris: Dervy, 2016.

Jansen, Jan C. "In Search of Atlantic Sociability: Freemasons, Empires, and Atlantic History." *Bulletin of the German Historical Institute Washington* 57, no. 2 (2015): 75–99. http://www.ghi-dc.org/files/publications/bulletin/bu057/bu057_075.pdf. Accessed 10 January 2019.

Kott, Sandrine. "Les organisations internationales, terrains d'étude de la globalisation." *Critique internationale* 52, no. 3 (2011): 9–16.

Laqua, Daniel. *The Age of Internationalism and Belgium, 1880–1930: Peace, Progress and Prestige*. Manchester: Manchester University Press, 2013.

Laqua, Daniel. "Transnational Intellectual Cooperation, the League of Nations, and the Problem of Order." *Journal of Global History* 6, no. 2 (2011): 223–247.

Ligou, Daniel. *Frédéric Desmons et la franc-maçonnerie sous la IIIe République*. 2nd ed. Saint-Martin-de-Bonfossé: Théolib, 2012.

Lubelski-Bernard, Nadine. "Freemasonry and Peace in Europe, 1867–1914." In *Peace Movements and Political Cultures*, edited by Charles Chatfield, and Peter van den Dungen, 81–94. Knoxville: University of Tennessee Press, 1988.

Maes, Anaïs. *Flamands? Wallons? Belges et Francs-Maçons! La franc-maçonnerie et la construction d'identités nationales au long XIXe siècle*. Brüssel: ASP, 2015.

Mandleberg, John. *Ancient and Accepted: A Chronicle of the Proceedings 1845–1945 of the Supreme Council established in England in 1845*. London: Q.C. Correspondence Circle, 1995.

Martin, Luis P. "El internacionalismo masónico: Génesis y conflictos (1895–1920)." In *La masonería española entre Europa y America*, edited by José Antonio Ferrer Benimeli, 351–365. Zaragoza: Gobierno de Aragón, 1995.

Martin, Luis P. "La Asociación Masónica Internacional (1921–1940) o la utopía pacifista." In *La masonería en la España del siglo XX*, edited by José Antonio Ferrer Benimeli, Vol. 1, 457–469. Toledo: Univ de Castilla La Mancha, 1996.

Mollès, Devrig. "L'Eldorado de la libre-pensée? L'Amérique latine comme objectif stratégique de la Fédération Internationale de la Libre Pensée (1880–1914)." *Revista de Estudios Históricos de la Masonería Latinoamericana y Caribeña* 7, no. 1 (2015): 17–36. http://revistas.ucr.ac.cr/index.php/rehmlac/article/view/19935. Accessed 10 January 2019.

Mollès, Devrig. "Le "Triangle atlantique": Emergence et expansion de la sphère maçonnique internationale: Une analyse statistique (1717–1914)." *Nuevo Mundo Mundos Nuevos, Débats* (2014). http://journals.openedition.org/nuevomundo/67498. Accessed 10 January 2019.

Mollès, Devrig. "Le système-monde maçonnique à la veille de la Première Guerre mondiale: Une analyse archéologique." *Revista de Estudios Históricos de la Masonería Latinoamericana y Caribeña* 6, no. 2 (2014–2015): 15–32. http://revistas.ucr.ac.cr/index.php/rehmlac/article/view/18196. Accessed 10 January 2019.

Naudon, Paul. *Histoire, rituels et tuileur des hauts grades maçonniques: Le Rite Écossais Ancien et Accepté*. 5th ed. Paris: Dervy, 1993.

Nolan, Mary. *The transatlantic century: Europe and America, 1890–2010*. Cambridge: Cambridge University Press, 2012.

Orzoff, Andrea. "Interwar Democracy and the League of Nations." In *The Oxford Handbook of European History, 1914–1945*, edited by Nicholas Doumanis, 261–281. Oxford: Oxford University Press, 2016.

Osterhammel, Jürgen. "Weltordnungskonzepte." In *Dimensionen internationaler Geschichte*, edited by Jost Dülffer, and Wilfried Loth, 409–427. Munich: Oldenbourg, 2012.

Paulmann, Johannes. "Reformer, Experten und Diplomaten: Grundlagen des Internationalismus im 19. Jahrhundert." In *Akteure der Außenbeziehungen: Netzwerke und Interkulturalität im historischen Wandel*, edited by Hillard von Thiessen, and Christian Windler, 173–197. Cologne: Böhlau, 2010.

Pegasus. "America ed Europa." *Rivista Massonica* 52, no. 8–9 (1921): 201–202.

Pernau, Margrit. *Transnationale Geschichte*. Göttingen: Vandenhoeck & Ruprecht, 2011.

Rosenberg, Emily S. "Transnationale Strömungen in einer Welt, die zusammenrückt." In *1870–1945: Weltmärkte und Weltkriege*, edited by Emily S. Rosenberg, 815–998, 1063–1078. München: Beck, 2012.

Sluga, Glenda. *Internationalism in the Age of Nationalism*. Philadelphia: University of Pennsylvania Press, 2013.

Snoek, Jan A. M. "Relationships between Grand Lodges." In *Handbook of Freemasonry*, edited by Henrik Bogdan, and Jan A.M. Snoek, 378–386. Leiden: Brill, 2014.

Süß, Wilhelm. "An die deutschen Freimaurer!." *Die Leuchte* 9, no. 12 (1918): 115.

Transactions of the International conference of the supreme councils of the 33rd and last degree of the rite held in Brussels from the 10th to the 15th of June 1907. Brussels: M. Weissenbruch, 1908.

Transactions of the Second International Conference of Supreme Councils, 33, Washington, D. C. 1912. Washington, D.C., 1912.

Tyssens, Jeffrey. "Freemasonry and Nationalism." In *Handbook of Freemasonry*, edited by Henrik Bogdan, and Jan A.M. Snoek, 461–472. Leiden: Brill, 2014.

Viton, Yves-Max. *Le rite écossais ancien et accepté*. Paris: Presses Universitaires de France, 2012.

Index

Note: *Italic* page numbers refer to figures and page numbers followed by "n" denote endnotes.

Adams, John 54, 87, 91, 93, 97
admittance of "coloured men" 133
Affiches américaines 71
African American freemasons 135
African American Masons 101
Agulhon, Maurice 74, 78
Ahiman Rezon 19, 22, 28–30, 32
"Alpina" 130, 135
American Freemasonry 17, 89, 92, 97, 100, 101, 113, 118, 123, 125
American German Freemasons 117
American lodges 120
American Masonic universalism 125
American Revolution 5, 7, 16, 19, 44, 45, 115, 125
American umbrella associations 130
American War of Independence 6
Americas: refugees and refugee lodges in 45–47
Ancient and Accepted Scottish Rite (A.A.S.R.) 118, 132, 138
Ancient Freemasonry 92, 98
Ancient Grand Lodge in London 19
Ancient Masonic expansion 19
Ancient Masons 19, 92, 96, 98
Anderson, James 2, 18
Anglo-American 133, 134, 136; race in 134
Anglo-British Atlantic Freemasonry 46
Anglo-Saxon race 133, 134
antagonism 31, 111, 114
antebellum period 112, 115
anti-clericalism 94
"anti-episcopacy" 103n27
antimasonry 16, 36
Armitage, David 88, 89, 141n20
Arthaud, Charles 71
"associational revolution" 4, 44
Association Maçonnique Internationale (A.M.I.) 137–140, 144n76
Atlantic exile diasporas 45
Atlantic French Freemasonry 49

Atlantic political culture 5
Atlantic revolutionary history 43–44
Atlantic world: eighteenth-century 15, 16, 24, 44, 51, 89, 98; fraternal associations in 1, 2, 19; freemasonries 7, 8, 48; freemasons around 8; international history of 141n20; masonic fraternalism 8, 67; political cultures of 3; post-revolutionary 3, 56; revolutionary period in 3, 45; shaped by fraternalism 3; social networks 4, 5; transatlantic salon 47
avant-garde or gravedigger: of transnational movements 137–139

Bainet: signatures from parish 75–80
Baltimore based refugee lodge 51
Barronnet, Pierre Louis 80
Barruel, Abbé 74, 91, 93
Barthelmess, Johann 122, 123
Baudry de Lozières, Louis-Narcisse 71
Beaurepaire, Pierre-Yves 44–45, 72
Becker, Heinrich 138
Before Haiti (Garrigus) 81
Belair, Charles 72
Belair, François 73
Belcher, Jonathan 20
Bell, David G. 17, 22, 25, 26
Bell, Madison Smartt 68
Benimeli, Ferrer 81n3
Berger, Joachim 6, 7
Bingham, Anne 54
black Atlantic freemasonry 7
black Mason 96, 101
Bolívar, Simón 81n3
Bonnet, Guy-Joseph 73
Bord, Gustave 74, 80
Borgella, Jérôme Maximilien 73
Bourdett, Oliver 31
Boyer, Jean-Pierre 4, 8, 55, 72–73, 77, 88–90, 92, 100; arrival in Norwich 88, 89, 95, 101; in Connecticut 6; foreign Masonry delivery

150 INDEX

98; higher degree systems 90, 98; Masonic effects 97
British Atlantic World 19, 24, 26, 28, 90
British freemasonry 16, 17–22, *21*, 33
British freemasons 15, 33–34
British-French schism 134
British Grand Lodges 15, 32
British North America: cosmopolitan fraternity 15; freemasonry 16, 17–22, *21*; Hiram Lodge No. 17 16, 17, 24, 26, 27; loyalist Masons 17–22, *21*; Masonic lodges in 16; political conflict 22–25
Brooke, John L. 92
brotherhood 1–2, 4, 5; Anglo-American 136; cosmopolitan 8; freemasons 8, 48, 135; masonic 17, 67, 116
Brussels conference in 1910 135
Brussels Convention of the A.M.I. 139
Buck-Morss, Susan 68
Bulkeley, Eliphalet 88, 90, 95, 97–99
Bullock, Stephen C. 17
Bullock, Steven 96
Bunting, William Franklin 17, 26, 30, 35

Campbell, William 22, 27
Cangé, Pierre Louis 79–81; signatures of *79, 80*
Cap-Français 48, 49, 52, 56
Carleton, Guy 23
Carleton, Thomas 24, 25
Caulkins, Frances Manwaring 88, 97
de Cauna, Jacques 68, 100
Cercle des Philadelphes 71
Certificate Laws 94
CFC *see* Committee of Foreign Correspondence (CFC)
Champion, Henry 98
charity: refugee lodges 51, 52
Choix des Hommes 77, 78
Christophe, Henry 73, 83n44
"cis-Atlantic" model 16, 88–89
Clark, Peter 4
Colonialism and Science (McClellan) 81n2
Combes, André 71, 72
Committee of Foreign Correspondence (CFC) 121–123, 127n42
congregationalism 91, 94, 103n27
"Congrès universel" 132
Connecticut: Atlantic dimensions of 4, 92; Federalists in 89, 91, 92, 94, 95, 97, 101, 102; Freemasonry in 93, 98, 103n27; grand lodge control in 102; masons 90, 91, 96
Connecticut Abolition Society 100
constitutionalism 32
The Constitutions of the Free-Mason (Anderson) 2
Cornwallis, Edward 19, 23
cosmopolitan fraternalism 3, 8, 48

cosmopolitanism 6, 16, 18, 19, 22, 34, 90, 93, 99, 101, 102; *see also* masonic cosmopolitanism
Craft 92, 95, 98, 100
"Craft Masonry" 132
Cross, Jeremy 102
cross-regional integration 44
Cuba: Freemasons in 47, 51; lodges in 54
Cuthbirt, James 22

decision-making process: of GLNY 115
Delahogue, Jean Baptiste Marie 93
Depas Medina, Jean-Louis 75, 79, 81; signatures of *76*
Dermott, Laurence 19
Desclaux 73
Descombaz, Gabriel 52, 53
Dessalines, Jean-Jacques 73
"diasporic freemasonry" 7
diasporic situation: of Saint-Domingue refugees 43–45, 49–51, 53–56
Dickinson, Tertullus 22
Dieudonné, Louis 73
Dixon, Francis M. 27
duc de la Rochefoucauld-Liancourt, François Alexandre Frédéric 47
Duke of Kent 35
Duke of Sussex 35
Dun, James Alexander 89
DuPeyrat, Bernard Guionnet 78
DuPeyrat, Pierre 78
Dwight, Timothy 91, 93

Eamon, Michael 16
Earl of Ripon 133, 134
eastern Connecticut: Freemasonry in 90, 93; Masons in 97, 98, 100
Efford, Alison Clark 112, 126n5
eighteenth-century Atlantic world 4, 44, 47, 51, 98
"Eklektischer Bund" 137, 138
emancipation 5, 6, 49–51, 90, 100, 101, 123, 134
émigré Freemasons 72
émigré reformers 114
English Grand Lodge 136, 139
The English lodge of Les Cayes 69
Escalle, Elisabeth 72
"escape clause" 22
European freemasonries 131, 132
European Freemasonry 54, 114, 123–124
European masonic bodies 135
European masonic umbrella associations 130
European migrants 44–45
"European" orientation 140
European schism 134
exclusive jurisdiction 6
exclusive territorial jurisdiction 114, 121

INDEX

fault lines 132–133
Federalists 89, 91, 92, 94, 95, 97, 101, 102
First World War 8, 131–132, 135, 139, 140
Foäche, Martin 70
Ford, Matthias 52, 53
formalism 124
Forty-Eighters, German 111–113, 117–119
France: Masonic authorities in 72; ritual system in 132
Franklin, Benjamin 2
fraternal associations and networks 2
"fraternal intercourse" 136
fraternalism 1, 3
fraternal organizations 3
fraternal web 90
fraternity 18
Frederick II 73
"freedom papers" 44
Freemasonic hypothesis 68
freemasonries 2–3, 6, 7–8, 26, 47–48, 90, 131, 134, 136; in the British Empire 5; with Catholicism 44; degree of elasticity 56; in eastern Connecticut 90, 93; elasticity of 19; free men of color and 71–74; in German 121; growth of 7; Haitian Revolution 48; "landmarks" of 140; in Louisiana 52; open membership 92; proliferation of 8; refugee lodges in action 48–55; revolutionary turmoil and displacement 43; in Saint-Domingue 69–71; Saint-Domingue refugees 44; scholarship on 141n8; transcendental basis of 134; transition in 26–33, 29; in United States 97; see also British freemasonry
freemasons 2, 16, 30; brotherhood 8; in Saint John 22–26; in United States 6; in US armed forces 135
free men of color: Saint-Domingue 71–74
French Atlantic Freemasonry 52, 56
French colonial Freemasonry 69, 71
French colonial trade policies 49
French Enlightenment 42
French Freemasonry 49, 69, 74, 94–95, 100
"frenchness" 97
French obediences 135
French refugee 52, 53, 55
French Revolution: refugees of 42
French ritual systems 46
French-speaking lodge: Philadelphia 42–43
French-speaking lodges 42–43, 46, 49, 50
"Frères Choisis" lodge 83n57
Funel de Séranon, Pierre-Joseph-Jean-Baptiste-Antoine 77, 78, 80; signatures of 79
Furstenberg, François 47

Garrigue, Rudolph 124
Garrigus, John D. 5–7
Gauvain, Pierre 50, 52

Genet, Edmond-Charles 91
Geneva Congress (1921) 137
Gérard 137
German American Freemasonry 114
German American Freemasons 112, 114
German-American Masonic relations: affiliation with GLH 115–116; German Forty-Eighters 111–113; German-speaking lodges 113–115; Pythagoras No. 1 vs. No. 86 117–119; racial segregation 119–123; secession from GLNY 115–116; territorial jurisdiction 116–117; trans-Atlantic Masonic communications 123–125
German émigrés 112, 113, 116, 119, 123, 125, 128n66
German Forty-Eighters 111–113, 117–119
German Freemasons 113, 115, 118, 123, 125; in New York 115
German-ness or "Deutschtum" 125
German-speaking lodges 5, 119, 130; in New York 113–115
German-US antagonism 124
Gervais, Charles Nicholas Donatien 50
GLH see Grand Lodge of Hamburg (GLH)
GLLi see Grand Lodge of Liberia (GLLi)
GLNY see Grand Lodge of New York (GLNY)
Glorious Revolution (1688–94) 18
GLS see Grand Lodge of Saxony (GLS)
GODF see Grand Orient de France (GODF)
Gouyon-Guillaume, Mariel 72
Grande Loge Provinciale 69
grand lodge jurisdiction 100
Grand Lodge of Alabama 136
Grand Lodge of Arkansas 134, 136
Grand Lodge of England 2
Grand Lodge of Hamburg (GLH) 113–117, 120–124
Grand Lodge of Iowa 136
Grand Lodge of Liberia (GLLi) 119
Grand Lodge of London 31
Grand Lodge of Louisiana 138
Grand Lodge of New York (GLNY) 6, 53, 113–117, 120–122, 124, 130, 133, 137–140, 142n50, 143n72
Grand Lodge of Nova Scotia 5, 20, 25, 32, 34
Grand Lodge of Pennsylvania 49, 52
Grand Lodge of Saxony (GLS) 120
Grand Lodge of Vermont 91
Grand Lodge of Virginia 133
Grand Lodge Pro Tempore 27
Grand Orient de France (GODF) 48, 69, 74, 83n57, 141n22
Grand Orient of France 89, 93, 132–139
Grand Orient of Italy 138
Grand Stewards 38n103
de Grasse, Alexandre Francois Auguste 93
Guillaume, Pierre 74, 75

152 INDEX

Haitian Revolution 6, 67, 68, 72, 73, 81, 97;
  Freemasonry 4, 48, 55; French white colonial
  Freemasonry 49; refugee lodges 50; refugees
  of 4, 42, 43, 45
Hake, Samuel 22, 26, 28, 29, 31
Halifax 19, 20
Haligonian Freemasons 35
Hall, Prince 7, 100
Hardy, Elias 20, 22, 24, 26
Harland-Jacobs, Jessica 16, 17, 19, 26, 34, 90
Harris, Reginald V. 17
Hayt, James 31
Hérard, Jacques 73
higher degree systems 90, 98
Hilton, John Telemachus 101
"hinge event" 26
Hinks, Peter P. 4, 6, 7
Hiram Lodge 26–28, 32, 34, 35; committee
  27; loyalist refugees 20; members of 22, 26,
  28–34; in Saint John 17, 22
Hiram Lodge No. 17 4, 5, 8, 16, 17, 24, 26, 27
History of the St. John's Lodge (Bunting) 17
Hoffmann, Stefan-Ludwig 123–124
Holt, Charles 93, 101
homogenization 114
Honeck, Mischa 112
Hubbard, Thomas 88
Huntington, Ebenezer 92, 98
Huntington, Samuel 92, 93, 98
Huskins, Bonnie 5, 7

Illuminati 91, 93, 94, 98
Imprinting Britain (Eamon) 16
Inginac, Joseph-Balthazar 72
International Bureau of Masonic
  Relations 134, 135
international conference in Antwerp (1894) 134
International Conference of the Supreme
  Councils in Washington 132, 142n25
international congress in Brussels (1904) 134
international freemasonry 3, 7, 49, 139
internationalism 131, 132
International Masonic Association 137, 139
Irish working-class Masons 18

Jacob, Margaret C. 18
Jamaica: case smugglers from 69; lodges in 48,
  55, 75–77
Jansen, Jan C. 4–7, 89
Jeffersonian Republicans 92, 102
Jefferson, Thomas 54, 93
Jensen, Jan C. 16
Jewett, David 87, 95–97
Johnson, Elizabeth 23
Joint Anglo-American High Commission 133
de Joly, Etienne 67
de Joly, Hector 75

Kenney, J. Scott 16
Kirk, John 24
Klages, Gregory 16
Knights Templar 77, 90, 95, 98–100
"Kulturkampf" or "culture war" 124

La Benignité 57n24
de Lafayette, Marquis 67
Laidley, Robert 34
Lamarque, François 72
Lambert, Pierre Antoine 43
L'Aménité 49, 50, 52–54, 58–59n45, 93
"landmarks" of Freemasonry 140
Lane, Hannah M. 16, 35
La Persévérance 59n50
La Réunion des coeurs lodge 48
La Sagesse in Portsmouth 46, 51, 93
La Sagesse refugee lodge 51
de Laujon, Alexandre 47
La Vérité lodge of Cap Français 46, 48, 52, 69
Law, Henry 22
Lawrence, Charles 19
Lebey, Andrey 136
LeBihan, Alain 71
Leffingwell, Christopher 92, 100
Les Cayes 75, 78, 82n40; English lodge of 69;
  Haitian lodge at 73; masonic lodge in 73
Les Frères réunis 57n24
L'Etoile Polaire 52
Levine, Bruce 112
Lewis, William 25
Lipson, Dorothy Ann 94, 103n27
de Lislet, Louis Moreau 51
"Lodge of Perfection" 93, 98
Longley, Ronald S. 17
Louisiana: Freemasonry in 52
Louverture, Toussaint 5, 6, 55, 67, 68, 72–75, 81,
  81n6, 87, 97, 100, 101
Loyalist Claims Commission 23, 27
Loyalist lodges 17
loyalist Masons 17–22, 21
Loyalist rebellion in New Brunswick (Bell) 17
Loyalist refugees 20
Loyalists 4, 22; cosmopolitan fraternity 33, 34;
  Freemasonry 30, 33, 36; institution 5, 15,
  17, 36; Masons 17–22, 21; in New Brunswick
  4, 5; political conflict in Saint John 22–26;
  refugees 5, 20; reintegration of 28

MacDonald, Stuart 17
McKean, Thomas 54
McPherson, Charles 24
McPherson, Peter 20, 22, 24
Macoy 124
Madiou, Thomas 73
Manning, Diah 92, 98, 99
Marcadier, Joseph 53

INDEX

"March revolution" 111
"Masonia" 118
masonic bodies 134
masonic brotherhood 4, 17, 67, 116
masonic certificates 4, 43–44, 49
masonic constitutionalism 31, 32
masonic cosmopolitanism 5–7
"masonic fever" 91
masonic fraternalism 7, 8
masonic internationalism 131, 132, 137,
  139–140; transatlantic dynamics in 131
masonic jurisdiction 116
masonic laws 117
masonic lodges 2, 44, 46–48, 53, 112; French
  colonial society 43; network 55; in Norfolk 42
masonic networks 5, 8, 16, 19, 55
masonic officialdom 16
masonic quality of honesty 30
masonic signatures 69, 70, 74–75, 78
masonic sociability 4, 44–45, 54
masonic universalism 117
Milbourne, A.J.B. 17
Milnor 116
Montgomery, Joseph 25
Montrose Lodge 22
Moreau de Saint-Méry, Médéric Louis Elie 42,
  43, 52, 53, 55, 71
Morgan, William 35
Morin, Etienne 75–77
Morse, Jedidiah 51, 91, 93
Mott, Samuel 92, 100
Murray, Alexander 95–97

Nagel, Daniel 112
The Napoleonic Wars (1803–1815) 111
"neo feudal oligarchy" 24
Nevins, David 92
New Brunswick 4, 23–24, 36; Freemasonry in 26;
  loyalists in 4, 5, 17, 20; masonic lodges in 36;
  political unrest in 22
New England 89, 91, 93, 95, 98, 100–102
New London 87, 88; masonry in 90, 98; masons
  in 95; Republican opposition in 101
New Orleans 43, 45, 46, 52; refugee
  movements 51
New York: bilateral normalization 138; émigré
  Freemasonry in 112; German Freemasons in
  115; German-speaking lodges in 5, 113–115;
  Pythagoras lodge in 113; refugee lodges 46;
  re-orientation of freemasons 139
Nolan, Mary 132
North American grand lodges 134
Norwich: Boyer arrival in 88, 89, 95; masonic
  identity in 100; masons in 90, 93; Somerset
  Lodge 92
Norwich Courier 88
Nott, Samuel 91

Nova Scotia: Freemasonry in 16, 17, 19;
  provincial grand lodge in 19, 20, 27, 28,
  31, 32
Nova Scotia Grand Lodge 17, 20, 26–28, 32,
  34, 35

"obediences" 132
Oliver, Sheriff William 24
Önnerfors, Andreas 5–7

Papers relating to the late occurrences in
  Pythagoras lodge No. 1 (1855) 118, 119
Parfaite Harmonie 77
Pasqually, Martinès 71, 72, 74, 82n20
Paul, John 22
Pennsylvania Grand Lodge 93
Pétion, Alexandre 73
Philadelphia: Atlantic French Freemasonry
  49, 52; French émigré life in 47, 89; French
  emigres and transients in 89; French-
  speaking lodge in 42–43; masonic lodges 54;
  refugee lodges 46, 50, 52, 53, 93; salons of 54
Philipps, Erasmus James 19
Pickering, Timothy 97
Pieret 73
Pitt 33
political alliances: versus religious-secular
  differences 135–137
political cosmopolitanism 5, 16, 34
Polverel, Etienne 67, 100
Port-au-Prince: freemasons of color in 73;
  lodges of 72
pre-existing lodges 46
Preliminary Peace Treaty 23
Premier Grand Lodge of Free and Accepted
  Masons 18
Prentice, David 22
pre-revolutionary Saint-Domingue 4–6, 50, 56
Prince Hall Grand Lodge 119–121, 123
Prince Hall lodges 55
provincial grand lodge: in Nova Scotia 19, 20,
  27, 28, 31, 32
The Prussian grand lodges 120, 122
Pythagoras lodge 116, 117; in New York 113
Pythagoras No. 1 5, 6, 8, 113, 116, 122–125; vs.
  Pythagoras No. 86 117–119
Pythagoras No. 86 113–115; affiliation with GLH
  115–116; vs. Pythagoras No. 1 117–119

Quartier-la-Tente, Edouard 135
Quasi-War 87, 95

racial segregation: in transatlantic conflicts
  119–123
Raible, Chris 16
Raimond, Julien 75, 81
refugee communities 44, 47, 53, 57n21

154 INDEX

refugee lodges 6; in action 48–55; in Americas 45–47; in danger of backfiring 51; diasporic dimensions 51; network 52; types of 46; in US East Coast 46
refugees 43; in Americas 45–47; of color 55; Freemasonry 43, 54, 55; of Haitian Revolution 4–5, 42, 43; Loyalist 20, 24; Masonic sociability 4; movements 51; population 42, 43, 47, 53; see also Saint-Domingue refugees
Reims: masons in 74
religious-secular differences: political alliances versus 135–137
Remougis, Claude 80
"republican craft" 25
Republican Masons 101
Réunion Désirée 72, 73
Révauger, Cécile 100
revolutionary and post-revolutionary: Atlantic world 3; Freemasonry 17
revolutionary Atlantic 43–44
Revolutionary Brotherhood (Bullock) 81n3
revolutionary events 6
Revolutionary War 16, 17
Rigaud, André 55, 73, 75, 81, 87–88, 93, 96–98, 100; signatures of 76, 83n60
Robison, John 91, 93
Royal Arch Masonry 90, 95, 98, 99, 104n47
Royal Gazette 25
Runifort, Jacques 80
Ryan, John 25

de Saintard, Pierre-Louis 70
Saint-Domingue 67; claimed freemasonry on 7; diaspora 7; free men of color 71–74; French Caribbean colony of 2; Masonic affiliation in 69; Masonic signatures 74–75; multi-racial Freemasonry in 68, 69–71; pre-revolutionary 5; signatures from Bainet parish 75–80
Saint-Domingue refugees 4, 43–46; in America 45–47; diasporic situation of 43–45, 49–51, 53–56; lodges 44, 45, 48; sociability and exile 47–48
Saint John: Freemasons in 22–26; Hiram Lodge in 17, 22; Masons 22; political conflict in 22–26
Saint John Gazette 25
sang mêlé 78, 80
Santiago de Cuba 43, 45, 46
Santo Domingo 43, 52, 78, 88
Saunders, Prince 73
Scottish Rite 75, 76, 89–90, 93, 97–98, 131–133
The Scottish Rite 76
Scottish Rite Freemasonry 71
Scudder, Townsend 137, 139
"Sea and Field Lodges" 137
Sedition Act 93
Selby, John 27, 28

Shreve, Thomas 34
Sidbury, James 89
Simmel, Georg 124
Sinnot, John 26–31, 33
slave emancipation 50–51
sociability 3–5; in Saint-Domingue refugees 47–48
Sonthonax, Léger-Félicité 100
Spaulding, Asa 92
speculative Masons 17, 18
The Spirit of 1848 (Levine) 126n7
Standing Committee of Hiram Lodge 28, 29
St. Domingue 6, 87, 90, 97, 98
Sterry, Consider 92, 94, 95, 98, 99
Sterry, John 92, 94, 95, 99
St. Jean de Jérusalem 48
Stoddert, Benjamin 95, 96, 104n33
Supreme Councils: conference in Brussels (1907) 135; of USA 132, 134
The Swiss Grand Lodge 130

Talleyrand-Périgord, Charles-Maurice de 47
Tangui de la Boissière, Claude-Corentin 50
Tempels, Pierre 135
territorial jurisdiction 6, 116–117, 125
"The First Twenty Years" (Hoffmann) 127n32
1723 constitution 22, 32, 33
'The Three Globes' 141n18
Torrigiani, Domizio 138
trade 49
transatlantic African slave trade 2
transatlantic antagonism 123
transatlantic conflicts: racial segregation issue in 119–123
transatlantic forums 132–133
"Trans-Atlantic history" 141n20
transatlantic lodge network 49, 52
trans-Atlantic Masonic communications 123–125
transatlantic Masonic relationship 115
transatlantic relations 132, 135, 138, 139–140
transatlantic salon culture 47
transnational movements: avant-garde or gravedigger of 137–139; and organisations 131
Treaty of Morfontaine 87
Treaty of Paris 23
The True Republican 94
Trumbull 87, 96
Trumbull, John 92, 97
Tyler, John 100

UGLE see United Grand Lodge of England (UGLE)
United Grand Lodge of England (UGLE) 33, 35, 119, 123
The United Grand Lodge of England 133, 134, 136, 137

INDEX

United Irish Rebellion 15, 26
United States: African American lodges in 121; Democratic-Republican agitation in 91; European lodges in 133; federal union 125; First World War 8; Freemasonry in 44, 45, 97, 114; freemasons in 6, 135–136; to League of Nations 139; Masonic interactions 55; as "new fatherland" 117; politics 112; racial segregation in 122; refugee lodges in 54; Supreme Councils of 132, 134; trade relations 49
universal brotherhood 6, 141n8
universal exhibitions 132
universal fraternalism 44, 112
"Universal Freemasons' League" 131
universalism 6, 44, 95, 113, 124
Unlawful Societies Act 33
"un-Masonic" behavior 53
unrestricted territorial jurisdiction: American doctrine of 134
Untersuchungen über die Formen der Vergesellschaftung (Simmel) 124
US East Coast: refugee lodges in 46
US Freemasonry 45, 119, 120

Vengeance 97, 121
"visiting brethren" 133
von Mensch, Friedrich August 120, 121, 123, 127n40
Von republikanischen Deutschen (Nagel) 128n66
"Vormärz" 111

War of the Spanish Succession 2
Washington, George 48, 54
Webb, Thomas Smith 102
White, Ashli 89
white colonial freemasons 7
white Mason 90, 101
whiteness 55
Willard 114, 116–118
Wilson, Woodrow 136, 137, 139
Winslow, Edward 24
Wittke, Carl 117
"world reconstruction" 137, 139

York, Neil L. 17
York Rite 102, 138